A
STRANGE
WAR

A
STRANGE
WAR

C.P. MILLS

ALAN SUTTON
1988

ALAN SUTTON PUBLISHING
BRUNSWICK ROAD · GLOUCESTER

First published 1988

British Library Cataloguing in Publication Data

Mills, Chris
    A strange war : Burma, India and
    Afghanistan, 1914–1919.
    1. Great Britain. *Army* — Somerset
    Light Infantry — History   2. World
    War, 1914–1918 — Personal narratives,
    British   3. World War, 1914–1918 —
    Asia, Southeastern
    I. Title
    959'.051'0922   D547.S5/

    ISBN 0-86299-377-6

Jacket photograph: On the road to Dera Ismail Khan.
Collection of B.G.L. Rendall.

Typesetting and origination by
Alan Sutton Publishing Limited.
Printed in Great Britain

In Memory of my Grandfather, Ernest Morely Chant.

ACKNOWLEDGEMENTS

AUTHOR'S ACKNOWLEDGEMENTS

This book would have been very much the poorer in the absence of help received from the following people. I owe them all a debt of gratitude.

Firstly I would like to thank Lord Montagu of Beaulieu for preserving his father's private papers relating to mechanical transport in India during the Great War. The papers helped rescue the book, which had been persistently dogged by the complete absence of any surviving documentary records. Lord Montagu was also kind enough to write the Foreword and supply some of the photographs. The Montagu Papers may be read at the Liddell Hart Centre for Military Archives, King's College, London. My thanks are due to the Trustees and staff of the Centre.

Warm thanks must go to Ollie Ewens for allowing me to use his grandfather's diary, 'A Cook's Tour of Burma and India'. The diary, pencil written on individual unbound sheets has, almost miraculously, survived intact since 1928.

I am also most grateful to Dr Jan Stovold of the Sound Records Department, The Imperial War Museum, who recorded Bert Rendall's memories. The tapes, made with Bert in 1985, form the basis of his account in this book. They may be heard at the Sound Records Department of the Imperial War Museum; Ref. No. 8745/23.

Lieutenant Colonel P.J. Emerson (retd) of the Indian Army Association provided encouragement, research suggestions and kindly proof read the manuscript for factual errors. Lieutenant Colonel R.G. Woodhouse (retd), DL, helped with material from the Somerset Military Museum, Taunton.

My thanks are due to Brian and Mary Hinder, for allowing me use of many photographs from the collection of the late Arthur Hinder, who also served with the 2/5th Somersets throughout the Great War.

I am much obliged to the staff of the following organizations; The Imperial War Museum, especially Mr D.B. Nash, Deputy Head, Department of Printed Books; the National Army Museum; the National Motor-Museum, Beaulieu; the British Library India Office, in particular Andrew Cook, Map Curator; the Royal British Legion; the *Western Gazette*; the Army Records Centre, Hayes and the Regimental Museum of the Royal Corps of Transport, Aldershot.

Most of the photographs were reproduced by Bryan Evans of the Walter Rendell Studio, Yeovil. The maps were drawn by Alick Newman, of University College, London, Department of Geography.

I am appreciative of the contributions made by the following individuals who have patiently advised, encouraged and helped in so many ways during the two years the book has taken from conception to fruition; Chris Pippard,

Jim Coleshaw, Jonathon and Kay Shepherd, Denzil Rankine and Clive Rendall. My sincere thanks go to Nessie Kinnis who patiently proofed and edited an extremely scrappy manuscript, teaching me much in the course of doing so. And I am obliged to Trevor Kingston whose savage literary criticism and encouragement shaped up much of my own writing.

Finally, and most importantly, I would like to thank Bert Rendall himself; without his boundless energy and his enduring memory the book would never have reached the stage of being even an idea in the air. It has been a privilege to work with him.

C.P. Mills

ACKNOWLEDGEMENTS FOR QUOTES

The quote from George Orwell's, *Burmese Days* appears by courtesy of the Estate of the Late Sonia Brownell Orwell and Secker and Warburg Limited.
The quote from Stanley Weintraub's, *A Stillness Heard Round the World* appears with the permission of A.D. Peters Co. Ltd.
The passages from Everard Wyrall's, *The History of the Somerset Light Infantry (Prince Albert's)* 1914–1919 are by courtesy of Methuen and Co.
The quote from Philip Mason's copyright, *A Matter of Honour* appears with the permission of Purnell Book Services Limited.
The short extract from Charles Allen's, *Plain Tales from the Raj* is reproduced by courtesy of Century, an imprint of Hutchinson Publishing Group Limited.

PICTURE ACKNOWLEDGEMENTS

The National Motor Museum, Beaulieu; 9, 10, 11, 12, 13, 43, 47, 67, 94.
The collection of the late E.W. Ewens; 24, 28, 30, 32, 48, 93.
The collection of the late Arthur Hinder; 5, 6, 7, 8, 14, 20, 21, 22, 25, 26, 27, 29, 31, 49, 50, 51, 52, 53, 66, 84, 91.
The author's own collection; 1, 2, 15, 16, 17, 18, 92, 95.
The collection of B.G.L. Rendall; 3, 4, 33, 34, 35, 36, 37, 38, 39, 40, 41, 42, 44, 45, 46, 54, 55, 56, 57, 58, 59, 60, 61, 62, 63, 64, 65, 68, 69, 70, 71, 72, 73, 74, 75, 76, 77, 78, 79, 80, 81, 82, 85, 86, 87, 88, 89, 90.
The photograph of Brigadier General Dyer appeared in *The Illustrated London News* on 17 July 1920, page 101 (83).
The photograph of 'A' Company the 2/5th Somersets appears by courtesy of Mr P.H. Shattock (19).

CONTENTS

FOREWORD

On 12 December 1914, a convoy of troop ships sailed from Southampton for India, carrying Territorial battalions who were to relieve regular units of the British and Indian armies for service in France. My father sailed as Commanding Officer of the 7th Battalion The Hampshire Regiment in the liner *Dunera*, his unit disembarked at Bombay and took up duties in Secunderabad. Another ship in the convoy, the *Ionian*, carried the 2/5th Battalion of the Somerset Light Infantry to Burma and on board was not only the author's grandfather, Private Morely Chant, but also Private Bert Rendall and Company Quarter Master Sergeant Ewens, on whose recollections of India and Burma in World War One this book is based.

Soon after arriving my father was appointed Inspector of Mechanical Transport in India, having been involved before the war with the newly emerging British motor industry and with improving British roads. He was shocked when he realised how backward India was, with only 12 army lorries on strength and an extremely inadequate road system. The struggling, disorganised and mule-dominated Indian army transport system certainly needed him.

Over the next four years he threw himself energetically into reorganising the whole system and when he left in 1919 there were 4,000 lorries, 75 armoured cars, manned by 7,000 men, and two driving schools set up specially to teach Indian Army personnel how to drive and maintain their vehicles in the future. Furthermore, there were over 1,000 miles of roads on the North West Frontier which had been made suitable for mechanical transport.

To help him in this priority work, he formed several Mechanical Transport Units and it was life in the ranks of the Second Mechanical Transport Company which is so vividly described by Bert Rendall, who also collected such a splendid series of photographs showing so graphically the everyday life of the company and its vehicles.

I was delighted to allow the author to consult my father's papers, which are necessarily of an official nature, but now for the first time they are suitably complimented by the memory of a non-commissioned officer who helped my father obtain his objectives.

Life in the army ranks in India during the First World War meant hardship yet it also provided adventure but certainly none of the miseries of those involved in the trench warfare in France. Nevertheless there were frequent actions against marauding tribes on the North West Frontier and for the first time mechanical transport and better roads played a vital part in ensuring the Army defeated the enemy and thus established a pattern of tactical defence which is still in operation today.

The men of the Somerset Light Infantry, the Hampshire Regiment and men from many other regiments who helped form the Mechanical Transport Companies had a significant role to play in modernising India's archaic road system, and the memories of those who served in these units tells us how and why. Now, seventy years later, this book is an invaluable record of an important contribution the British made in improving the land communications of India.

Lord Montagu of Beaulieu

PREFACE

The Preface to the Book of Remembrance of the 5th Battalion (Prince Albert's) Somerset Light Infantry.

In a recent article by that eminent military historian, the Hon. Sir John Fortescue, based on a newly discovered daily order book of the Richmond (Yorks) Militia when embodied and quartered in Newcastle in that year of Victories, 1759, he said: 'While its pages were slowly filling up, news had come in that Knox had stormed Masulipatam, that Barrington had conquered Guadeloupe, that Ferdinand of Brunswick had beaten Contades at Minden, that Wolfe had beaten Montcalm at Quebec, and that Hawke had vanquished Conflans in Quiberon Bay; and little though they suspected it, these Militia men had borne their share in these victories by liberating the Regular Forces for service overseas.'

That is the opinion of the greatest living British Military historian, writing in the cold light of history 170 years following the event and long after the glamour of the victories themselves had passed away.

So from 1914 till the end of the Great War those Territorial battalions who did not take an actual part in the fighting line also did their share by setting free the army from the duty of maintaining peace and order throughout His Majesty's vast Empire, and so contributed to every victory won.

Those battalions which went to Burma released the Line battalions who then formed part of the immortal 29th Division whose services in the Dardanelles will never be forgotten while military history is read. The 2/5th Somerset Light Infantry can be well proud of the fact that but for them, and the other Territorial battalions in Burma, that magnificent Division could not have been formed.

The 2/5th Somerset Light Infantry arrived in Burma at a critical moment. A rising of some of the hill tribes in the north had taken place; serious indiscipline had just occurred in Rangoon, and worse was to follow in Singapore within a week or two. With their arrival it became possible to concentrate a formidable force at Myitkyina in the extreme north of Burma causing the rebelling tribes to hastily submit; and at the same time it enabled a battalion to be sent to the assistance of the hard pressed government in Singapore.

From the moment of their arrival the 2/5th Somerset Light Infantry, which was composed of men of fine physique, set energetically to work to perfect themselves in all branches of military training, spurred on, no doubt, by the hope that they in their turn would eventually go to the fighting line. Although that hope never materialized, they soon made themselves fit in all respects to take their place with credit and distinction on any battle-front. Meanwhile they did their part in the War by guarding great camps of Turkish prisoners and by the strength and confidence they contrtibuted to the Government of

India through those anxious years, until the crowning victory, made possible by them, at length arrived.

I am glad this record of their services has been compiled and only hope that their fellow-countrymen in Somerset will realize the important services rendered by them.

Major-General, H.A. Raitt.
Commanding Burma Division 1914–18.
December 1929

THE BACKGROUND

'The history of Captains and Kings is written down and will last forever but the history of the Common Man dies with him.'

THIS BOOK OWES its inspiration to my grandfather, Ernest Morely Chant who served in the 2/5th* Battalion (Prince Albert's) Somerset Light Infantry, a Territorial force unit which was raised for the First World War. He was with the battalion from the outset of the war until late in 1918 when he was attached to an Indian Army formation; the 3/9th Bhopal Infantry, as a sergeant instructor. During those years he served in Burma and India and for him the war ended with the Bhopals in Mesopotamia. Morely Chant returned to England in the spring of 1919 where he was demobilised from the army on 15 May. with his war service completed he went back to his hometown of Yeovil and returned to his pre-war trade as a table glove cutter.

The book contains little of the overall political and military sweep of that war, it is more concerned with the experiences of the two men whose lives it touched. Both served in 'C' Company of the 2/5th Somersets with my grandfather. It is, therefore, a very personal story, the telling of which is founded upon an intangible feel for the lives of those men which I can only hope to convey to you by way of an apparently sentimental account of my relationship with Morely Chant. It is not intended to give that impression but I do consider it necessary to the overall value of the book to explain the feeling with which it has been written.

One of my earliest memories, at the age of 2½ was of discovering my grandfather's old army tropical helmet, high up in the rafters of his potting shed. I ran to find him in the garden, anxiously wanting him to fetch it down and show it to me. From that time onwards he was to foster in me a very keen fascination for all things old. He was an anachronistic man who enchanted me as a child: he always wore dark three-piece suits with a gold pocket watch and

---

* Pronounced 'second fifth'.

fob chain, high lace-up boots, shirts with detachable collars held on by gold studs and he shaved with a cut throat razor. His small terraced house in Yeovil was full of curios which I associated with great age and history.

In the front room of that house, a room quietly full of books and ticking clocks, there was an engaging paradox. A sepia photograph there expressed itself in the form of an imperious young man in army uniform, a sergeant, staring down from the wall. This was my grandfather, who was by then an old man in the next room, reading his newspaper and wearing his gardening suit. I wanted to know what had passed between the two images.

Morely Chant's speach was liberally decorated with Indian words and I delighted at how many people he would term a 'wallah'; there was the milk wallah and the bread wallah, the insurance wallah, the post wallah and so on. He was self-educated in the army during the Great War (he had left school at the age of 14) and campaigned throughout his working life for the Labour Party and the Trade Union Movement. He was an intensely gentle man who loved his rose garden and his allotments, yet was capable of working himself up into the most tremendous furies over politics and would make rousing speeches at trade union meetings. As I was growing up I spent many hours with him hearing mysterious stories of Burma and India, of Ghurkas and ruby mines, rupees, tigers and snake charmers. Never a very fit man after the Great War he suffered recurrent bouts of malaria and retired in the early 1950s after contracting tuberculosis. In 1971, after a long and spirited fight with cancer, Morely Chant died.

At that time I was too young to appreciate the full significance of the loss of my grandfather; I did not understand that on his death almost all the knowledge of his early life had gone forever but in the ensuing years I became absorbed in his memory. I began to realise how the years that he had spent abroad in the Great War shaped and influenced his character. Those years dominated the rest of his life.

After spending much time with my grandmother talking about him, my interest crystallized into a compelling wish to know more of his service in the First World War. Unfortunately, my grandmother knew precious little about this; they had not met until after the war and she had little interest in that part of his life. The rest of my family had only vague and sketchy knowledge of his wartime years. Very few mementoes had survived; a single photograph of him in Calcutta, 1918, a group shot of 117 men taken earlier in the war, his medals and two picture postcards sent from Port Said and Burma.

Three years ago I set out to research his Great War service with the intention of writing something or other on the findings. But after following every avenue of enquiry open to me, over a year, I had discovered virtually nothing that was not already known. The prime source of information would have been his army record papers but most soldiers' records from the 1914–20 period were destroyed by the German bombing of London in 1940. Apart from these papers little was ever recorded of private soldiers and NCOs, though it is possible to discover more of officers. So that was it, nothing.

Then, quite by accident, I came upon the man about whom much of this book is written. My brother, a furniture maker, had received an order for a small coffee table from an old man in Yeovil. On meeting him it was obvious from pictures in his house that he had served in the army in India during the First World War. It turned out that not only had he been in the same platoon of 'C' Company, the 2/5th Somersets, as Morely Chant: (this was a remarkable coincidence, as at the time of writing I am aware of only two surviving veterans of the whole battalion) but Mr B.G.L. Rendall remembered my grandfather well enough, having last seen him in Burma in January 1917. In due course I met Bert Rendall and this book has arisen from our resulting friendship.

With the discovery of one of Morely Chant's fellow soldiers many facts which had previously been hidden behind the veil of years, reappeared from Bert's living memory. Before we met Bert we did not even know for sure in which battalion of the Somerset Light Infantry Morely Chant had served. Neither were we able to recognise him in the group photograph of 'C' Company (he was sporting a moustache, with which we were previously unacquainted). Bert Rendall was able to fill in so much for us.

When I met him, Bert was having his memories of the Great War recorded by the Sound Records Department of the Imperial War Museum. The majority of his account in this book consists of those recordings: edited, expanded and rearranged into the written word. His memory is quite tremendous for a man of his age and in the course of researching the book I have been consistently impressed by his accurate recollection of detail. Nevertheless, it must be borne in mind that Bert was 88 years old when the recordings were made and that the material therein covers a period 68 to 73 years ago.

The other soldier with whom we are to be concerned was Edward William Ewens, another Yeovil man, who died in 1962. He left a comprehensive written account of his war entitled, 'A Cook's Tour of Burma and India. By one of the Tourists.' It appears to have been written up in 1928, probably from rough notes made in the war. The Diary is vivid and caringly written and, together with Bert Rendall's memories, the two accounts provide a unique view of a Territorial battalion in Burma. The two tales are told many years apart but concern the same events.

The book falls into two halves: Bert Rendall was with the Somersets only until January 1917, when he was transferred to an Indian Army unit which had been formed in 1915: the 2nd Mechanical Transport Company. He was then to see service on the North West Frontier of India and in the Third Afghan War of 1919 as a Leyland lorry driver. After January 1917 we follow him away from his battalion. It is then left to Company Quarter Master Sergeant Ewens to complete the story of the 2/5th Somersets.

The researching of this book has generally been a sad story, of discovering that nearly all documentary evidence of the existence of both the 2/5th Somersets and the 2nd Mechanical Transport Company, has been destroyed. Many of the units raised specifically for the duration of the Great War, having had no existence prior to the war and being disbanded afterwards, saw no point in keeping detailed records of their existence. Even in 1927 the official historian of the Somerset Light Infantry found that, 'Of the 2/5th Somerset

1

THE BACKGROUND

1
Sergeant Ernest Morely Chant, Calcutta 1918 after joining the 3/9th Bhopal Infantry.

2
B.G.L. Rendall, 1986, aged 90. Bert Rendall is the last known survivor of the 2/5th Somerset Light Infantry, who sailed to Burma on 12 December 1914.

Light Infantry there are few written records.' [1] It was even more difficult to find anything out about the 2nd Mechanical Transport Company or the 3/9th Bhopal Infantry; most Indian Army records were left in India when the country gained independence and those that weren't destroyed are inaccessible.

There has been one exception, not everything has been lost; the private papers of John, 2nd Lord Montagu of Beaulieu, Mechanical Transport Adviser to the Government of India in the Great War have survived. These papers have provided the background to the 2nd Mechanical Transport Company and mechanical transport generally in India during the Great War. In the absence of the present Lord Montagu having preserved his father's papers and generously making them available to the public for study, it would have been impossible to have discovered any of the operational details of 2 MTC.

The 2/5th Somerset Light Infantry and the 2nd Mechanical Transport Company are shrouded in historical obscurity and the first hand accounts of CQMS Ewens and Corporal Rendall today remain the most complete records of those units available to us. Much of the historical wealth of the individual and collective experience of the men who served their King and Country during the Great War is utterly lost to us now, as are most of the men themselves. This book has been written with the aim of preserving the knowledge of history available to us today in a form which will remain for future generations for as long as it may take them to chance upon it.

C.P. MILLS.
London, 1987

---

1. *The History of the Somerset Light Infantry (Prince Albert's)* 1914–1919 Everard Wyrall, Methuen & Co., 1927.

THE CALL TO ARMS

'. . . it's Special train for Atkins when the trooper's on the tide—
The troopship's on the tide, my boys, the troopship's on the tide.'

RUDYARD KIPLING. *Tommy*

THE KING'S COLOUR of the 5/5th Battalion (Prince Albert's) Somerset Light Infantry hangs in the parish church of St. Mary's, Ilminster, where it has remained undisturbed since it was placed there and consecrated on 9 September 1920. Such colours were presented to every new battalion of the British Army which served overseas in the Great War 1914–1918. A faded and tattered flag today, it commemorates the overseas service of a battalion which was raised, as hundreds of others like it, at the outbreak of war in 1914. It was disbanded soon after that apocalyptic war. The Colour is one of the few memorials to the men of that battalion.

No records exist today of the activities of the 2/5th Battalion Somerset Light Infantry, and nothing has been written about the unit except the memorial book of the 5th Battalion. This encompassed the 2/5th and its sister battalion, the 1/5th, and it was published privately in 1930 by a committee of the battalion's ex-officers.[2] The tribute was possibly written in reaction to the official historian's treatment of the service of the 2/5th; the official history devotes no more than a few lines to the battalion.[3] This apparent neglect has its causes partly in the fact that most official and authoritative works in the immediate post war years tended towards the jingoistic and the battalions which saw no active service were not considered worthy of any real attention. This is illustrated in the official historian's view of the 2nd Battalion which, '. . . *unfortunately* was one of eight regular British battalions stationed in India throughout the course of the Great War 1914–1919'. A second and more forgivable reason was that, in the course of compiling the sheer bulk of the

2. *The Book of Remembrance of the 5th Battalion (Prince Albert's) Somerset Light Infantry,* Chiswick Press, 1930.
3. Ante Cit.

history of that war, historians understandably had those army units which saw no active service low on their lists of priorities.

Yet the service of this battalion encompassed the collective experience of over a thousand men, all volunteers, most of whom were to leave their homes and families in December 1914, bound for an unknown destination from which they were not to return until 1919. Some, of course, were not to return at all. Theirs was to be a strange war, wholly spent on garrison duties in Burma and India; though they were spared the horrors of the Western Front, the discharge of their duty towards King and Country was no less valid. They had no choice in the matter of where they were sent. In many respects their experiences of the Great War would be personally very significant indeed; most of the men had probably never been abroad before, some indeed had possibly never left their home county. They were mostly young men and they were to spend the next five years thousands of miles from home, amongst the peoples, the enigmas and the heat of the Far East.

The British Army of 1914 was of a similar composition to the army of today; there was the small Regular Army made up of full time volunteer soldiers and the Territorial Force, which was comprised of part-time volunteers. The Territorials, like those of the present day, did their training in the evenings, at weekends and at annual camps. Initially, at the outbreak of war in August 1914, the Territorial Force was intended to have the role of Home Defence only; but, as the situation in France rapidly deteriorated, and the tiny British Expeditionary Force looked in danger of being completely overwhelmed, the strategic role of the Terriers was reviewed. They were asked to volunteer for overseas duties immediately despite not having had the six months training period promised them. Very few Territorial soldiers refused and in February 1915 there were 48 T.F. battalions serving alongside the regulars in France.

The desperate expansion of the army in 1914 brought hundreds of new battalions into being; Lord Kitchener's legendary appeal to the British Nation had set out to raise some 500,000 new recruits by the end of August. It was to be the best acclaimed war in British history and men joined up in vast numbers; many for varied and disparate reasons but equally as many for no particular or well thought out reason at all. It was for most of them simply the right thing to do and it had to be done.

The 5th Battalion Somerset Light Infantry was descended from the 2nd and 3rd Volunteer Battalions SLI, and had been brought into existence in 1908, under the Territorial and Reserve Forces Act 1907. The Battalion Headquarters was at Taunton and it maintained other detachments at Pitminster and Bishop's Lydeard. Further companies were spread throughout Somerset. In September 1914 each Territorial battalion which had volunteered for overseas service was empowered to raise a sister battalion for Home Defence duties. Thereby under Army Order 399, the 5th Battalion was split into two; the 1/5th and the 2/5th. The latter was initially known as the 5th (Reserve) Battalion.

Recruiting in Somerset had been brisk during August and September; 916 recruits had been absorbed into the 5th Battalion by the end of August alone.

There were more than enough to fill the ranks of the nascent 2/5th. By October the new battalion was in billets at Taunton and the task of training the men, the majority of whom had no military experience whatever, into fighting soldiers had begun. Officers and NCOs were in great demand but in equally short supply; being transferred from the parent battalion and otherwise drafted in from any available sources. Training progressed through October and November.

One of the new recruits to the freshly formed battalion was Bert Rendall, a Yeovil man now aged 91, but then not quite 18. He was born on 20 October 1896 and when the First World War dawned he was in the early part of an engineering apprenticeship at the Petter's Engines, Nautilus works in Yeovil. A military career was very far from his aim before the Great War exploded into his world. That his youngest son should join the army to go off to war was even further from the intentions of his father. Herbert Rendall who had, in the 1880's, served six years as a regular soldier in the Gordon Highlanders, seeing some savage actions in Egypt and the Sudan. Nonetheless on his third attempt, rejected twice previously on account of his youth and diminutive stature he was given the King's Shilling and became a private soldier in the 2/5th Somerset Light Infantry. In order to do so he had to lie about his age; the minimum age being 19, he was not yet 18 when he was attested in September 1914.

PRIVATE B.G.L. RENDALL

I started my apprenticeship about the middle of 1912 and in September 1914 I sloped off to the Great War. It was a lovely sunny morning and at the time I was working under a definite fitter. Each fitter had two boys doing their apprenticeships. I well remember this Monday morning when my fitter, named Down, shouted to Davis, the fitter on the next set of engines;
"I believe it's coming boy, there isn't going to be much doubt about it."
With this the iron door in the shop opened, this was a door set into a big sliding door. "I'm buggered, we're at war boys, we've got it." And that was it. So I said to Downie, "Well, I'm damned if I know," He said that it won't last long, give it a couple to three months. But it wasn't was it?
So I had my back to the bench. Time went on. Alfie Syrrell, another boy my age was missing. Ernie Gandon was missing, he'd gone and so on. One morning my fitter looked at me and said, "You'll damn soon be missing I suppose!" These were his words to me unknowing that I had already had one go and got turned down, and got hold of by the ears by my Father, to look face to face at him. He was calling me one of the biggest blasted fools in the nation. Here I had a job; no reason to go. He told me all about his hellish days in the Sudan and the Relief of Gordon and that hadn't done me had it? My Father had found out that I tried to enlist and had got turned down because I wasn't big enough. This recruiting sergeant and a Major Batten agreed. This major sat at the table taking them in by the hundreds. We were all lined up eight o'clock at night. "All right sergeant, this kid just won't do." Well, I just went back to work. My Father was very angry and just next door to giving me a good hiding. The reason was that they were going in such thousands. Everywhere was queued up just like going to the theatre. The recruiting officers were just overworked and they had to get reliefs for them.

3

WORLD WAR   AGE 17 LATE
ONTH AS A
I ER

THE CALL TO ARMS

3
Private Herbert Rendall,
1st Battalion Gordon
Highlanders, 1886.

4
Private B.G.L. Rendall,
September 1914.

One evening my brother Harold said, "Let's go to the pictures, Bert." We tapped our clothes for any coppers that we might have and my brother said to me on the way there, "A few acid drops Bert?". A good idea. I well remember the shop and we both trundled up the town and went in Joey Axe's, a fine home made sweet merchant. Now Harold took a few steps in the doorway. I just went like a madman; I had to go four or five hundred yards and I was in the recruiting office again. Major Batten had seen me twice before and said, "Put him in, Sergeant, it's that bloody kid again." I came out a soldier. I went to Taunton Barracks the following day. I was sworn in again down there, signed up, three or four forms, and was then sent back to Yeovil to be called for. Mother cried, Father was spellbound and he said to me one or two words, "I can't give a soldier a hiding, can I ?."

They had me again at Taunton and I went from there to Salisbury Plain. Prior to all this I drilled in Yeovil for three weeks as one of the 'broom handle straw hat boys'. They had no rifles then. We were just in our 'civvy' suits and we used to march up to a field under an old timer sergeant in Yeovil and do a few odd drill-ups learning the rudimentaries of what the rifle would be like. There were thirteen thousand of us on our side of the Plain alone. We were pursed up and fixed eight to each bell tent. Preparing us for the old Kaiser's gun fodder, that's all you could call us really. I suppose it was the same on the other side.

Once or twice we came home to Yeovil on weekend leave. They weren't too hard on us to begin with but on the third time they rumbled and this is what happened; there was a pile of red uniforms flung down in a heap and they were old SLI uniforms in our encampment. Stood beside this heap was a sergeant and he said, "Try it on lads, some of you will get long trousers and short legs, some short trousers and long legs, but if you look bloody respectable enough you'll be able to go home on another leave for a weekend and God knows what will happen after that." They were rough and ready in those days, mind. I searched and changed and chopped and picked it up, tried it on. There happened to be a bit of sun so we could do this on the dry grass and the heap gradually disappeared. Four hundred of us had been rigged out in red and white piping.[4] The sergeant looked us over with a critical eye as we went from the heap because he had to inspect us. "You'll do," he said, "you can get in the train with that, you won't stop the bloody thing." That's how they took us. I went back to my bell tent.

We learnt the rifle on the firing range occasionally, anything to do with the army. Halt, form platoon, on the left, at the halt. Different marching orders all day or all morning long. We were up at four, five, six in the morning. It was mid–winter and almighty cold was it in those bell tents. We had a board that formed a floor. After a while we had some wet weather; the mud inside the tent was as much as the mud outside, especially where everyone came in.

All over the Plain far and near were thousands of buglers and the sound was a charm which took you out of this world; you'd hear all the various calls, calls to feed the horses, calls for the post, calls for the cookhouse, calls for the guard.

All those buglers all over the Plain. You could hear a bugle, make no mistake, for damn near three miles. They were all learning the various calls

4. Khaki uniforms were in great shortfall in the early months of the war and many soldiers had to be kitted out in old uniforms whilst waiting for their khaki issue.

*and orders, far and near, because everything that was in the army was bugle
controlled. We even learned the gallop and the charge. Even for the bayonet
charging the bugle sounded and that was it.*

In the course of their anticipated role as a Home Defence unit, the 2/5th were
ordered at the end of November 1914 to proceed to the outer defences of
London, near Guildford. On the eve of their departure the Commanding
Officer of the battalion, Major J.R. Paull, was called to the War Office where
he learnt that his battalion was being sent to India, with Burma as its ultimate
destination. This came as something of a surprise and the 2/5th were set to
follow their sister battalion, the 1/5th, which had sailed for India on 9
October. The men were not told their destination until well into the voyage.
On the morning of 12 December 1914 the battalion travelled by train, in two
groups, from Taunton to Southampton where the troopship *Ionian* was
awaiting them.

PTE B.G.L. RENDALL

*All things have to end and one day this happened. We were disbanded and
sent home on five days foreign service leave which meant we were going to
France or God knows what destination. This was the start of my travels
around the World. I went back home to Yeovil and on the sixth day after my
leave reported back to Taunton where all the regiment was. We were stationed in various parts of Taunton and we were all drawn together on this
morning, never to go back to our billets. We then got on the train. On the
morning that I left Yeovil to go back to Taunton the only persons to see me
off were poor old mother and father. I heard after I got back that my father,
an old soldier, turned to my mother and said, "You won't see him no more,
Hannah, for five years," and he was right. We trundled along until we got to
Southampton. We arrived there on the morning of 12 December, still 1914, on
one of the lousiest days I can recollect.*

*From the outset we saw our beautiful home of abode for God knows how
long. The* Ionian, Ionian Trooper. *We looked up at her massive size of three
funnels and saw she was an ocean-going liner. We formed up and marched
up the gangways but as we got up the gangways we were detailed to come
back down on the opposite side of the bows to report for duty. We didn't know
what that duty was but soon found out, the cranes were roaring away and
working the massive great square platformed carriers with their four chains.
These were dropping down into the hold, and this was all artillery shells.*

*There were 7 tons to get aboard. We also had the 16 Battery Royal Horse
Artillery; they had six guns, thirty six horses and the horses were put on four
decks down. Next aboard came the Dorset Regiment. With the artillery, the
Dorsets, the Somersets and the Devons, there wasn't much room for playing
about on the decks.*

*We reported to the Staff Sergeant on the quay. There were 24 of us. The
sergeant pointed as cool and calm as you like, "There's a little bit of cargo
here boys that's got to be taken aboard so get going. Two to a box and there's
three and a half tons of .303 rifle ammo to be carried up the decks and right
down below. Each trip will be a bloody nice trip for you. You'll know the way
up and down before you finish."*

We started off, when we came to go down the massive iron gangways, the first flight of steps were about twelve, then another two flights of twelve. We walked along and stacked these boxes in the hold. When doing this you had to be vitally careful as the back man, because the box sloped down, hellish down the stairs, and it was liable to catch the heels of the poor kid in front. That happened. The kid went down. I was paired up with a Lance Corporal. I never did know his name nor see his face properly. You had paired up, come along, and picked up a box, sooner the better to get it aboard. With the box that I had I somehow stumbled and it caught his heel. There were two more in front again because at no one time were there less than three different pairs of two on the steps going down. We were a regular procession behind one another, the faster the better.

This box went down and the poor kid that was with me held onto the box and pulled me with him. My hand was dashed off the handrail and I went down. I let go the box and the damn thing went trundling on down over his head, back and neck. These boxes were about nine inches square and near on a half cwt each. The box went on and stopped on the nape of this poor kid's neck, jammed between the box and the edge of the stair by his mouth and nose. When they picked the poor kid up he was gone. I have never, ever forgotten that. He was just put aside and they said they'd put him ashore and that was that. The sergeant said, "You're in the army now boy, and you've joined the army for anything." That was the answer I had. He said that I'd be bloody lucky if I didn't get something like that before we'd finished.[5]

That night, after a couple of stops for a quick snack of army food on the quayside, we were all on board by six thirty, seven o'clock. I couldn't face going down below yet. I smelt the engine rooms. I smelt the heat. Up on deck was a filthy, dirty black drizzle. As yet I didn't know it, but there was a little boy almost my own age each side of me. We were all kids, when suddenly some dim figures came along the quayside. It was like looking off a church tower from her bows down to the quay: first one little lamp lit, then another little lamp lit, and another and another. We could then distinguish the field service caps and Salvation Army caps on the quayside. They undid their paraphernalia in the filthy, blowing wind and played us some wonderful cheerful stuff. A song that was the only one I knew; 'God be with us till we meet again, may his presence guard and guide you. . .'

This was a Saturday night send off from Southampton. Then a few minutes to nine o'clock it started and we heard noises and we could dimly see the tugs in the distance just about one to two hundred yards off. One of the kids nearby said, in his Somerset way, "Look the gap's widening," and I turned to him and said, "Where the hell for?" I went down below and looked around. I was on 'D' deck, four decks down, well down. I came up with all my equipment on, the lot. We were detailed then. I was detailed for 'D' deck which was 50 men. Each was given a hammock irrespective of rank: CQMS, CSM, Sergeant, excepting officers. We were all mixed in one big heap. They just wanted to get us aboard ship. I stayed on deck for an hour and by this time, looking back, saw Southampton fully lit up. There was no such thing as blackouts then. Only at sea because of submarines.

---

5. This soldier does not appear in the *Book of Remembrance* as the first casualty. He probably survived after being put ashore.

Also with the troops on the *Ionian* were No.1643 Private Ernest Morely Chant, who was 20 years old in 1914, and another Yeovil man, who at 39 was one of the more senior recruits; Company Quarter Master Sergeant Edward William Ewens. Prior to the war Ed Ewens had worked for his father who owned a gloving factory in the town, which also employed Bert Rendall's father, a master leather stainer.

The newly raised battalions of the British Army, both of Lord Kitchener's New Army and of the Territorial Force, were desperately short of experienced officers and NCOs. To help obviate these shortages any volunteer with experience of handling men in any capacity was singled out for higher rank. Ed Ewens, with experience of factory management was an obvious candidate for rank; quite apart from the manifest advantages of being much older than most of the other volunteers. A company quartermaster sergeant was responsible for equipping his company and maintaining its stores. There was one per company and the four sergeants were responsible to the Quartermaster himself, who in the case of the 2/5th, was Lieutenant T.H. Hood. CQMS Ewens had travelled before, having lived in the United States between 1898 and 1900 and during the Great War he was to keep a record of his experiences.

CQMS E.W. EWENS

The reader will find in perusing this diary that the narrative deals largely with number 3 and later 'C' Company the 2/5th Prince Albert's Somerset Light Infantry. The writer has only recounted the doings of other companies as they came to his knowledge whilst with them, temporarily or otherwise.

Wednesday December 9th 1914 found us in billets, in St Andrew's Hall at Clifton Lodge, Taunton. It became known on this day that the battalion was under orders for the East; near or far, not specified, and that we should be sailing shortly. Thursday and Friday of the same week, we of the Quartermaster's Stores were busy issuing the necessary articles which go to make up a Tommy's kit and being civilians we got into a muddle with the buttons(brass) and the brass(buttons) and similar items on the issuing sheets. In fact it was not until an old sweat came along that we could tell t'other from which with the usual swear word accompaniments.

On Thursday night we were given a farewell supper at St Andrew's School by the inhabitants of Taunton and it was quite a nice todo but the one fly in the ointment was that our Company Sergeant Major was missing from same. He was still absent from early morning parade on the Friday; to the great consternation of our officers, who knowing very little, (and we less) had to take us and it ended in our soon being dismissed for breakfast. The prodigal turned up at breakfast time no questions asked, but one or two of us knew that he had been home for a last farewell to the Missus and kids, without leave and in civvies. The rest of the day was pretty full as we had then received orders to parade at 6.30 am on Saturday December 12th in full kit. Shades of military orders as we knew them afterwards.

We were sent away without any inspection whatever and various articles got lost or flogged as time passed and it could never be proved that they were issued, so the lucky ones came in for a free second issue. That Friday evening three of us had a night out and finished at the Cherry Grove at 11 p.m. The landlord

5

6

7

THE CALL TO ARMS

5
Soldiers of the 2/5th training on Salisbury Plain, October 1914.

6
A group of 2/5th men in Yeovil, Autumn 1914.

7
Training continues on Salisbury Plain.

8
Private Arthur Hinder (on the left) and other 2/5th men on Salisbury Plain. No more than boys, really. Note the old red uniforms.

then kindly invited us into his private room and after various healths and have anothers, we found ourselves outside of Clifton Lodge at about 1 a.m. without any means of getting in and the doors locked, barred and bolted. About 70 of our fellows were sleeping on the floor in this house and when we eventually found the window on the ground floor could be forced open, it was soon done but the first one to step in over the sill put his feet on the lower part of a sleeper's anatomy, which caused a most unearthly yell and for quite ten minutes pandemonium reigned. Everyone there seemed to make some sort of row and I am sure the air turned blue all over Taunton. By the time quietness reigned we were snugly rolled up in our blankets and, as we believed, were never suspected.

Saturday morning, December 12th 1914, we fell in at St Andrew's School in full marching order. What a time we had that morning trying to get our new web equipment together. A Chinese puzzle wasn't in it; there was hardly one in the whole company that knew how to proceed. Belts, braces, bayonets, frogs, pouches etc were mixed in the most awful confusion, out of which there seemed no way and at the fall in, if we had been inspected, some caustic remarks would sure to have been passed by the Inspecting Officer. As it was, one of our own officers had to carry out the job, and he, never having done it before, did not know anything whatever about web equipment; possibly it was the first time he had seen it. It passed off all right however, and later the remark of the old Tommy aforesaid, 'Fred Karno's Ragtime Army on Tour,' though not appreciated at the time, was seen and laughed at as its truth became known. In fact the saying stuck in the Company for years.

We were then issued with a bag of eatables – biscuits, cheese and pork pies for the train journey. We marched to the station and left with the first half battalion about 9.15 a.m. The second half was following about an hour later. Arriving in Southampton we were taken to the docks and embarked upon the *Ionian* Allen Liner and after a lot of apparently useless waste of energy and temper by our Quartermaster, baggage and ammunition was stowed away and the second party arrived and embarked. We were ready to sail at 6 p.m., having on board the 2/5th Somerset Light Infantry, the 4th Dorsets and half of the 4th Devons. On the opposite quay to us, some 'kilties' were embarking for France and a few ribald jokes were exchanged across the dock.

It appeared that our boat was short handed for stokers, so about 12 of our fellows volunteered for the same, being paid about £7 for the trip, Waspby of Bridgwater being one of the first to shovel coal. We were then told off in messes and issued with one hammock and one blanket per man and moved off at 9 p.m. Going down Southampton Water the search lights were playing all around and the night being a bit rough, nearly everyone turned in on the boards. They wouldn't risk getting into the hammocks as it was too risky for most, they tried hard enough but finished on the deck and stayed there.

Next Morning, Sunday 13th, was nothing but wind and rain and an angry sea in the Channel. Quite 95% of our fellows were down and out, couldn't even face the upper deck. By midday we were off Strait Point, having passed and recognised Portland at about 8 a.m. and caught a glimpse of Lands End as the day was ending.

What thoughts of home; should we ever see England again, and how many of the present Ship's company would be left behind on foreign soil? Thoughts such as these were passing through our minds and were not pleasant. We left Lands End astern and made for our rendezvous with the rest of the convoy.

Dinner time on Sunday at 74 Mess, there were only two not feeling the effects of the tossing. They made their way to the galley armed with a dixie and cover and the following dialogue ensued: Cook, as orderly corporal was hopeless. Mess number? Answer: 74. How many in mess? Don't know, but we only want enough for two. Damn you take enough for 20! And the forlorn ones had to. They picked out the best pieces, had a decent meal, offered what was left to the others lying about and got soundly cussed for their trouble. They eventually put the remains through the porthole, cleaned up and went through practically the same performance at tea time, although the dixie of tea did a few of the sick ones good.

Monday morning broke worse than ever and about noon we came up with the rest of the convoy, consisting of the *Dunera*, the *Saturnia*, the *Arragon*, *Caledonian* and *Nile*, escorted by HMS *Talbot* leading and two destroyers on either flank. We took the second position in the line and stood across the Bay of Biscay. That night the Ushant Light was discernible ahead of us on our port bow. Still everyone in Mess 74 was in a mess and wanted no grub or even thoughts of it.

Tuesday 15th December we were well into the Bay of Biscay and the weather had moderated a bit. 'King Sol' doing his best to break through the clouds, but a devil of a sea on. Everyone was feeling better by dinner time and most were now very peckish but still one was missing from 74 mess. As it did not occasion much surprise, the orderlies went to fetch dinner and one carrying the dixie of soup descending the companionway, through the pitching of the vessel, missed his step and landed at the bottom, soup and he together. Another mess and no soup for one table with the usual recriminations, but we got over that by each of the other messes feeding one of the luckless.

That evening was devoted to a few boxing matches, as by then the weather had cleared and only a slight roll on the boat. According to the official records beer was supposed to have been issued on this day, at one pint per man; but the troops saw nothing of it. If you want to know where it went, ask the Quartermaster. It did not go over the side, in fact it was several days after this before we got a taste.

Cape Finistere was passed today, very low down on our left, not unlike the last sight at Land's End, but as we were standing in more for the coast we hoped to see Portugal more fully.

Wednesday 16th dawned beautifully. The coast of Portugal with the sun rising over it, appeared in the mist, which disappeared as the sun rose in the heavens, and the sea was a picture. Everyone was now enjoying the sun, except the boy who was missing. The Lance Jack in charge of the mess had not reported it yet – a more inefficient Lance Corporal never left England's shores; no doubt he was given his stripe because he was a sergeant in the Boy's Brigade before joining up at the age of 18, and yet in his mess were men who were 15 to 20 years older, and had done a greater number of years in the old Volunteers and Terriers. They had to tell him what to do in most cases and in others he had to look out for himself. Similar was one or two of us sergeants, because they joined as school-masters. Before they left the attesting table they were handed three stripes, yet they were not fit to handle men, only kids.

How fine the lines of Torres Vedras looked topping the cliffs at Cape Roca and what desolate rocks the Barlinga Islands are, which we have just passed. Towards evening a little commotion was caused as a strange warship was sighted hull down, and well out to sea from us. All the line then started zig-zagging and moving in more towards the coast. HMS *Talbot* moved seaward to intercept the stranger, but it turned out to be a Portugese man of war. All being well, we resumed our usual course. Singing was indulged in that night on deck, accompanied by a banjo and mouth organs and all went well.

Thursday December 17th broke fine and clear. We are now in sight of Spain and very early passed Cape St. Vincent, recalling memories of Nelsonian times. Nothing doing in the morning as the other battalions have the deck, so four of us proceed to search for our missing one. And after a couple of hours search we find him, huddled in the bow of a boat, more dead than alive and so weak as to be unable to stand without the help of one each side of him. No sick bay having been yet appointed, we decide to see what we can do for him and eventually succeed in getting some dry biscuits into him and half a mug of water. At tea time we got him to eat some bread and butter and another half mug of tea, then put him as comfortably as we could to bed in a corner of the deck. Next day he was feeling better and there we will leave him.

At 2 p.m. we sighted another convoy of one large four-funnelled cruiser and nine troop-ships coming towards us but about two miles off. The opinion was that they were the first contingent of South African troops for France. What a splendid sight they made steaming in line, the foremost of the troopers looked like the *Mauretania*. Our wireless reports today that Jerry has been having a go at Hartlepool etc. The expressions passed on board were not favourable to any Germans – the cowards.

Today we were issued with canvas shoes, some white, some brown, but they are better for shipwear than ammunition boots. We now turn in expecting to reach the Rock early tomorrow morning.

Friday December 18th. We were up before daylight as an old salt, a member of the crew, advised us to be about at sunrise and we should see a sight never to be forgotten; as the boat was likely to be at a certain spot at a certain time and we should see the sunrise behind the Rock of Gibraltar. On our starboard the lights of Tangiers were plainly visible and the dark coast of Morocco. To our left the Serifa Light was showing and to the port and in the east the outline of the Rock was thinly visible against the greying sky of dawn. In less than half an hour the sun was straight behind the rock which seemed to lie directly in our path; like a lion, couchant, and barring our way to the East. The whole dark outline of Gib was lit up with a wonderful golden halo with the sun at Europa Point to where it suddenly dropped away at the isthmus connecting it to the mainland of Spain. A truly wonderful panorama. As we put in toward the harbour in the rapidly strengthening sunlight, we were met by a French destroyer, which must have brought despatches to the *Talbot* for in a short while signal flags were fluttering from the masthead, the purpose of which appeared to be that the convoy would separate here and make the best of their way singly to Malta.

The *Ionian* immediately turned away, without putting ashore our mails, for the straits, which were like a silver strand connecting Europe with Africa, caused by the white horses risen by a freshening breeze from due east. As we rounded the point a few gun embrasures could be detected and knowing it was honeycombed by galleries and gun platforms it gave one the impression of great strength and certainly it is the key to the great inland sea. The *Dunera* put into Gibraltar and succeeded in convoying into collision with a large schooner, but we saw nothing of it.

Now ensued a race between the transports to reach Malta first. The Sierra Nevada Mountains were clearly discernible on our port bow, with their tops covered in snow, the base of them being seared and seamed with deep gullies and with the sun shining it gave a lovely contrast of light and shade. On our right was the forbidding, burnt out and scorched coast of Morocco, looking like a gigantic heap of cinders with sparse vegetation near the water's edge.

This was the first full day on which beer was issued to the 'sets; the men were lined up along the deck and the orderly corporal was on duty to see that each man got one pint, and did not come up for a second time. Up came a sergeant with four mugs. He was asked by the two striped wallah why he wanted four pints and he explained; one for the Sergeant on Guard, one for the Sergeant on Cookhouse, one for Orderly Room Sergeant and one for himself. The four pints were issued. In about 15 minutes another sergeant appeared with the same yarn, and so it went on until the four sergeants concerned had four pints apiece. By that time the fifty sixer was out. The corporal tumbled to it, but being just promoted did not like to say anything before the men. He spoke to the sergeants concerned afterwards and got cussed for his pains and told to keep his ruddy mouth shut.

This evening orders were issued that no lights were to be used, but that did not stop the usual community singing on deck, though it was not known by that name in those days. Porpoises were around us, and the officers were having a bit of revolver practice at them, but by the splash of the bullets they could not hit the proverbial hay rick. In fact, with their actions and frightened appearance when the bang took place, it must have been the first time some of them had fired a firearm of any description. The weather was now perfect.

Saturday December 19th. One week at sea and fairly settled down to sea routine. Something happened that was very irksome to the 2,000 troops aboard. This boat had a forward well deck and one aft well deck. Between the two, but higher and approached by companion ladders, was the promenade deck which comprised roughly two thirds of the length of the boat. This deck was now reserved entirely for the use of the officers aboard. They numbered considerably less than 100 and yet the 2,000 men were packed in a space of about half the area which was allotted to 100 gents. If you messed in the stern of the boat, or in the front, woe to you if you were caught crossing the sacred piece of deck between meals, at which time there was a right of way allowed for about half an hour. It was not generally known at the time but it was nearly instrumental in causing a mutiny onboard as the men were packed in like beasts in Taunton Market on a Saturday. The older hands succeeded eventually in soothing things over a bit and the discontent died down.

Today at noon Algiers was quite visible. It gave one the appearance of an amphitheatre placed in sunburnt hills with one side open to the sea, the buildings arising from the water in tiers, topped by a large tower or monument. The native boats about here brought back memories of one's school days and the Sally pirates. We heard via our wireless today of some more damage done by the German Fleet at Scarborough and the general wish was expressed that we shall have a chance to hit back for the loss of the women and children of that place, and of Whitby.

A bit of rifle drill took place today, using the old Martinis. Talk about cows handling muskets. This was the first experience of scores of our men, or rather boys, who, barring the carrying of them to Taunton station, had never handled one before. To add to the confusion in the well decks, there were several limbers and wagons for the Australian force which had just reached Egypt and we were supposed to drop same at Alexandria. We eventually unloaded them at Port Said and we were thankful when they were gone. Their room being preferable to their company.

Day after day sunrises and sunsets in the Mediterranean were gorgeous. No artist could even paint the vivid colours placed by the hand of nature across the heavens. Cloud effects were marvellous, looking at times like fleeces of cotton wool suspended by something unseen, and at night, high up in the heavens, dark red sky with variegated clouds and curtains of velvet appearing to hang from them until dissolved in the dark mist which enshrouded the Eastern horizon, and so on to another day.

PTE B.G.L. RENDALL

We came on around Southampton Water and as far as I know, left the Isle of Wight on the left. We went down the Channel towards Biscay. I dared to say to one of the crew, kid like, forgetting all my soldiering; "Where do you reckon we're off to, Joe?" "Keep your mouth shut, son, and don't ask anybody else if you don't want trouble. There's a bloke up there on the bridge who knows where we're going and that's the lot. I don't and I'm one of the anchormen." I said no more.

On the following night I felt a bit queasy. When you are slung up in a hammock it's one of the worst sicknesses there is aboard ship. You're about a foot below the deck above, and you swing all the time to the roll of the ship, and the more she rolls the more you do. I jumped out of the hammock at 4 o'clock in the morning; stuck on the white daps we'd been issued with and ran. I didn't go below decks again for four days. I was floored, flattened and done, seasick. They were around us like flies. I always remember a pair of ammunition boots right up against my face because another kid was lying that way. We were all just out. There was no sickroom, what didn't go over the rails came down on the deck. The crew was raving mad.

We had well and truly got into Bay as they called it, which was Biscay. On my second morning I saw a sight that made me sick. I never thought a human being could do it. We hadn't lowered the jibs over the holds, which are poles which are used between the masts, they are like telegraph poles that you can swing in and out. Now these, coming on board are chained and wired down to sockets. For some unknown reason they'd been left out but now they'd suddenly taken a fit to draw them in board. There was a kid next to me who I could see sideways on my left and he was laid, neck and head right up against a winch bracket under the cocks of the winch. This lout knew the cocks were open. You started a steam winch just the same as a pair of cylinders on a railway engine. This lout pulled two levers and away clattered the gears. This bloke near me had the full blast of boiling steam in the head and neck. He felt it and I saw him come over; his neck was red, he fell sideways and brought some more up. I couldn't catch the winchman's face because I couldn't move myself. It only lasted a while and the poles were down. He knocked off and pulled a couple of levers and by luck he walked to one side a couple of steps and between the hatches. I couldn't get a view of him. I screamed out and somebody came and took the kid away. It was two first aid blokes. We all had our ambulancemen aboard ship, they were called first aid men. Every regiment got them; stretcher bearers we called them. He was taken off.

It was four days later when I struggled up on my hands and knees and found by holding the rails I could stand up. From that day I let go the rails bit by bit. I felt as though I was on roller skates.

On the fifth day out we were heading towards the Med. I could walk

*about on deck and take more notice. We were gradually gathering our wits
together on board. When we went down under for a meal the everlasting,
indispensable sergeant was there; "You on this table, you on that table, you
on the other side of the deck." We were all sorted out on our deck, thirty two
to a mess, sixteen to a side.*

*Then it happened. Out came the Fray Bentos, bloody bully beef. It came
in large doses – seven pound tins. We ate so much of it going towards the Red
Sea. They were going straight down the bloody mess table and we found at
the porthole the tins were tapered and they'd just go through the porthole to
flop down and we listened to the plop as they hit the water . Then they
changed it to bread, cheese and onion. We had enough corned beef to last us
for ten years. It was just the same with the plum jam; we saw enough plum
jam to last the rest of my life. I've never fancied jam from that day to now
and I'm gone 88. I've still got a job to eat a jam sandwich now. At tea time
we'd get a nice slice or two of bread, and a crown of butter in a round dish,
that's what it was called then; a crown of butter. You helped yourself to the
bread and butter and the inevitable jam. The name of the firm; Crosse &
Blackwell, everlasting jam.*

*The dixie came round and tea was made with seawater. We had to drink
it but it tasted salty. When we told the crew, they said wait till you get the
freshwater tank shook up. It will be as red as blood itself, but it will be
alright. The tanks are over the main engine room. These tanks stored about a
thousand gallons each and were fed through the water system.*

*No treatment was received for seasickness. You were left to recuperate and
revive. I didn't know one who went west. It's one of the most hellish jobs I
ever had though, to be sick on an empty stomach; some had stomach strain
and you never forget that. We had our own medical officers who were doctors
in civvy life who had joined.*

*We had to parade in batches for physical training. To keep us supple we
had to run around the officers' promenade deck which was right around the
superstructure of the boat deck. The rest of the day we roamed about or lay
and sat about. As we got towards Gibraltar all signs of seasickness cleared
up. We were all sailors and could walk the decks then with our hands in our
pockets. The yarn is that if you get seasick it clears the way for you to walk a
rolling deck. If you weren't seasick you never felt safe to let go the rail. It
was a kind of passport to being a sailor.*

*The voyage to Gibraltar took roughly five days. One day one of the old
soldiers who had seen it all before stood up on deck and said, "Here we are,
here's Gib." It looked like a little sandheap stood up. One of the sailors
nearby said he had good sight because we were damn near fifty miles off yet
and we wouldn't be there before morning. He was right. At nine o'clock in the
morning we saw the people on the beaches like flies. That was Gibraltar; we
didn't dock at Gibraltar. No one told us where we were going but we guessed
it was the Suez. About a fortnight out from England we got to Alexandria and
then entered Port Said.*

3

AN UNKNOWN DESTINATION

THE SOMERSETS ABOARD the *Ionian* comprised less than their original battalion strength of 1077 men; with their destination being Burma, the number required of them was that needed to make up an Indian Field Service Battalion. Thus they were 29 officers and 800 men, with those remaining in England forming the nucleus of the 3/5th Somerset Light Infantry. The 3/5th became a training unit which was to supply reinforcements throughout the rest of the war.

By the eighth day out from Southampton the *Ionian* had passed Gibraltar and was steaming steadily into the Mediterranean. The ship itself, a civilian liner prior to the war, had been built at the end of the 19th Century, entering service with the Allen Line. She was 8,000 tons and she had been requisitioned for use as a trooper in the Boer War and again in 1914. She did not survive the Great War, being sunk by a torpedo in 1917.

The men had, by now, mostly recovered from the sea-sickness and were settling down to enjoy the new scenery.

CQMS E.W. EWENS

Sunday 20th December. The day broke with a clear blue sky. In the morning a church service was held in the after well deck conducted by our Colonel as no chaplain was aboard and the singing of hymns, especially 'Eternal Father Strong to Save', was well rendered. About noon we passed a French convict establishment called Galacia. A most sterile and desolate looking island. Nothing but a mountain of rocks and not a sign of a dwelling. Very few guards were wanted here, and yet another wonderful sunset. During this night we had wind and rain, the old *Ionian* rolled and pitched rather badly, but sleeping in the hammocks we went to the land of dreams without knowing much about it. Those who slept in the lower deck had rather a bad time of it. According to the swear words, interspersed at intervals, the Mediterranean when bad, *is* bad.

Monday 21st December. Wind and rain had disappeared by the time the sun appeared but there was still a nasty choppy sea on and a few fed the fishes once more. At 9 a.m. we sighted the island of Gozo low down over the horizon. It appeared to be shimmering in the heat which was no doubt the effect of the sun's rays dancing on the waves, and so on still Eastward to Malta, which we reached about midday. We stood in towards Valetta harbour and gunboats came out to sea to meet us, but to theirs and our disappointment, we turned once more towards the East without stopping. Today our Indian sun helmets (topees) were issued; but no puggarees with them. Possibly the Quartermaster was under the impression that no one knew how to fold them. Why couldn't he have found out from the officers who so neatly did theirs, and then some poor Tommy on sixpence per day for self and sixpence per day for the missus at home could have made a few extra bob for himself. No, rather give it to the durzai when we reach our destination which is now rumoured to be Burma. As the wind was pretty fresh today, and being without chinstraps, several of the new issue were soon floating astern and their late owners were mulcted in miscellaneous stoppages.

Tuesday 22nd passed without anything untoward happening, chief interest being centred in the race with our other ships to Port Said and today we sighted the nearest—we believe that we're in the van – the *Dunera*, about five miles astern and gradually overhauling us. By then our stokers were going all out and we were racing neck and neck till night closed down and shut her out from view. Today we had out first lifeboat parade or lifeboat drill, being told off to stations. What a farce it appeared. One of our fellows reported sick today and was placed in a bunk called the sickbay. Pretty bad we believe. Various rumours as to the cause and only married the day before we left Taunton.

Wednesday 23rd. Wind still strong and more topees overboard. Later came an issue of chinstraps and not before they were needed. Our sick fellow was much worse today and diagnosed as ptomaine poisoning. It appeared to be the result of eating tinned salmon, or that is the rumour passing through the ship. We expect to reach Port Said tomorrow evening and the *Dunera* cannot be seen. Did sing-song on deck at night with mouth organ accompaniment and so to the close of another day.

Thursday December 24th. Nearing Port Said. A cloud of sadness comes over the ship this morning as the sick one has passed away during the night.[6] This, the first in the battalion for England's cause, it makes one ponder on how many more and who will be the next. The most heartfelt sympathy was expressed by all the ranks for his bereaved relatives in Taunton, especially the young widow.

On our right lay the low coast of Egypt and the town of Danyetta and at 11 a.m. we were passing the light called Pharos at the entrance to Port Said and the Suez Canal. A large convoy was in the harbour with troops aboard, which eventually formed the famous 29th Division at Gallipoli. The Tommies aboard were now lining the sides as we were and many a bit of repartee and wit passed, such as "Where are you bound?" and the answers "Burma"; reply "Then God help you." This was from the Munster Fusiliers who had left Rangoon and whose place we eventually took. Another from the 4th Worcesters, whom we had to relieve at Meiktila and Shwebo, telling us we were going the wrong way. Our thick khaki serge, topped by topees without puggarees elicited various

6. Private E.C. Williams of Taunton, who died early in the morning and was buried the next day in the English cemetery beside a Private Williams of the 2nd Highland Regiment.

remarks which were not to the credit of the issuing authorities, but then we knew no better and the others did.

Port Said is a place full of interest but filthy dirty. Flies, well we had our first taste of them here; dirt and filth were everywhere. Bumboats were soon around us, plying their trade by the means of baskets and twine and only a very few men were allowed on board. We supposed they had squared the Quartermaster somehow. Our mails were landed and a few of us were allowed ashore. When night fell we were still moored to the buoys, with no sign of moving yet and understood that we had to coal before proceeding.

Christmas Day, December 25th 1914 found us at the same spot. The first thing to note this day is the funeral of our late comrade. Arrangements were made in the morning and he was buried in the afternoon. RIP. At dinner that day things did not go at all well. While we were feeding and gracing who should show themselves on the lower deck but the Colonel and Quartermaster and enquired about the food. A general murmur of disapproval was heard. The Quartermaster looked round and said, "Why this, you are feeding a damn sight better than you do in your own homes." One Tommy, whose voice we well knew, but who could not be seen by the officers, answered, "What do you mean, that we were ruddy well brought up in the workhouse?" and they did. No Christmas duff came our way after that. We were given to understand that the Dorsets, on the deck above, pinched it as they had a double ration. But some of us were of the opinion that our share was sold to their Quartermaster.

The rest of the day passed quietly, but as we were about to do some carol singing on deck in the evening they started coaling the ship. What a row, why, the coal heavers, all asiatics swarmed from the lighter alongside, entering one door in the side of the liner with baskets of coal on their shoulders and out of another with the baskets empty. We noticed one peculiar individual amongst them – at first we took him for a down and out European, but later came to the conclusion that he was an Albino. The coaling started about 7 p.m. and finished about 1 a.m. [7] For us who slept near where the black diamonds were dumped down the chutes to the bunkers, there was no sleep; so nearly all of us adjourned to the upper deck and lay down for a doze where we could. About a dozen still stayed down below, and in the morning their mothers wouldn't have known them. Neither should we, if it hadn't been for the uniforms they were wearing. Every part of the vessel near the chutes was covered in a black filthy mess of coal dust; a thing to be experienced before believing. We were also supplied with fresh water, but that was no trouble; hose pipes being laid on the water pump from the lighters to our tanks. The numbers of troopers, liners and tramp steamers that we saw in an almost endless procession all day and even during the night as well, truly gives this port the name of The Gateway to the East.

PTE B.G.L. RENDALL

As regards the climate, we left Southampton on a dirty, filthy, winter's night, the worst you could wish to have. Within three days we were in the sun which baked us, but we didn't know anything about it. It just got warmer and warmer, drier and drier. We could look back towards England and see the massive clouds about. We were about one hundred and fifty to two hundred miles away, it was like going to Majorca in the middle of winter and finding summer.

---

7. During which time 1200 tons of coal were loaded.

As we approached Gibraltar we handed in our field service caps, etc and we had the forage cap, a little side cap, similar to the type worn by the RAF. They were worn angleways, bow and stern as we used to call it. We also had deck slippers and were issued with these white knicks and singlets. We queued down around the ship and got our suit of this and wore it with a thin khaki shirt with epaulettes where you wore the shoulder badges. Ours was 2/5th SLI, T (Territorials) and also a badge. We also transferred these badges to our forage caps.

We arrived in Port Said and on the way, it was broad daylight about 4 or 5 o'clock in the afternoon, when all the excitement was on. There was a lot of floating rope about on the ocean bed and we couldn't make this out. Our ship ploughed on through and we stopped engines and her own weight took her on for the next four or five hundred yards. The mystery was solved. We were looking down about one hundred and fifty feet. There was a sunk French Destroyer with bodies still wedged in the rigging. She'd been sunk a few days before, some said by the first German submarine that got round there in the mouth of Port Said, some said a German sub but they weren't going by there then; some said by overpowered boilers. Either way, eight to ten feet of mast was still above water. The rope was various mooring ropes kept aboard for use fore and aft.

We anchored and everything was quiet, not a sound. On the other side of the bay, almost a mile, right against the quay was another troopship. Then a voice called out, "Who are you?" we replied, "2/5th Somersets, 4th Dorsets, 4th Devons." They were the Worcesters. "Where are you off?" "Bournemouth." – "You're not going anywhere," between the two ships. We found out afterwards that she was the Guildford Castle. There was a lot of music and our ship joined theirs and the whole harbour echoed with thousands of soldiers. The ship was almost keeling over, the decks were packed with the weight of soldiers, almost two thousand seven hundred – two thousand nine hundred. We were overcrowded.

We had some food and it was getting dark. One of our pastimes was to fling pennies (we still had our English coinage), down into the sea and black kids would dive right under the ship and come up with the coin in his mouth or hand. My Dad had told me about this in the past. One of the crew flung a dinner plate down as hard as he could. But it rocked backwards and forwards under the surface, it took half an hour before we lost sight of it. This is what happened to the pennies and why it was so easy to retrieve them.

The Algerians, Turks, Arabs, any nationality you could name around the Suez, all had their boat loads of fruit which rolled alongside our ship like a native bazaar. Us kids were seeing this for the first time, they were below us and although they were loaded up we were still a good height away from them, about sixty feet. They would call "All on board this ship 2d., all on board this ship 2d.". We still had English money, ten shilling notes and such, but I had plenty of change. I picked out one particular boat which had some type of little oranges. I didn't then know the name of them. I called out to him for the oranges and flung some pennies down into the boat. At the bow end there were little, tiny baskets which held about twenty or thirty oranges. The chap would climb up very close with the oranges, which were really tangerines that had a very loose skin and the quarters just fell apart in your hands. The M.O. was walking around and took them all from me except two and said they were enough to give the whole regiment dysentry. Someone else had two bananas. We were told to eat them very steadily or we would be in the sick bay by nightfall. The rest of the oranges rolled along the deck.

In my father's day I heard him tell about the coaling boats. By the evening we felt as though we were being attacked by the savages of a foreign island. Why they waited until dark we didn't know, but they clambered over the ship like rats and used a bamboo-type scaffold similar to the ship's ladder which was called the Admiral's Walkway. There must have been forty or fifty coaling boats. We had orders to go below and shut down and hide everything possible. We realised the natives were leaving their boats and coming up in chains. Each had a coconut-oil lighter on the front of their heads, held on by some sort of tape. Each man had this light and there were thousands of them. Each boat held between ten and fifteen. Each had a sack of coal. They were chanting, "All–ah, All–ah". It was like Hell. About two hundred of them were around us, and all through the night they were letting the coal roll from one end to the other. She was blacked out. I shall never forget; we were in a black sandstorm. It was very fine, powdered, going down in a stream, hundreds of bags to the hour. It gave us some idea of the two thousand tons needed to make Bombay. Eventually, everything was over and all the junk was taken off the side and once more Port Said was sober.

We had no leave, we had to stay aboard. It was full of vice, disease and filthy corruption. It was Christmas, but we had nothing to celebrate on, we may have got a lump of plum duff from the cook, perhaps. They tried to make dumplings but you could play tennis with the damn things – nothing broke them.

The ship gave three blows to warn we were leaving. We turned and entered Suez. There is a place called Ismailia. There are two vast lakes there and I think through blunder, someone had entered the other end who had pref-erence, so we turned to the right (starboard) into what was called the Bitter Lakes, which were miles in diameter. It would take an ocean liner. You could go through the neck into the second one. The cause of the trouble was the Italian destroyer Guillihoi making her way through the Suez, and she was not to be turned back no matter what happened. We were in the Bitter Lakes roughly twelve hours.

There was a bang and a crackle and a roar and up opened the decks in the bows. Up from below came twelve barrels. They contained sour flour which couldn't be used. They had been overlooked from the last transport journey. They went over-board and it was thought that they would eventually float ashore. This didn't happen. Prior to the barrels going overboard there was talk about being able to bathe in the harbour. The Army authorities were stopped because small sized sharks, octopus and different kinds of fish were apt to be about. When the barrels were thrown overboard, we didn't know what it was, but it must have been some kind of shark, a pair of jaws closed around one or two of these barrels and they splintered to dust. It was like putting powdered cement in a pool of water, half will come back up with the dust, the rest slowly sinks. Whatever it was, porpoises or whatever, must have been very big to splinter a barrel (they were all three quarter sized ones) like that. For some reason the engines were stopped and we slowly cruised around because of these jaws that appeared to be stood upright and looked twice their normal size, their insides were blown out; we still didn't know what they were, but they weren't full size sharks. The sailors themselves didn't know what they were because we were ten to twelve miles in. The Suez led directly *to the sea so they could have come in just like a big ship.*

As we approached Aden, it was getting much hotter, down around the Gulf of Babel Mandeb, which is the entrance of the Red Sea to the Indian Ocean. We had to travel another two thousand miles across the Indian Ocean to Bombay. On reaching Bombay, about nine o'clock one morning, we had a short, snacky breakfast, as much as the cooks could get together. At twelve o'clock we left Bombay in four trains, all of us, officers the lot, just the SLI (we were disbanded from the Dorsets etc). After we had eaten our meal the trains ran right alongside of us. We went to a water tank at the other end of the quay to wash our cups up and then we fell in again. Companies A, B, C and D. Each company of 200 were split up into each of the four trains, which had six to eight coaches. We still didn't know then what was going on. But within an hour on these trains, driven by white and black drivers, we were off. Two, two and a half days later, stopping at various places and eating, we finished up in Calcutta, in a compound called Fort William.

When we landed in Calcutta we were put under canvas in the Maidan. This was our week's rest before we didn't know what. The Army announced that those who had not been innoculated/vaccinated would not be allowed into the city; "You will pass through an inspection post with the M.O. and don't try it. Anyone who is innoculated from the time I am speaking to eleven o'clock tonight, we're extending it, may go into the city and look around." Quite a few went and had it done, I remember I had it done but it didn't take. One or two of the poor fellows that had it done had three or four sores come up, as big as a one pence piece, and they were sometimes knocked off on board the ship in the crowd. These innoculations were for any type of fever abroad; to make you immune from typhoid, sand fly fever, enteric, and for when you went amongst the native bazaars; all that holocaust and mess where you could bring back anything from the Far East.

We didn't know much about Calcutta but there were a few regulars amongst the Lincolns in Fort William. The others had been sent to the mud and blood of France: they were on that trooper that we'd passed, the Guildford Castle.[8] We wandered around and saw exactly what you are seeing on the TV; we often stepped over a bloke, dead on the pavement or another one dying. They were dying in the roads and pavements just like flies.

In our party there was a young corporal of the Lincolns with us, (they'd been stationed in Fort William for over a twelvemonth preparatory to being sent back to England) who said, "The Black Hole of Calcutta is over here." We didn't know what he was on about. There were about eight to ten of us and we went up and there it was by the side of the pavement in a wall and by kneeling down you could get a perfect photo of it; ". . . wherein incarcerated 123 Europeans and only 23 came out alive."

We returned and after a break in Calcutta for a few days one morning we had a fright; I turned to the staff sergeant and remarked on the huge great ship alongside. He said it was only a small one and that a bigger one would be coming for me. With this the ship sounded and steamed on out, perhaps it had the wrong mooring. In came this great ocean liner and it was called the Thongwa. *It was years after I came home that I discovered that Thongwa was a town in Burma.*

8. A Union Castle liner, she was to meet the same fate as the *Ionian* in 1918.

*This was a Burmese named ship still owned by P & O.[9] All aboard
again but not quite for so long. We started boarding her at nine o'clock
the next morning, by eleven o'clock we were all aboard. No ammunition to carry, no shells to shove on, just our regiment and off we go.
By this time as a kid who'd never been on a ship before in his life, just
the same as my father, I began to wonder where the hell the world
ended. There I was already nine thousand miles out from England
and still going strong. (On the way down through the Red Sea I
didn't realise it at the time but I passed within fifty miles of Dad's
first old battlefield, Tel El Kebir. The first battle for Dad in the Sudan
in 1882.) Day came, night came, day came. Within a few miles of Rangoon.*

CQMS E.W. EWENS

Saturday December 26th 1914. We were up and about early, washing and
scrubbing and trying to make everything spick and span. This occupied the
whole morning and at 1 p.m. that day we cast off from our moorings and entered
the Canal, passing on our way the palatial buildings which are the headquarters
of the Canal Company. Things we saw now were very interesting to some of us.
The left bank going south appears to be nothing but a sandy desert, in fact it is
the Desert of Sinai. On the right was more vegetation, but not a lot and every
kilometre was marked. At various points there are what may be called sidings;
places cut out of the bank large enough to moor a liner to allow another
homeward bound boat to pass.

Another and very pleasing feature was the sight, at fairly regular intervals, of
the bungalows of the engineers employed on the upkeep of the canal. Some of
these houses were a picture in the arid wastes around, with flowers and well kept
shrubs such as you would never find in a much more cultivated and cooler
country. Sea planes and air planes (sic) were continually patrolling the canal and
reconnoitering the desert as the Turks were not far away. Again on the Eastern
Bank of the canal were encampments manned by Lancashire and Manchester
Territorials and native Indian troops. These were enclosed by barbed wire
entanglements; in fact these latter ran nearly the entire length of the waterway.
We grounded two or three times during our passage and with the electric
searchlight not working properly, we anchored about midnight off Ismailia in
the Bitter Lakes waiting for daylight. Phew – stinking hot, most of us slept in a
blanket on the upper deck to get some fresh air if possible.

Sunday December 27th. At daybreak we were up and stirring. Anchored
not far from us was a French cruiser. A hazy mist hung over the lakes and the
visibility was bad, but as the sun rose the mist disappeared, giving way to
exceptional clearness of the atmosphere and intense heat, which was not even
mitigated by a slight breeze. The water was like glass and reflected the sun's rays
and heat till it was almost dazzling. There seems to be nothing in this lower half
of the canal to break the monotony of desert sand and scarcely a rise in the
ground until we are approaching the Port of Suez, when barren hills are seen at
the back of the town, to us, going south, although they turned out to be the most
eastern shores of the Red Sea.

We reached the town at about 5 p.m. and stopped just off the port, putting
ashore the canal pilot and his crew. The ubiquitous bumboat was soon seen
alongside, but nothing doing as we were to start practically at once. This same

9. Actually owned by P & O's subsidiary; the British Indian Steam Navigation Co.

boat was nearly swamped as The *Ionian* gathered way at 6.30 p.m. Being in front of the accommodation ladder and coming under as it floated off, it was only the promptness of our crew in hauling up the ladder that saved it. Just in time as water was beginning to come over the side of the depressed bumboat. All's well that ends well and she, and her crew of two, floated away astern like a cork as soon as freed, amid many shoutings and recriminations.

On the passage to Suez we again had to moor in a siding to allow an Orient liner from Australia to pass. The sides of the boats did not appear to be more than about six feet apart – too close to be pleasant for vessels of this size but we, being stopped, and she going dead slow, perhaps there is not much reason for the alarm caused after all. It appears that homeward bound boats have the right of way and outward bound boats must receive their instructions as to when and where to tie up by signal from the bungalows mentioned.

As the day ended we were fairly on our road to Mandalay, steaming down the Gulf of Suez with Africa on our right, high barren and burnt out looking hills and Arabia, with Port Tewfik and its desert of low lying land on our left. The desert sand was like the waves of the sea, only still – no doubt caused by high winds at times. Everybody appeared to sleep on the upper deck now, to see the troops lying down and asleep it reminded one of sardines in a tin – all space on the deck and hatches being covered by recumbent, snoring humanity. No slave deck could have been packed more thickly.

Monday 28th.   The day broke fine and hot and by midday was unbearable. You must remember that we still had our 'Blighty' serge suits on. Awnings were rigged over the fore and aft well decks to protect the men from the sun's rays. The sea was just like a looking glass, hardly a ripple or breath of air, but such as was caused by the passage of the boat. We seem to be much nearer the Asiatic shore and toward midday a large mountain came into view on this side, which one of the crew informed us was Mount Sinai 50 miles away, but quite discernible on account of the clearness of the atmosphere. This brought back memories of our Sunday School days as we must have passed the spot in the Red Sea where Pharaoh and his host were engulfed, and the rugged mountain reminded us of Moses and the Ten Commandments and the water which the Israelites got in this desolate spot, by the smiting of the rock by the rod of Moses. Thinking of your past days, what wonderful memories those things are which you read of in the Bible then and never pictured correctly. Travelling and observing in the east gives one a different conception altogether of the scenes in the great book and thereby enables one to read with greater and broader views and more understanding.

The Isle of Sharon was next sighted on our starboard. The day passed away at last, but left its mark in the shape of insect bites. Where they came from goodness knows. Came aboard at Ismailia no doubt, skeeters, sand flies and that ilk.

Tuesday December 29th.   Another hot morning. Today the Island of The Brothers, low and very barren, was passed on our port side, with a lighthouse on the southern end of it. Pity the lighthouse keepers on a place like this, but how useful they are on a dark night. A British Man of War patrolling the Red Sea signalled us today but we did not get near enough to see her name, neither did we hear what the signal was. The troops are now wearing only their shirts and trousers – everything else discarded because of the heat.

The Medical Officers attached to the three battalions were busy with innoculations and vaccinations and looked as if they thoroughly enjoyed it with their tunics off and their shirt sleeves turned up. Everyone, officers and men who were not done before leaving Taunton had to go through it. Another good

9

10

11

12

13

4

AN UNKNOWN DESTINATION

9
The *Dunera*, Port Said,
Christmas 1914.

10
Over-crowding on board
the *Dunera*.

11
The usual monotony of
sea-life; nothing to do and
nowhere to do it. On board
the *Dunera*, December
1914.

12
Unloading at Port Said.

13
The tarpaulin bath on the
Dunera.

14
The *Ionian* steaming
down through the Suez
Canal.

concert tonight, by all aboard taking part. Our adjutant sang 'Thora' and 'On the Road to Mandalay' and the colonel gave one or two of his favourites including 'Out in the Open'. What a kind, fatherly gentleman he appears, not a bit like the martinet one expects as a Commanding Officer. But this must not be forgotten – we are only Territorials called up at our country's need – amateur soldiers, not soldiers by profession, but still keen on doing our best with as much esprit de corps as any regular battalion that ever left England. Intent on doing our bit and share wherever we were sent, to uphold the name of Somerset.

Wednesday 30th December.　Not much happened today. The usual monotony of sea life with nothing to do and no room to do it in. The wind freshened and made quite a choppy sea, but by this time we were pretty good sailors and welcomed the cooling breeze. It was dead ahead, and so cooled the 'tween decks nicely and made things more bearable. A bit more arm drill today for the NCOs, on the sacred promenade deck for some, on the boat deck above again for the sergeants under the Regimental Sergeant Major. This boat deck was also used as a guard room for the men on guard and thankful they were for it because in this spell of four hours on duty they were allowed to full range of this deck and it was also allowed for use by the sergeants instead of mixing too much with the troops in the well deck.

Thursday 31st December 1914.　Still very hot, more than half a gale blowing and a good sea running. Tonight is New Year's Eve and a few sergeants were successful in getting an extra pint or two today, stored away for later in mess tins to enable them to toast the New Year at midnight when five bells were struck on the ship's bell. They then retired to their hammocks and a bit of horseplay went on, some of the hammocks being cut down at the end and so depositing their inmates on the deck. Feet first as a rule although they sat down with a bump a second later.

Friday January 1st 1915.　The day broke fine; a very beautiful sea again, like a mill pond. At 7 a.m. we were in the Straits of Babel Mandeb and passing the Island of Perrin. Not a large place by any means but a certain amount of verdure was discernible. The first we had seen since leaving the Suez Canal. A large tramp steamer was leaving the harbour as we passed. The Isle appeared fairly low behind it, with a large lighthouse and buildings. A large shark now trailed behind our boat, its dorsal fin was plainly seen at times. He followed quite halfway across the Arabian Sea. We supposed it was the same one as he was always about the usual spot astern. At noon we bore in towards Aden, of which at 1 p.m. we got a passing glimpse. Another pudding basin, a small opening to the sea between two high cliffs, one on each side, it gives the appearance of being strongly fortified with a fort occupying a spur of land commanding the entrance.

We had a good view of HMAS *Sidney*, just inside the harbour, plainly seen with the naked eye. She had just been on escort duty with the Australian troops we passed in the canal and had returned to coal and revictual at Aden. She bore no marks, as far as we could see, for her recent scrap, the smashing up of the notorious sea raider *Emden*.　This　was　six weeks previously, not a pleasant place this to have to reside in for duty, weatherwise. Nothing but a baked, dried up cinder was the impression it gave us and we were thankful it was not to be our destination. A lot of our fellows said it was the last place created, but others said it was the first because of the improvements shown in the other places we had passed. Shoals of flying fish were seen today. They are about the size of a small mackerel and appear to skim the surface of the water with the help of large fins for so small a fish and then plop back underneath again. These and the porpoises have now become our everyday escort, with the sinister gentleman astern.

Sunday 2nd.   What beautiful mornings here in the Indian Ocean. The sea with a slight swell on, not enough to rock the boat, just a gentle sway on her, blue-green colour; the sky also blue towards midday, turning to a steely blue, which to the onlooker looks like heat and a nice cool breeze blowing which tempers the day as the awnings act as a draught. It was three weeks ago we left Taunton and now approaching the 5,000th mile from home. Far away on our southern horizon Cape Guardofui is noticeable, but only in outline as the distance is so great, and further to the east the Island of Socotra. The day passed as usual with our escort still with us. Beautiful moonlit nights.

Sunday 3rd January.   Much cooler now than the Red Sea and perfect weather. By the records again the Somersets were supposed to have been issued with their khaki wear for India today, but not so. We received it later on Calcutta Maidan. Divine Service was held in the morning, our colonel again conducting the service. In the afternoon, no doubt because it was Sunday, another boat drill farce. It makes one shudder to think what would occur if anything unforeseen was to happen such as a collision or fire. Homeward bound boats passed today and salute us. And so another day of rest ends on our 'Cook's Tour' as the voyage is now dubbed on board.

Monday 4th January.   Still rolling across the Arabian Sea and this day passed uneventfully. We discovered that a large bath had been rigged up towards the stern of the boat near the galley. It was made of an immense tarpaulin and you had to climb in over the sides. This was a treat and there appeared to be occupants in it all day. It was quite a refresher. One of the Company Sergeant Majors aboard, who did not care for the troops to see him in his natural uniform or bare skin, took a dip about midnight to the amusement of the guard. He was not aware that they were enjoying themselves at his expense. Medical officers were still busy with innoculations etc, and also another inspection today, in one door of a cabin, and out another, re-adjusting your dress, what there was of it.

Still the porpoises and flying fish and our usual companion, waiting like Mr. Micawber for something or somebody to 'turn up'. Another fine concert at night with community singing. We fairly lifted the roofs (awnings, I mean).

Tuesday 5th.   Much the same as yesterday. In fact all early mornings seem alike in this latitude. We are now 18 degrees above the equator and have risen 6 degrees since we left Perrin, which is about 12 degrees north. Our wireless seems silent since we left Suez – why? Is the war finished or are there no stations this way from which we may hear any news. We had a few showers of rain in the morning, which were welcomed as it cooled everything on top deck a bit. Another grand sunset tonight due to the few rain clouds about.

Wednesday 6th.   Still rising slowly north of the line. It does not appear at all certain as to whether we are bound for Burma or somewhere else, as we have had no instructions about disembarking at Bombay. All troops aboard were very busy today, getting equipment in order. We were quite expert at the job now and spent most of the time polishing and cleaning. Rifles were still in the ship's armoury and would be taken out tomorrow. The Dorsets and Devons received definite orders to disembark but the 'sets were still in the dark as to their future. That Bengal Blanket, the sun was now setting once more and we expected to sight India later tomorrow afternoon. Everyone was keen to get a leg stretch after four weeks cooped up aboard. The officers on the promenade deck can have a walk about of quite 100 yards but we could not walk a step without dodging or bumping into somebody. The 6,000th mile out from home was passed this evening.

January 7th, Thursday.   Everyone up betimes, no laggards now as we were nearing land, but yet no sign, only the heaving sea. We understand that the convoy is still racing as to who will get in first and it appears we lead, with *Saturnia* astern, just above the horizon. In the late afternoon land became visible on our left, front first in soldiers' language, and later right in front of us. We were about 45 miles off and many glasses were brought to bear on the Brightest Jewel in the English Crown. But by the expressions passed the title did not seem to be borne out. We arrived in Bombay Harbour at about 8.30 p.m. Searchlights from the defences were continually playing on the boat on entering and as we got further in the brilliantly lit promenade, known as Bunder Abbas, was plainly seen. And so we anchored to spend our last night aboard, as we were given to understand, in the sweltering heat with no breeze stirring.

Friday January 8th.   The day broke awfully hot with the sun pouring down its rays unmercifully when it reached a very high altitude. Our view of Bombay was not very enticing. True there were a few palatial buildings on the side of the King Edward dock and a few could be seen further away in the city, but on that side we seemed to be shut out by the go downs and sheds on the wharves. Here, a conducting party from the 4th Worcesters left behind to show us the ropes, informed us that we had to disembark and proceed across India by train to Calcutta. At once we were all hustled and rifles were re-issued from the armoury and the men were strictly enjoined, shortly before leaving the ship, to take what rifles were found lying around as it appeared possible that some of our men, in the haste and bustle, would leave them behind. This collecting of rifles, we understood, was left to number 3 Company as our comrades in other companies were in the act of landing, leaving the Dorsets and Devons on board to disembark later.

By now we were proceeding slowly to our discharging dock, with the help of tugs. At 2 p.m. the actual work started and the baggage parties were told off for various jobs, unloading and transferring luggage, ammunition and the necessary, and in some cases unnecessary, impedimenta of officers. Something was wrong ashore as it was almost impossible to make our way to the train in a siding adjoining the dock on account of the crowd of hawkers around our fellows, but we did get ashore at last and onto our train, not forgetting our orders re rifles, and upwards of fifty men walked ashore with two. When the RTO gave us permission to proceed, it was quite dark and 8.30 p.m., so we were not able to see much of Bombay. But one good thing to the eye was the vegetation and palm trees that we occasionally got a glimpse of, by the aid of arc lights nearby. We were on a train, coaches supplied by the Great Indian Peninsular Railway, but we took, after leaving Bhosaval, the Bengal–Nagpur route.

Our first stop was at Kalyan Junction, of which more anon, to change engines to a special 'Ghat' type engine, here attached to the train for the climb over the Western Ghats. The view over this range in the daytime must be exceptional and for those that kept awake there would be the full tropical moonlight; and then we turned in. The coaches consisted of compartments as in England, with corridors on entering, one seat each side. Just above, suspended by chains from the roof and hinged to enable it to be folded up flush with the side in daytime, is another rack for sleeping on. Five to a compartment, two on the seats, two on the racks and one on the floor. The sanitary arrangements were awful, consisting of a recess and a hole cut out of the floor in the coach and no water. Sometime during the night the engine was again changed and we arrived at Bhosaval Junction for breakfast. Our first Indian cooked meal. The journey across India was uneventful; except for lack of water. As we got to a station scores would leave the coaches and make a raid on any water about; it was a marvel several did not suffer from typhoid. It was an everyday occurrence for about 20 of us to shave in half a pint of pawnee and no wash.

At Raipur on the Sunday afternoon, there were some horse troughs outside the station at which we stopped and in no time the place was alive with half-naked Terriers with towels enjoying the souse up. This shortage of water was obviated latterly by the Sind Desert Affair.

On Sunday 4 June 1916 a troop train left Karachi to cross the Sind Desert for Peshawar on the North West Frontier. Daytime temperatures in the desert in June reached 130°F; at night it cooled to 105°F. The troops were packed into old third class native coaches with corrugated tin roofs, thirty eight to a carriage. They could do no more than sit, there was no room to lie down or move around. There were no punkahs, no ice and the only water available to the men was that in their water bottles.

When the train pulled in at Rhori Station on Tuesday 6 June a large number of the soldiers were sick and some were dying of heatstroke. Seven had died on the journey and their bodies were decomposing in the vicious heat. More men died on the next leg of the journey, despite punkahs having been obtained at Rhori. A carriage was set aside as a mortuary.

On its arrival at Montgomery, ice was obtained and urgent telegraphic messages raced ahead of the train. At Lahore a team of medics and nurses bundled the sick men off to the cantonment hospital. More of the sick and dying were taken off further along the line at Rawalpindi. Still more were removed on the train's arrival at the ultimate destination of Peshawar.

Altogether thirty-seven men had died and between 300 and 400 were badly affected by heatstroke, many of whom never recovered their health and died later in India. The affair was the result of totally inadequate arrangements by Staff Officers with regard to the provision of ice, water and punkahs. The military authorities later tried to hush up the catastrophe, even suggesting that the soldiers had brought it on themselves by being drunk.

CQMS E.W. EWENS

The country we are now in is full of interest, tea plantations at Nagpur, cotton, paddy, sugar cane fields and an immense amount of jungle and very little grass. The land after passing the Ghats has been fairly level, with rises here and there. At 2 p.m. on Monday 11th February we arrived at Nagpur. This town is to the Bengal–Nagpur Railway what Swindon is to the Great Western Railway. We were expecting to reach Calcutta before night. Here a wire overtook us asking for the number of rifles we had taken with us, as the Dorsets were about 50 short on landing. It eventually transpired that we had 48 or 49 too many, which belonged to them. That was our repayment for pinching our Christmas duff at Port Said. 'C' Company said nought and handed them over to the QM for return to their rightful owners.

Scores of animals, strange to us, were seen daily, including baboons who raced the train for a mile or two, samburs, jackals, zebus and draught oxen and the ever present pariah (dog). Birds of different plumage and hues, and last but not least, the natives in their many coloured saris, but mostly of white cotton.

We arrived at Howrah station at about 6 p.m., detrained and marched over the famous Howrah Bridge, built of pontoons, which rises and falls with the tide in the Hooghly, and headed by the band of the 10th Middlesex marched to our camp about two and a half miles away through the streets of the capital to the Maidan at Fort William and into tents for a few days.

The sergeants of the Middlesex entertained our sergeants that night in their mess and should this happen to catch the eye of one of our hosts please accept our thanks once more for such a meal. It is praised often now when reminiscences are being spoken of amongst us. That fact and the years between will show how it was appreciated.[10]

10. One of several instances in CQMS Ewens' account which seem to indicate that he intended it to be published in some form. His son and grandson know nothing of the origins of the account or Ed Ewens' intentions in writing it.

4

THIS IS BURMA

'This is Burma, and it will be quite unlike any land you know about.'

RUDYARD KIPLING. *Letters from the East* (1889)

THE BATTALION WAS to spend nearly two and a half years on garrison duty in Burma. Nowadays Burma is an independent and insular Socialist Republic, but in 1915 Burma was a backwater of the British Empire. The British had annexed the country in three stages, each with its inevitable small war; the First Burmese War of 1824, the Second of 1852 and finally gaining overall control of the country after the Third Burmese War of 1885. From then, until the country was granted its independence in 1948 Burma was ruled by Britain as an adjunct of Imperial India.

Burma lies to the south of India and China, sandwiched between the two, with its long coastline stretching down the Bay of Bengal towards Malaysia. To the east lie Thailand and Laos with Kampuchea and Vietnam close by. Burma is dissected by the great Irrawaddy River, which runs north–south for almost the entire length of the country, emptying into the Gulf of Martaban and the Andaman Sea. The Irrawaddy Valley forms the bulk of the country's land mass, for to the west, north and east there are mountain ranges which form a horseshoe cutting the country off from its neighbours.

The climate is tropical and ranges from comfortably warm to almost unbearably hot and humid, especially for Europeans not yet acclimatized to such weather. There are three identifiable seasons; the hot season which runs from February to May when temperatures of up to 114°F occur. Then from May until the end of October the monsoon rains fall, but it remains very hot. Lower Burma is generally wetter and more humid than the northern plains, which get the higher temperatures. Then, from November to February, it is cooler and dry, with average temperatures being about 60°F.

In 1915 the population of Burma was comprised of the indigenous, mongoloid Burmese, who accounted for about 70% of the total and a number of minority groups who tended to inhabit the mountainous regions, away from the plains and the south of the country. These groups included the Chins, Karens, Shans and Kachins. There were also large numbers of Indians who had drifted into

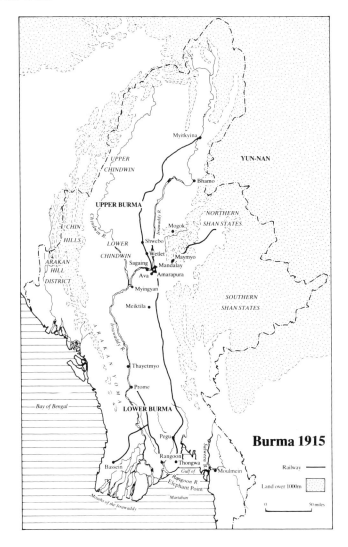

Burma since the British assimilated it into their own country; and also a number of Chinese.

Burma shared the same administrative system as India after the British abolished the Burmese Monarchy following the Third Burmese War. The country was divided into roughly forty districts each handled by a deputy commissioner. The deputies relied on the Burma Police and the army, to back them up should their authority be challenged by force. The army in Burma also came under the direct control of the Indian Government. The military structure of the Indian Army in 1914 had its headquarters at Simla. Its Commander-in-Chief was General Sir Beauchamp Duff and he had at his disposal 75,000 British soldiers and 150,000 Indian sepoys. These were divided into two armies; the Northern Army with its headquarters at Murree and the Southern Army which was based at Ootacamund. The Southern Army was comprised of five divisions; 1 4th (Quetta) Division;[11] 2 5th (Mhow) Division; 3 6th (Poona) Division; 4 9th (Secunderbad) Division. 5 Burma Division.

The Southern Army was under the overall command of General Sir J.E. Nixon with Burma Division having as its Commander, Major General T.D. Pilcher. Major General H.A. Raitt took over this post early in 1915 for the rest of the war.

Prior to the arrival of the 2/5th Somerset men, there were three regular battalions of British infantry in Burma and two companies of artillery; 4th Worcesters, 1st Border Regiment, 1st Royal Munster Fusilliers and two companies of the Royal Garrison Artillery. Before the Great War each regiment of the British Army normally had two regular battalions, one at home and one on station abroad, usually India.

Somerset men were not unknown to the Burmese, the 13th Light Infantry had fought there in the First Burmese war where they gained the battle honour of 'Ava'. They were there again as the 2nd Battalion Somerset Light Infantry in the war of 1885. But why were they sent there in the last days of 1914? Although the British Army in India and other parts of the Empire had its numbers cut to a minimum in order to reinforce the Western Front and other active theatres, it was unlikely that the political and military authorities would leave the far flung reaches of the Empire ungarrisoned. So the 2/5th were to find themselves in a peculiar position; in a war for which all their men had volunteered and which was to claim the lives of up to a million British and Commonwealth soldiers, they were to spend the whole war without firing a shot at the enemy.

The battalion left Calcutta and crossed the Bay of Bengal on the S.S. *Thongwa*, again the men were packed onto a ship of inadequate size and the journey across to Burma was an uncomfortable one. In the approaches to Rangoon the battalion was transferred to an Irrawaddy River Flotilla (effectively a paddle steamer with two flat barges attached to it) for the journey up to Northern Burma. Near Prome the 2/5th lost their second soldier; Private Fred Board of Dowlish Wake who was drowned in the main stream of the river when the men were allowed in for a bathe. February 1 1915 saw the battalion reach Meiktila where its HQ was established with 'B' and 'C' Companies. The remaining two companies proceeded up to Shwebo, a jungle station some 40 miles north of Mandalay. However, 'C' company was not destined to remain in Meiktila for very long; for on 16 February, 'C' and 'A' Companies were ordered down to Rangoon to replace the King's Shropshire Light Infantry which had been sent to Singapore where some disturbances had broken out.

Meanwhile, Ed Ewens had not yet reached Burma; at Calcutta he had been picked out for a musketry training course. Along with four officers and three other sergeants he had gone to Satara in India. He rejoined his company six weeks later, sailing from Madras to Rangoon where he unexpectedly found 'C' Company, (having expected to rejoin his comrades in Northern Burma).

CQMS E.W. EWENS

On Wednesday this week four officers and four sergeants were told off to attend the musketry course at Satara and would be likely to proceed at any moment. The four

---

11. This division included the regular 2nd Battalion Somerset Light Infantry.

15

THIS IS BURMA

15
'C' Company, the 2/5th Somerset Light Infantry, Rangoon, 1915. The Signal pagoda can be seen in the background.

16
CQMS E.W. Ewens. (2nd row from front, 8th from right.)

17
Private B.G.L. Rendall. (4th row from front, 7th from left.)

18
Private E.M. Chant. (4th row from front, 5th from right.)

sergeants, one from each company, were fitted out by the Quartermaster and made to look presentable. Later the rest of the battalion were issued their khaki drill and puggarees. It made them look much smarter indeed and they felt more like soldiers then before in their topees and English khaki serge.

The next day, January 14th the Satara party left late in the afternoon; four officers, four sergeants and four bullock carts with baggage, not one eighth of which was the NCOs, but they were told off by the Quartermaster to escort the carts, one to each, with fixed bayonets. They learnt different afterwards, but such were the amateur soldiers imposed on at times by men who should have known better. Howrah was reached and the journey across India started again. We will follow the officers and sergeants for a while, leaving the rest of the battalion in camp. Allahabad and Jubbulpore were both passed and they arrived at Kalyan Junction on the Saturday morning, where they had to change for Poona. Baggage was got out and stacked on the platform and the sergeants were ordered to mount guard over the same, two at a time, two hours on, two hours off, while the officers went on a shooting expedition in the vicinity. We never heard they shot anything and the whole party entrained for Poona late at night, changed for the Satara road and eventually arrived at their destination via a tin lizzie and bullock tonga on Sunday evening.

Another party was sent to 'pindi for a course in platoon drill under the double company system, but did not benefit much as they knew as much as the West Ridings to whom they were attached because the new double company arrangements were not yet installed for the troops in India.

On arrival at Satara and having a good rest for a few days, they made themselves well acquainted with their surroundings. Later they were placed in squads under instructors, two of which, to their great delight were 2nd Somersets, Tibby Ryall and Bill Buckley, who were quite pleased to have their Terrier proteges with them. Old Bill, and one of our sergeants, won the four-hand billiards sweep in the mess and the same 2/5th sergeant walked away with the Satara Spoon for being the best shot on the course, which comprised officers and sergeants from nearly every unit of the army in India. This course was a Regular course and not the modified Terrier course which came later. All the Somersets passed out as fully qualified musketry instructors and, in six weeks, left again to rejoin their unit via Madras.

The country here is very hilly, seemingly like some gigantic eruption, hills in straight, basaltic columns to a great height. Hereabouts is also the Kistua, with burning ghats for the disposal of bodies which was an everyday occurrence. It was peculiar to see the natives bathing in the river and in their midst two Salvation Army lassies from home. About 1½ miles west of the school were two Towers of Silence for the disposal of Parsee remains. Numerous weaver birds nests in this locality, with their bottle-neck entrances hanging earthwards. Here the Somersets experienced their first flight of locusts and also the Banyan tree with its innumerable trunks.

On the way to Madras, and near Arkonam Junction, for several miles the telegraph lines by the side of the railway were covered with thousands, nay millions of swallows, no doubt congregating for their migration northwards to cooler climes.

The battalion, meanwhile, had left Calcutta and proceeded to Rangoon on the B.I. Boat *Thongwa*, transferred there to a river steamer and two flats attached for the journey up the Irrawaddy, B & C Company to Meiktila, A & D Company to Shwebo. The sergeants at Madras were in Fort George waiting for a boat to Rangoon. Had a good look round, especially at the damage done by the *Emden* at the oil tanks and harbourmaster's house, which was hit clean in halves. The oil tanks were nothing but a heap of scrap now.

Left on Monday, no officers' baggage guard now for the sergeants, they had learnt something from the regulars at the school. By the *Fusalla*, not sorry to get away as Madras is by no means a picturesque place and extremely hot and uncomfortable. Plenty of flying fishes around in the Bay of Bengal and one little yarn of the crossing; one evening the sergeants were sitting by an open skylight smoking and the saloons below were laid with officers' dinner. Directly they came in and took their places. They were in full view of the sergeants who, in the darkness, could not be seen above and the native bearers started serving the khanah. After a little while, one officer, who was born in India, but left at an early age, was trying to practice his knowledge of the Hindu language on the Tamil boy. The boy looked very dull and stupid and made the 2nd lieutenant wild; the other gentlemen began smiling. Presently the bearer could not stand it any more and quietly and politely said in good English; "Sahib, if you speak English I will understand," to the consternation of the young lieutenant and the general laughs of his companions and the three-striped wallahs about the skylight.

Friday morning early the Andamans were passed and soon after the current of a great river was noticeable in the sea, although quite ten hours from the main. The *Fulsalla* arrived in Rangoon River, one of the mouths of the Irrawaddy, just at dark and anchored there for the night to await the tide. Weighed anchor at sunrise and proceeded upstream, low lying banks covered with bamboo and jungle clumps on both sides and as they neared Choka Fort the immense dome of the Shwe Dagon Pagoda came into view, like burnished gold in the morning sunlight and later as Syriam was reached the whole low lying parts of Rangoon could plainly be seen.

What a sense of the East. Great ocean liners, tramp steamers, oil tankers at Syriam, Chinese junks in Pozoondaung, trigs taking in rice, the sampan with its queer bow and stern plying everywhere.

As they landed at the quay two officers and two sergeants were ordered to proceed to Sale Barracks, Rangoon, and the other four up country to their companies. This was a great surprise; we had no idea of any Somersets being down here. On rejoining them, the reason was known; the 126th Baluchis had mutinied in Rangoon native cantonment, and that had meant the bringing down of the 'sets two companies from up country. They had been safely rounded up and the revolt quelled. Seven ring-leaders were shot at Choka Fort, just over 100 were escorted to Thayetmayo Military Prison and later to the Andaman Islands, a penal establishment, and the rest and quieter ones disbanded.[12]

PTE B.G.L. RENDALL

> *The following night towards six o'clock the sun was dying down and we were then approaching the Gulf of Martaban, if you look at your map you'll find that's just outside of Rangoon. It's where the tributaries of the Irrawaddy river join the northern end of the Bay of Bengal, which we were travelling across. Here we spotted a brilliant colour, it was like the sun going down and, kid like, we said again to these blokes who had travelled time and again on these ships that we wanted to know what it was. One of them said it's what they call the Shwe Dagon Pagoda. It's a great golden temple in Rangoon, and we're still a good eighty to one hundred miles from Rangoon yet. We won't be pulling into Rangoon river until nine or ten o'clock tomorrow morning.*

The Shwe Dagon Pagoda, the centrepiece of Burmese Theravada Buddhism, rises 326 feet above Rangoon. Bert Rendall was later to while away seven years of

---

12. CQMS Ewens is confused on this point. He connects two unrelated events. The Baluchis had actually

19

THIS IS BURMA

19
'A' Company, the 2/5th at
Battalion H.Q., Meiktila,
1915.

20
Private Ernest Hillard,
Burma, 1915.

his spare time, during the Second World War and after, making an impressive model of the Shwe Dagon.

PTE B.G.L. RENDALL

We pulled into Rangoon river, in other words it was Rangoon Docks or in other words again, Bar Street Jetty. (Little did I know, but I was going to have more connections with that before I'd finished.)[13] We had another fright, we were not to go ashore and to our surprise a massive great barge was pulled up either side of us, attached to a river steamer and we had to transfer down through, over these two gangways, straight onto the river steamer. The second barge was then brought in next to the paddle-steamer's side. We weren't there more than half an hour when, chug, chug, chug, off starts the massive great engines and we were off four hundred and eighty miles up the River Irrawaddy, a thing of which I've never seen the likes of before.

Now and again the paddle wheels would catch a whirlpool on a bend and they simply skidded round just the same as a whirlpool, in the air. The wheels would go round, hit nothing, go right round, halfway perhaps, then the other wheel pulled her out and vice versa. We got up to a place called Prome which is just above the Yenanchoung Oil Wells where they allowed us to have a break. (The Japs fought so hard for it years after I left.)

At Prome they allowed us to go into the river and there was one hell of a bungle before we woke up to it. One of our blokes was caught out too far and he got caught in a quicksand, whatever they did he went down. There was no way out.[14] In the meantime I knew nothing of this, it was only the party that went to try to get in and have a bit of a bathe. They soon called them out when they realised. We had regular sergeants with us, but they had omitted to tell ours in charge that to do such a thing would be treacherous. It was done before these regular sergeants who were escorting us told us not to get in rivers.

CQMS E.W. EWENS

On proceeding up the river we unfortunately lost a man bathing, thus keeping up the native legend that, ". . .every English battalion that sails on the Irrawaddy has to pay the toll by at least one life lost." Whether or not there is anything in this superstition such events do happen but it was the general opinion that it was just as likely to occur anywhere else with such a large body of men. Considerable bravery was shown by our officers and men in diving to try and get him in this treacherous river of quicksands and eddies but all proved unsuccessful.

---

mutinied earlier than this in India, apparently in fear of being sent to fight in the war. They killed their major and other officers. The majority were sentenced to penal servitude for life and a number of them were being taken up country on one of the flats attached to the Irrawaddy River Steamer which was carrying the 2/5th. They were eventually dropped off at Thayetmyo. The mutiny at Singapore occurred on the 21 February 1915 when the Punjabi Muslim 5th Light Infantry and the 36th Sikh Battalion rebelled. The rising was firmly put down and thirty-seven Indian soldiers were executed, a further forty-one being transported for life.

13. Two years later Bert was to return here on his way to the North West Frontier.
14. Private Fred Board.

PTE B.G.L. RENDELL

*In the meantime I was wandering up the main street of Prome, a
flattened out dust track called a road, which led to a pagoda. On the way
there, there were all us kids, there were all these fruit stalls. I went up to
one and we'd learnt a little bit, and asked for some bananas (in the dialect).
In his broken English he said he wanted change. With the same I felt a tap
on the shoulder, one of the white engineers of the ship said not to have that
because there was 16 pice to two annas, and one anna is divided into eight.
Pice they called them. "You go over there and that white man there will
change all your Burmese money." I walked back with my handful of coins,
on average as big as one of our farthings or a halfpenny piece. I pointed to
them and he pulled the stalk down and there were about fifty bananas on this
stalk. I asked the engineer;" "What the hell do I do with this lot?" He said,
"You'll have to take them on board, he won't take them back. You gave
twopence for them and that bloody lot's yours, and don't forget half of those
are in the green. You won't see many of them, you've got a surprise coming."*

*We trundled back, me and my pal, up the gangway back on board ship.
"Oh yes, yes, yes, oh boys, we have some fruit now!" I was told to take the
two off that I wanted. We looked so sheepish. We were again told to take the
two that we wanted and the rest were certain death. Everyone was told to
help themselves, no more than two each. Clean it up and they did. They came
round like a shower of pigeons. However he was quite right; had I eaten
more than two of those it would have been disastrous. I wasn't fully
acclimatised, Christ knows what could have happened.*

*We were issued with Burmese currency on board the troopship. We were
coming across the Bay of Bengal and the English currency was still valid, but
we were changed into Indian currency as we had spent our English money.
As we spent English money, like a ten shilling note, we would be refunded on
board to that amount in Indian coinage. The money in Burma was all the
same as Indian because India and Burma were as one and the same to our
government. The Burmese coinage and the Indian coinage were all the same.
We had no shore leave, only one week's stop at Calcutta, but after that we
crossed the Bay of Bengal as I said.*

*From there we pulled into the Gulf of Martaban and without being allowed
to land we transferred straight to the river steamer. The whole of the regiment
went up the river towards Mandalay, right up the Irrawaddy, four hundred
and fifty miles to a place called Myingyan, forty miles from Mandalay,
further up. We started marching from Myingyan to a place called Meiktila
towards Mandalay. Then we went into wooden barracks at Meiktila. You will
find that's just above Mandalay the opposite side of the Irrawaddy River.*

5

SOLDIERING ON ISOLATED

'The War rolled on, like a storm beyond the horizon. The hot, blowsy country, remote from danger, had a lonely, forgotten feeling.'

GEORGE ORWELL *Burmese Days.*

PTE B.G.L. RENDALL

THE MIDDLE OF FEBRUARY 1915 saw 'A' and 'C' companies of the battalion installed as the British Infantry Garrison of Rangoon, the Burmese capital. Duties were to be strenuous for the Territorials, wartime reduction in troop strength throughout the Empire made this inevitable. The two companies of recently trained volunteers had taken the place of a full regular battalion of infantry which consisted of four companies. Consequently, there was a constant shortage of men for the various duties which had to be performed. This is reflected in the official photograph of 'C' Company, taken early in 1915 at Rangoon; out of the full company strength of 200 only 112 men could be mustered for the shot. The rest were on various duties, guards and in the sickbay.

A month after arriving at Meiktila we had orders for Rangoon, which was what we wanted. We went down to a place called Sale Barracks, Rangoon. Now Sale Barracks is named after a General Sale. They had Elphinstone Road named after General Lord Elphinstone, the hero of the Kabul Massacre – 1879. They had Parade Street named after Colonel Parade. It was a place never to be forgotten; always on garrison duty. Whenever we went and took over different barracks it was to give us all a turnaround. Again, not long afterwards I left to go to the North-West. We travelled by train from Meiktila to Rangoon. There were two different railways, one ran down one side of the river and the other went down the other side. We had to cross the river in order to transfer onto the other railway.

Whilst we were in Rangoon we had little news of the war; it was so far away and distant that it was only occasionally that we got smatterings of what was happening on the Western Front. We knew very little: we were practically clear of the war, about 9–10 thousand miles away, almost halfway round the world.

We never received English newspapers, but sometimes we got the Rangoon Times, *this was a company all over India and Burma. There was the* Calcutta Times, *the* Burma Times *and so on. It appeared to be one massive company that practically ran the Far East news. Occasionally it reported happenings on the Western Front, if there was a very big push.*

We had letters from home about once a month. When the troops came out they brought the mail with them. Whilst we were at Rangoon and the mail boat pulled in, a single gun was fired to let us know that the mailer, as she was known, had turned from the Gulf of Martaban into Rangoon River which, as I told you, is where we embarked on the river steamer. I had very few letters from home; I don't think I had half a dozen in all. The main three were from my girl at that time and you didn't expect much war talk from a girl. She was about 18 and it was only when I got back that I heard quite a few things about the war.

Whilst we were in Rangoon we felt really out of it. Just because there was a war in Europe didn't mean we could have one in Rangoon. We were really on a peace footing. But at anytime you could be back aboard a trooper and on the Western Front in no time. There was the gravest chance we could be sent back and we did hear about Kitchener's quote "Your Country Wants You" and he wanted at least 200,000 more men and we could hardly see our way clear with this kind of game: guarding the Far East. There wasn't only disillusionment amongst those of us who had enlisted. I don't really know how I felt. I would hardly say, "Take me back to France, dears and get me shot", could I? If you understand my meaning I wasn't going to ask to go to France, was I?

They had their chance when they shoved me aboard and down through the Bay of Biscay and off out. I had no say in where I went. There were 8/10 other regiments all over India and Burma, Sussex, Surreys, Kents, Wilts, with garrison duties. As I said before, my luck was well in as a kid just right for France, an able-bodied youngster, and there were quite a few more in the regiment posted out abroad.[15] We weren't going to stop the troopship in the Suez and say let's have a smack at the Turks, along with the Aussies and all those that were there. We weren't going to ask for the battlefield of war. Although I volunteered for Mesopotamia whilst I was in Rangoon, but for some unknown reason my name was lost off the list so really my luck was in. All our volunteers, twenty of them, all got caught with Townshend in Kut al Amara. They asked for volunteers, this was in about 1915. We were told that Turkey had joined in the scrap against us and the idea was to get around that area. I don't know why I volunteered, why do we do these silly things? Why did I join up? I have no answer.

CQMS E.W. EWENS

Early in 1915 saw our first draft leave for Mesopotamia. All volunteers, and if they could, the whole battalion would have gone. Out of the 40 that marched away, only two ever rejoined us, most gave up their lives before and during the siege of Kut al Amara. One who rejoined us was wounded at Shat al Arab and another was an exchanged prisoner of war whom the Turks captured with the notable garrison of Kut.

There was to be a constant demand on the soldiers of the battalion to provide

---

15. There were four other Somerset Light Infantry battalions in the Far East; the 1/4th, 1/15th, 2/4th and the regular 2nd Battalion.

volunteers for the various units in need of reinforcements throughout India and the Empire. This draft for Mesopotamia was to form the bulk of the battalion's casualties. They were attached to the 1st Battalion Oxford and Bucks Light Infantry and fought with them in General Townshend's advance up through Mesopotamia. On reaching the heavily defended Turkish position of Ctesiphon, Townshend retired to hold Kut al Amara owing to the large number of casualties suffered in the advance. There followed a long siege and eventually the garrison surrendered to the Turks. Of the forty volunteers from the 2/5th Somersets thirty became casualties or prisoners of war.

PTE B.G.L. RENDALL

We heard about Gallipolli whilst we were in Rangoon. We just heard smatterings of this, there were no war pamphlets to read or any official news of any sort. We soldiered on isolated. We weren't really worried because there was nothing we could do. We had no idea of what was going on. Occasionally someone would say, "Oh, they've knocked us back another 20 miles, right back to Arras". Nine out of ten of us didn't know where Arras was. We didn't know where they were when it was spoken about.

After a while in Rangoon, where we had quite a good time, I found my first scorpion. Me and another young sentry were on what was called No.2 post, there was a flat recess leading down the side of the Shwe Dagon Pagoda, like a platform of earth that we were on, with a little shelter, like a bus shelter. Every hour there was a call, "No.1, all's well, No.2, all's well," and so on. It was a moonlit night, typically eastern. The sentry with me said, "Did you see that?" I said "What," the grass moved, ". . . someone's in there", we didn't know what it could be in a place like this so he gave it a poke with his bayonet. Nothing happened. We continued to look at this spot, again the grass moved, we fixed our bayonets onto our rifles for extra length. My mate moved back, I moved as well and we poked until we found it.

At last, out of the grass came the loveliest black scorpion: the tail was up and he'd caught our bayonets. It was a dirty, vivid purple, a fair drop running down over the bayonets which were polished to the nines. The other chap gave the scorpion a tap. Wherever the bayonet went its tail struck, then there was a tap, tap, tap. "We'll have to kill the damn thing", he said. We took the bayonets off our rifles and hit the scorpion with the flats of our bayonets. He didn't seem to take any notice of it, all six legs were moving perfectly and he looked ready to start. The tail was up 4 or 5in. easily, a full grown scorpion. Wherever we put those bayonets, within seconds he was facing them, we hit and hit the scorpion which looked like a black lobster and was just as hard. We had to find the join between the body and the head, we turned the bayonet edgeways and after a few attempts took the head nearly off. The back part of it still reversed into the grass. The head went forward on two legs and just fell over. The sight of that thing, Tommy or not, gave me nightmares. All the time you felt it was a poison about to spring; it was a weird feeling.

CQMS E.W. EWENS

March 3rd 1915. We were turned out by an alarm at 2 in the morning. Something wrong in the native quarter. From the time the alarm sounded until we marched away fully equipped but not clothed, took eleven minutes. We saw nothing of it, being detailed for the defence of the brigade office and the arsenal. One of our officers in flourishing his revolver, waving it up and down in his excitement, lost it. It was never found again. Jolly good job it was not a man's rifle.

Duties in Rangoon were heavy. Here you had a half battalion of inexperienced Terriers doing duty for a full battalion of regulars whom we relieved. In fact we relieved the King's Shropshire Light Infantry who took over from the Munsters and when we arrived from up country they went on to Singapore.

Our men were one night on guard and one off to give you some idea; 'C' Company were for duty and at the parade that morning, (guard was always mounted at 5 p.m. overnight), was one corporal and two men. The officer commanding, after waiting 15 minutes, before he went onto the parade ground, looked into the company orderly room and said to the Company Quartermaster Sergeant, "Quartermaster Sergeant, where the hell is my company this morning?" Looking out of the window and pointing to the three men he said, "That is all that's left of them, sir." Officer Commanding, "Where are the others?" Quartermaster Sergeant, "On guard sir". Officer Commanding, "And that's that, tell them to dismiss", and it was done. The guards that had to be found were the arsenal, magazine and government house guards and, for a short while, one also for the treasury while the disturbances were on. The whole of 'A' Company for guard one day and 'C' Company the next and the inlying picket the day the company was off.

This fact surely accounted for the battalion's renowned smartness in guard mounting a few years later in India. We had been well schooled in the intricacies. One day 'C' Company was with the General Officer Commanding on the Maidan, the monsoons were now on. After waiting for an hour and then company drill for about two more in the alternate sunshine and rain and in heat that was suffocating, we were marched back to cantonments. On the way over twenty of our fellows dropped with dysentry and diarrhoea caused by the miasma from the ground.

Our cantonment at Rangoon was known as Sale Barracks, still a name connected with the Somersets and our badge: for was it not Sir Robert Sale in command when Jellalabad honours were gained? They are built on a raise and overlook nearly all the city, especially to the south and the east. The living bungalows were high, well ventilated for this climate, airy, being built on struts twelve feet above the ground to keep out the innumerable crawling devils that are about this place, snakes, great black and white ants, scorpions etc.

The Shwe Dagon Pagoda lies north of us, with only a road between so you may say we are in, and dominated by its shadows and size. This is an immense pile approached through an archway, the carving around which is most grotesque and elaborate, and standing between two leogryphs, up a flight of stone stairs, worn and polished like glass by the feet of countless pilgrims for hundreds of years to an inner platform, around which there are different shrines devoted to Buddhism. In the centre there is an enormous edifice like a great dome which tapers towards the top. Surmounted by the htee (umbrella) and its hanging golden bells, the whole over 300 feet high and covered with gold which is simply dazzling and wonderful in the bright sunlight and with the green foliage and the tall feathery coconut palms around its outskirts completes a picture which once seen is never forgotten.

The Royal Lakes in Dalhousie Park are another beauty spot in an eastern setting. Here the elite of Rangoon promenade in the cool of the evening listening to a first class band. Two boats are kept on the lake by the government for the troops in the cantonments and many a pleasant hour we spent on its water rowing when off duty.

We had not been in mess long before somebody thought that they would like a haggis for dinner one night, perhaps it was the mess secretary or the sergeant major. At any rate the bobberjee was told to get a sheep's innards clean and the way to cook it. The haggis was eventually dished up, cooked like a large football, all steaming hot. No one appeared to know the way to start carving it so Beefer said, "Here goes", and put his knife across and through it. Phew, everybody left the mess for fresh air. The native cook had only cleaned the outside!

The German spy scare was as bad at Rangoon as anywhere, several Germans being rounded up and sent to Ahmeduagar for internment. One day in the early spring two sergeants of the Burma Military Police arrived with a Jerry who was accused of inciting the natives in the Shan States and placed him in the guardroom. The sergeant in charge that night was of a windy nature and behind the guardroom the ground fell away rather steeply, a drop of about 40ft. to the road on which were electric lights. The windows of the cells overlooked this embankment and road.

After it was dark one of the guards noticed a light flickering like dots and dashes coming from the road. At once he notified the sergeant. He had a look and hearing a tap, tap, tap, tap, tap, formed the opinion that someone was trying to signal to the man in the cells. He at once took a file of men and went down the dip to investigate and found a man up an electric light standard, flashing an electric torch and apparently tapping the standard. He arrested the man and marched him to the guardroom and placed him in the cell next to the German and would on no account listen to the man trying to explain. The sergeant in due course reported to the orderly officer who decided to wait until daylight. Sequel – devil of a row next morning. the man turned out to be a mechanic, sent to mend an important break and then, to his employers seemed to disappear into nowhere and the break was not mended. When the manager of the works called at the guardroom on the off chance that it was his missing employee, the language between the officer commanding the detachment, the manager and the sergeant was lovely. This caused a general laugh throughout the barracks and was the means of infernal leg pulling afterwards. The same sergeant now occupies a piece of ground near Mesopotamia, which is and will be forever England.

We were extremely friendly with the European sergeants of the Rangoon Police and were welcome visitors to their mess in Moghul Street. Sammy and Joe were returning from there one day to go on duty and, being pushed for time and no taxis about, hired a rickshaw. It was a long pull back to barracks,and being uphill the rickshaw puller couldn't make much pace so Sammy, a bit of a Barbary wallah, cut him across the stern with his cane and the next instant Sammy and Joe were on their back in the dust, which was inches thick. The rickshaw man let go of the shaft and scooted. A good job for him he couldn't be seen when they arose and shook the dust out of their eyes, otherwise two sergeants would have been late for parade. They had to walk back, and as it was arrived just in time to clean up and turn out.

The food at Rangoon was by no means good and often not palatable and this caused a round robin signed by 96 privates of 'A' Company being sent to their commanding officer. These men were at once ordered the Orderly Room and given three days confined to barracks. At 6 p.m. defaulters call that evening they were there to answer their names on till 9 p.m. It proved to be such a farce. Provost Sergeant was at his wit's end the next day, it was washed out.

Not long after this, a few months in fact, the messing allowance for all Terriers in India was raised by another 3*d*. per day. Thanks to the agitation in the house by the late Lord St. Audries. Was it possible that his son, the present Lord, who was with us as an officer, had something to do with this? For it was our opinion. We may have been wrong.

Company training was at somewhat of a discount in Rangoon on account of the multifarious duties to be done. Besides the guards mentioned before, men were supplied for various signalling and other duties at different points of the Rangoon River down to its mouth at Elephant Point around 25 miles away. Soccer football was played and 'C' Company entered the Burma Junior Cup and won it. Medals may now be seen around Yeovil with the Shwe Dagon Pagoda on the obverse of them. Senior football here was quite good stuff but very little rugby, which was the forte of 'A' Company, Taunton.

It was with great regret in June 1915 when the instructors from our regular battalion the 2nd (Prince Albert's) Somerset Light Infantry, received orders to rejoin their unit. These good fellows had been attached to us for about six months and generally liked. They not only instructed in all phases of company drill but helped considerably in every other way – running of the sergeants' mess, canteen, sports etc. The night before they sailed for Calcutta they were entertained to a farewell dinner in the mess. It was a memorable occasion. They were known to us as Reevo, Ernie Powies, Billy McLeod, Flossy Todd, Charlie Poore and Duffy Moore, although the latter was ill most of the time and in dock. He was nonetheless appreciated and they must have taken a great interest in their Terriers.

Towards the end of our stay in Rangoon a few sergeants of the 13th London Rifle Brigade were attached to us on their way to the Andaman Islands for garrison duty. They were all old soldiers from the National Reserve at home. The RB's have more honours than any other regiment in the British Army and the same is reflected on their badge. Pat picked up the cap belonging to one of them one night and said, "Why, all these honours, Sidney Street Siege, South Wales Coal Strike?" He got no further – they were all on him like a ton of bricks and a rugby scrum ensued for possession of the cap, but all in great part.

PTE B.G.L. RENDALL

The barracks at Rangoon weren't near the centre but at the far end away from the city. A city I'll never forget. The first time we went down we had to go across the entrance of the Shwe Dagon Pagoda, one and a half miles down the Strand where you turned in any of the side streets which you cared to name and jump off. All trams were free. On the way down you passed the Soldiers Home, the YMCA and the YCA (Young Christian Association.) In either one of those you could have a walloping good supper for two annas as a Tommy, a civilian would pay 20. Everything was run by the English, with native help. There was a white supervisor, male or female or perhaps a pair, over the lot who had their own quarters up over. In some rooms there were a couple of lovely billiard tables, but there was enough going on in the city not to worry about that for a bit.

They had four or five different cinemas there: the Empire, Cinema de Paris, Globe, Elphinstone and the World. One of which was a playhouse where the Burmese girls would come and dance, stark naked. I don't need to tell you

22

23

SOLDIERING ON
ISOLATED

21
CQMS Ewens, on the right, with CSM Gibbs, Rangoon, 1915.

22
Private Arthur Hinder.

23
Lance Corporal William Hillard, 'C' Company.

24
A machine gun section, Meiktila, 1915.

the rest do I? For a little bit extra you could go out the back when the show was over. We were allowed to go into Rangoon when we were off duty, there were no restrictions but we had our Red Caps who were the military police. It was the case then when a private could arrest a sergeant, if he had gone too far, e.g. a drunken fool who had started to knock the natives about.

They had the Royal Lakes where we had the boats of the Regiment, they had Victoria Gardens, they had Cantonment Gardens where the Band of the Inniskilling Fusiliers played wherever the crowd was largest. They were really weird lakes. You went under a mass of pretty little bridges and you had to lie down to go under several. It was a very pretty place, so clear was the water, the grass grew to two or three feet on the banks. It wasn't rotten or stagnated. We had our own boathouse and when our regiment came to Rangoon, the badge of the last regiment was cleaned off and the badge of the Somerset Regiment was put on each side of the bows. There were four boats and never once did we quarrel. Those boats were always in use and we got on well. What we often used to do was get a bloke who had no ear for music, except for tin can muck of the day and he would row three or four of us out in the boat, bring it back again and pick up another party. Or, if another boat was in, another party would come across. We'd get up on these little islands round the bandstands and sit in lovely seats.

In Victoria Park there was a massive great statue of Queen Victoria with a lovely chain guard all round it only 150 yards from the barracks. We used to go down the back end of the barracks and we were there.

There was a large shop in the Strand called Whiteaway and Laidlaw and they sold everything possible from gramophones upwards and I personally met a Whiteaway man. I was in Rangoon Gardens by myself and a lady came along. She was the wife of the Bishop of Rangoon, but I didn't know. She asked my how long I had been out there and how was I faring. I replied that it was my first year. She asked me to tea but I declined and we were approached by Mr Whiteaway and he joined in our conversation. I realised that instead of being in the mud and blood of France I was, in comparison, on a picnic, but I couldn't help that could I?

I was talking to this Whiteaway, and not mentioning the regiment's name, but at that time, years before I had ever seen or heard of Burma, they had been discharged with ignominy out of a certain regiment, Whiteaway and Laidlaw. The lady suddenly got up and left, said she must be going and that it would soon be tea time at the barracks. Whiteaway asked what the state of it was over there. I told him it was a holocaust in France.

We were in Rangoon for nine months. I was there long enough to join Rangoon choir. The Bishop of Rangoon notified the Regiment that they could do with two or three men, could the Regiment do anything? Captain Ward Jackson was a good one and Captain Spurway was the son of a parson out at Petherton and this was just his cup of tea. So on a main parade they suddenly sung out; "Volunteers wanted for the church choir. Anybody who thinks he can sing can go down to Rangoon Vicarage." I was number one out of eight. We all went down, I was brought up in a musical house and I knew what music was. In no time I was tapped on the back and asked if I'd go back on Sunday. There were another two fellows from Bridgwater. That was the end of guard duties and sentry duties. Every Sunday we had a damn good spread before we had to go back to barracks. If we passed the guard room at 10 o'clock no one asked why we were late. Your guard duties started in the evenings, but I got out of these and so did the other two on the understanding, with our captain, that we went down and did the choir practice at the Cathedral, we just had to walk down there, it wasn't far.

Guard duty in the evening lasted from six to six. They used to pick out one guard that did no guard, he was the cleanest, best done up boy of the lot. They would then dismiss him, and that left the right number of guards, as it should be. They would pick this one out who was called a stick guard who would go back to barracks and have a comfortable night in bed. Next day you reported to the Orderly Room and ran about different parts of the barracks with notes and that type of thing; all the odd jobs. Besides that there were four men who came off duty and went and drew the rations for the day for the rest of the barracks. It was a form of early leaving guards. We did the guard through the night when there were extra ones on. By day there weren't so many on. Some had the one some had the two.

I was on sentry guard one night on the Viceroy of India's residence in Rangoon; it was called Government House. Now there was a gun each side of the doorway with a massive great portal up above with two massive pillars. Each soldier had to stand beside these Indian Mutiny guns until they decided to signal to start marching across one another (I go to the left hand side, he comes to the right) and we'd change in the middle between the two guns and take stations again, just for a change of venue on sentry duty. We'd heard these awful damn great things and seen them. They were damn great flying beetles, half the size of a walnut and they'd whack this light, bang, and come round in a kind of dirty spiral and fall down like a moth would.

Now it was an exceptionally hot night and I dared the consequences by loosening the neck of my tunic which was fixed in front by two double hooks. When the other bloke saw it he said, "That is some idea, nobody will be about here. Anyway it's 12.20". We were on 12–2 a.m.

These things were flying about, but it had to be me and when they were coming down they made as good a hum as any plane I've ever heard, but get them on their backs and they were filled with crawling, lousy black and brown bits of mites that wanted some seeing with the naked eye. To give some idea of their size we actually saw them walking on the beetles legs. One of them hit the lamp up over. I wasn't aware of this. Now at night you wouldn't be wearing the great helmet. I had on what was called a forage cap, now that is a cap that fits on the side of your head, like a boat turned upside down.

This thing came down and passed the back of my head, right wallop into my tunic neck. I felt the thing hit like a piece of stone and like a fool I made a grab but pushed it further down. Twice I had a go. Frightened to call the other sentry, I bent down. I'd lost all sense of nerve when I felt a hell of a sting. It had bitten me. Eventually it caught hold my finger; I didn't catch hold of him. I flicked it out, wallop on the ground, you daren't tread on them, only by accident and then it was like cracking a walnut. Five minutes after this I felt pain, and it was a pain too; a nasty surging pain. So much so that I pulled a couple of tunic buttons open and what we did was fatal for a guard on Government House. We got together and he looked at my neck. I'm wondering how the hell I was going to get through a guard duty like that when up came two captains, a lieutenant and a major-general and they walked up the driveway, swords occasionally clanking.

One of the captains came up to me and he said, "What is all this then, unseemingly dressed?" I told him to have a look at my neck and that one of the great beetles had dropped into my tunic. He said, "You had your tunic neck open then?" I had to confess I did. He told me it was against all regulations. He called Captain Wilson and told me this was the Viceroy's personal surgeon. He came over, gave me the order to quick march around the side of the house and I went into another place where there was a little bed and what have you, everything a surgery would have.

Within seconds he had my neck open in four, like a hot cross bun, he had a handful of cotton wool and he was giving my neck a twist, it was agony and it took a month for my neck to heal. But what he showed me wouldn't have come out of an ink bottle any blacker. Bloody horrible stuff. He further said that if I had been in the jungle I'd have gone and that I'd had a lucky escape. Without any more ado he picked up the telephone to the guard room and I was relieved and had to go back to the barracks and, whatever happened I had to be on sick parade next morning.

Our own M.O. Captain Ingston looked at it, he said it was well on the mend and it would be alright. But just for safety's sake he put a little bandage on my neck. "You won't be on any duties nor wear a tunic for a week." That was that. It healed and even today I've got the lump just like a very small boil. This is getting on for 65 years since I left Rangoon. We were told of the dangers of being bitten by insects as each soldier enlisted, according to where he was going, even then we were all given Kitchener's Regulation Handbook and in there was all the dangers from the Far East and you know the rest, playing with women etc.

'C' Company and 'A' Company remained in Rangoon until 6 September 1915, during which time they coped well with the rigorous duties normally carried out in peacetime by twice their number. The battalion had been re-armed (they had come out to Burma equipped with the Martini-Henry rifles of Boer War vintage) and improvements had been made in its organisation. Many officers and NCOs had benefitted from various training courses and specialist machine gun and signalling sections had been formed. During this time the remaining two companies had been in Upper Burma, at Shwebo and Meiktila, where the Battalion had its headquarters.

CQMS E.W. EWENS

Will any of our fellows ever forget their feelings and thoughts of home when the mail flag was hoisted on the flag staff on the Signal Pagoda, and the answering gun at the Arsenal booming out to all Europeans that the mail steamer had arrived with its good, and sometimes bad, news from Blighty.

A REMOTE JUNGLE STATION

*'By the old Moulmein Pagoda, lookin' lazy at the Sea,
There's a Burma girl a settin', and I know she thinks
o' me; For the wind is in the palm-trees, and the
temple-bells they say: 'Come you back, you British
soldier; come you back to Mandalay'.'*

RUDYARD KIPLING. Manalay (1887)

ON SEPTEMBER 6 1915 the 2/5th Companies were turned around; the two companies in the north came down to Rangoon. 'A' Company was sent up to Battalion Headquarters at Meiktila to relieve 'B' Company and 'C' Company went up to the remote jungle station of Shwebo, swapping places with the men of 'D' Company. 'C' Company was to remain at Shwebo until the battalion was sent to India in May 1917.

PTE B.G.L. RENDALL

After a while we left Rangoon and went back north again, to Shwebo just to change stations. Shwebo was a jungle station, not greatly unpleasant but there didn't seem much point having a full company of men there, but there it was and we were near Mandalay.

Our duties consisted of guarding Burma. Burma was ours, we had our stations there just as in India. Every town of any repute in India had its garrison. Put us all together and we were fairly mighty army. If we were called to one bad spot in India or Burma we could mass hundreds of thousands all told. If I started to mention the names of places where we had garrisons, it would be never ending: Bangalore, Ishapore, Calcutta, Rangoon, Dinapore, Mandalay. We were never called out for anything violent, only in later years when I was up around the North West Frontier, in the Lahore, Punjab riots.

In Shwebo, it was more or less a country place. It was here that a bit of the Song of Mandalay comes into it now. I was going down to Shwebo Bazaar which was a long lane of bodge-up huts which sold everything. Every week I bought a few postcards of Burma to send home. We had to dress to go out of the barracks and my friend had gone on ahead. I went off down the road and glanced at a little girl wearing a pair of slippers, no heels, dragging her feet just

*like the Burmese do, she was aged roughly 18. Without any hesitation she said,
"You, young British soldier?" I said, "Yes" and that wound up, "Come ye back
ye British soldier, come ye back to Mandalay." I won't tell you what happened,
we'll leave it there. But I was very late down at the bazaar when I met my
pal.*

*There wasn't a lot to our daily routine of duties owing to the hellish heat. You
jumped out of bed at 5 o'clock. At 5.30 Parade, PT, at 6 rifle drill, 6.30
marching and at 7.00 a quiet sit down doing what was called finding the range.
You worked at the distance on the clock. A sergeant would say to you, "Point
your arms in the direction that I've been talking about." There was a clay
building on the left at 10 o'clock, "Line your rifles up with that." He'd go round
each one in turn and we had to say how far away it was. It was a form of
musketry drill. Twice a week we had a rifle inspection, where we familiarised
ourselves with the parts of the rifle and rounds of ammo. We were then
dismissed for the day, at eight or nine o'clock.*

*It was while up in Shwebo that I got this awful trouble; it was what they
called a whitlow on my finger. That gave me three of the most awful nights of
agony. The M.O. put it down to fixing bayonets, there was no other way to
squeeze it and somehow it jammed between the rifle and the bayonet ring. A
ring closes over this rifle muzzle and the clip fixes down in the frame. Somehow
I misfired and squashed my finger between the rifle muzzle and the bayonet. I
took no notice at the time, as I think I was mounting guard. We did plenty of
it in drilling in the barrack square. When I pleaded sick the mucus was already
thick under my fingernail. A whitlow is caused by the skin being compressed onto
the bone, the flesh then stays compressed and generates a nasty growth. There is
the black whitlow and the white whitlow; I had the white type.*

*I paraded the barracks all night, in a pair of white daps. They were sleeping
all around me and awoke as I was in pain. "Stick it son, we don't give a
damn." During the second week the pain had eased off a bit and I was on the
sick when this medic said, "We'll have to give you the jam jar treatment,
Private Rendall, and then we'll get this lot out." I could put my hand up in the
air and the mucus would run right down my wrist if I stretched my hand
upwards. I found myself sat on the steps to the detaining ward. Every hospital
in India and Burma had a detaining ward; they put you there for observation
or final treatment before discharge. From somewhere two natives got a jam jar.
They were carrying the jar with a cloth round it and in my innocence I thought
this was to keep the dust out. Instead of that it was because the water was
damn near boiling, how the jar didn't break I don't know. The big Sikh got hold
my arm, "Jar Sahib, Jar Sahib, doctor want." and I pulled back from him.
Within seconds the other native reached over, there was no way out and my
finger was nearly boiled. When it came out it was nearly twice the size.*

*One of these Sikhs shouldered me into the surgeon's room. As he caught hold
my hand he said, "You needn't look", and I felt a tickling sensation. Then they
started to work their hands down. But we'll finish with that. For nearly a
fortnight my arm was in a sling, so bad was it, so I had a very good start in
Shwebo. It was in a military hospital attached to the compound.*

*All the barracks were gathered together in a military compound and this was
a sort of colony on its own. We had our own hospital and cookhouses for each
platoon, each platoon had two cooks. Each barrack room had a platoon of men.
We were 'C' Company stationed up there. The other three companies were
stationed at different parts of Burma, but when the split up occurred I don't*

know. I fancy it was when we landed as a full battalion at Myingyan. One company, I can't exactly remember which, went right up near the Chinese frontier.[16] *Another company was at Rangoon, I don't remember where the fourth company was. We were 'C' Company at this place called Shwebo and there were numbers 9, 10, 11 and 12 platoons in four barrack rooms. Each barrack room held fifty men, that was a platoon. Being at war strength there were fifty to a platoon.*

They were wooden barracks and we had our first lesson as to what a sandstorm was. We'd done the third day's parade and were settled in barracks.Towards evening, the natives got worked up, really and truly. They called us out of these barrack rooms, which were all of a wooden construction, mighty strong beams and the like. They were tiled roofs and the lamps hung from the ceiling on a long bent bar like a meat-hook, crooked at each end in order to hold the lamps. They were lit by the room orderly. Each man in turn was room orderly and they had jobs such as cleaning the barrack room.

On this particular day these natives had us out and they were worked up and excited, "Sahib, sandstorm come, Sahib, sandstorm." We didn't know what the sandstorm was, these natives on their own initiative gave us the hint by running round and shutting the doors. In the barracks there were six sets of doors each side of the room, which could be bolted and there was no time wasted bolting these. The first we heard of it was the roaring and it got blacker and blacker. Suddenly it hit us like a tidal wave and the whole barracks was shaking. Although they call it a sandstorm it was really a mighty fine dust, and there was no way to keep it out. We were told to keep our kit boxes shut and all we could do was lie on our beds. There was nothing else we could do. It came in all on one side of the barrack room, the side facing the storm. In the middle of this came peals of thunder and that really frightened us. About half an hour after the sandstorm was over it was nearly dark and the lightning was going in eight or nine different places in the sky and the guns of thunder were as good as France. It shook the barracks, the lamps, the lot, and the wind gradually abated. Then we felt the drive of rain, yes, rain came after this. So hot were the barrack roofs with the heat, that the tiles were actually heard to hiss slightly. I'm talking about 120°F heat.

It roared down the barrack gutters, down the roofs and chutings, which were about a foot wide but still couldn't take the deluge. The drainpipes were six inches in diameter and ran away from the barracks under the Shwebo Road. The sandstorm lasted roughly 20 to 25 minutes of dust and cloud and then it brightened. Then behind it came the rain. It wasn't a monsoon, it only lasted a matter of five or ten minutes. It was enough to drive the scorpions, tarantulas and everything up out of the ground. We used to stand out on the veranda rail and point out those coming up because of the muddy ground, all moving they worked and wormed their way back up the top.

CQMS E.W. EWENS

At the end of August 1915 we left Rangoon for Shwebo, exchanging stations with 'D' Company and the train journey for the 600 miles was much better than the previous one across India. The Supply and Transport were responsible for meals and supplied us with tea at Toungoo, the CQMS taking on sufficient

---

16. 'B' Company, which went to Bhamo in 1916.

bread and several Edam cheeses for another meal in the evening. The country we passed through was not picturesque, being for the most part flat and nothing but paddy fields. Very monotonous, and as the sun went down, the ridge of the Arakan Yoma Mountains to the west could plainly be seen. One thing that struck us particularly before darkness set in, were the enormous tufts and clumps of bamboo, a plant which supplies the Burmese with nearly everything except food and even a little of that in the shoots. They use this plant to build their huts and for most of their tools used in husbandry. By their peculiar way of splitting male bamboo they get quite a sharp instrument necessary for different uses; this wood is exceptionally hard, but not to be compared with iron or steel.

At Mgohoung Junction, four miles from Mandalay, we were supplied with a good breakfast and there met a conductor, a Warrant Officer in the Supply and Transport Corps, who was an old Somerset. He was quite pleased and said how good it was to see the old badge once more.

We next proceeded through rich foliage and undulating countryside to Amarapura. This was one of the old capitals of Burma and is well known for its manufacture of silk fabrics for Burmese dress. Lingyis and lungyis are all made on very primitive hand looms. A large number of creeper-covered ruins, telling of its bygone greatness are here discernible. We stopped on the banks of the Irrawaddy and transferred to a river steamer for crossing the ferry, which is about one mile wide, to Sagaing Shore. Our baggage car was run straight onto the boat and landed on the other side and again attached to our train. Innumerable hills cover the western bank of the stream here, not very high, but every one of them seemed to be topped by a pagoda – a very pretty sight. The trip across was soon over and we entrained again and proceeded north to Shwebo through Ava and other small places. What contributed greatly to the pleasantness of this trip was the goodwill of our officers and though we may joke at their expense later, there was no company in the British Army with better officers than we had. We (NCOs) thoroughly understood them and by this time the men trusted them.

The rest of the year 1915 passed quietly by, with a movable column or two to Ombock and the surrounding countryside. Company training was now fully entered into and the men got smarter every day because they gave their minds to it.

On Christmas day the 'Ghadrite Rebellion' broke out in India and we had a week's picket duty round the natives, expecting a revolt. We marched out and took up our positions at night and returned to cantonment at daybreak. The native military police, Sikhs mostly, took over the day duties. The trouble passed away in time. 'B' Company, who had been moved to Bhamo had a month's march to the disaffected hilly country on the Chinese frontier. The trouble was supposed to have come from Yunnan but nothing untoward happened and they returned to Bhamo.

The two companies in northern Burma were to spend most of their time at musketry drill and company training. In Rangoon the men of 'B' and 'D' Companies continued with the demanding guard and picket duties which had been carried out during the previous seven months by 'A' and 'C' Companies. The situation in Rangoon got progressively more serious towards the end of 1915, the rebellion in India had its knock-on effects in the Burmese capital. Reinforcements were needed: there were not enough men in two companies to handle the situation. On 5 January 1916 the Somersets in Rangoon were replaced by the 18th London Rifle Brigade, a Territorial Garrison Battalion. 'A' Company promptly returned to Meiktila, together with a large number of Turkish prisoners of war who were destined for internment at Thayetmayo. Guarding of the Turkish prisoners of war was a further task given to the 2/5th, as soon as they reached Meiktila the men of 'A' Company were ordered back to Thayetmayo where they were to remain on these duties until 17 August 1916. They then returned to Headquarters at Meiktila.

'B' Company, as CQMS Ewens mentions, had been sent to Bhamo upon being relieved at Rangoon. There they went into barracks which had been unused for a few years. This followed a week's journey up the Irrawaddy on the R.I.M. steamer *Bhamo* from the town of Khaukmyoung. The various frontier tribes in the north eastern region of Burma had shown signs of disaffection and it had been decided that a show of force in the area would be expedient. 'B' Company was chosen and on 29 February 1916 a force of five officers and 131 men with their transport, elephants and mules, and native camp followers left Bhamo and began a march which was to take them into the Kachin Hills and to the Chinese border. Their first objective was Namkham, a market town in the north of the Shan States, where they put on the requisite show of strength by marching through the town with fixed bayonets. They then followed the Namwai river and marched for five days, their ultimate destination being Loije in the Chinese province of Yunnan. With their objectives achieved the detachment retraced their steps back westward to Bhamo. No opposition had been encountered anywhere and the whole exercise was adjudged to be successful. With this, their main reason for being sent to Bhamo, completed, they returned to Meiktilia in April 1916.

During this time 'C' Company remained at Shwebo undergoing routine company training. There was always the possibility that the battalion would be sent to one of the active theatres of war, such as Mesopotamia or German East Africa where the small guerilla army of Von Lettow Vorbeck was tying up large numbers of British troops. Training was based on the assumption that active service was just around the corner.

In February 1916 'C' Company received a visit from the General Officer Commanding Burma Division, Major General H.A. Raitt.

CQMS E.W. EWENS

In February 1916 we had to undergo a General Officer Commanding Inspection, the colonel and adjutant having arrived from Meiktila for the same. On the day of the inspection, a day which turned out to be full of humourisms, we were drawn up in line awaiting the GOC Division when the colonel told us not to be flurried as the general was only a man, like ourselves and would not eat us. At once we heard the purring of the motor car bringing the gentleman. Around turned the colonel calling for the adjutant by his surname three or four times and said, "He's coming, he's coming, whatever shall I do?" Poor old chap, he was the most flurried of the lot of us.

As the officer who was driving the general's car got out he gave a smart chuckup and said, "May I rejoin my company, sir?". "Certainly, certainly," was the reply. He then turned very smartly and with his first pace forward at the double, he measured his length on mother earth. Some said his sword caught

26

27

28

25
Private Arthur Hinder,
Burma, 1915.

26
A wireless signals section
on manoeuvres, Burma,
1916.

27
Shade from the sun.

28
The wooden barrack room,
Shwebo.

between his legs. There was no knowing but it started a suppressed titter amongst the men, who were now at attention awaiting the command for the general salute.

This came along in time, the old man had mastered his nervousness and read the orders from his cuff where they were supposed to be written. It passed off okay and we were put through the movements of company platoon drill, finishing up by marching past in line, which we did like a brick wall, earning the praise of the General Officer Commanding. We were then told off for various duties. Company platoons – we will follow number 11 platoon for bungalow inspection. As the entourage passed through the bungalow, the colonel, who was nearly the last noticed a smart, clean soldier who was standing beside his cot and engaged him in conversation as follows;

Colonel – "How do you like this country my man?"

Man – "Not bad, sir."

Colonel – "Let me see, you came out with the last draft."

Man – "No, sir."

Colonel – "What, not the last one? Oh no, you came with Mr Beachy's lot."

Man – "No, sir."

Colonel – "You didn't? Why, when did you arrive then?"

Man – "With you, sir."

Colonel – "Sure you did, my man, I ought to have known."

He then passed on and overtook the others, but it was good for army discipline that he did not hear the laughs and remarks in the bungalows as soon as he was clear.

About ten miles south of Shwebo there was a large jhel or lake called Wetlet and many a fine bit of sport our officers got there in their spare moments. The place teemed with wildfowl of all descriptions and the Sergeants' Mess always received their share. Elephants were also in the surrounding jungle, several being shot from time to time by our captain. On these shooting expeditions they were almost invariably accompanied by a shikari named Maung La Gyaw, a peculiar little fellow who could always take you to whatever kind of game you wanted, large or small. He was supposed to be an old Dacquoit chief, placed in the position of thana or headman of a neighbouring Burmese village by a benevolent British government. Set a thief to catch a thief and well 'twas done too.

The Orderly Corporal one day after taking the sick parade, returned to the cookhouse for his breakfast which had been reserved for him. As he emerged from the cookhouse with a platter containing steak, chips, bread, and 2oz of butter piled on it in one hand and his mug in the other; down swoops a kite-hawk and collars the butter. The bird hovered aloft trying to get the sticky mass from its talons. The corporal noticed it and placing his platter and mug on the ground, looked around for a stone. He saw one about two yards away and fetched it, but when he got back to his khanah other hawks had boned the lot and he had to do without. The flight of these birds is wonderful and this calls to mind various acrobatic stunts that they did every day of their lives; wheeling, banking, swooping and even at times, flying on their backs when trying to snatch a morsel of food from another bird's claws.

In the next spring, of 1916, 'B' Company joined us from Bhamo and the company rivalry which then ensued in all sports was healthy and though both companies were as keen as mustard to win all they could, there was never any bad feeling. 'B' Company was comprised of men from Bridgwater, West Somerset, Minehead, Watchet, Williton etc.

The duties at Shwebo now covered a prisoner of war camp, barbed wire enclosures having been erected, which enclosed about 100 Turkish officers and their batmen who numbered more. What our troops could not understand was why these Turks (the men) should be supplied with 17 different rations and they only 7. Amongst the Turks' issue, a packet of cigarettes per day and one box of matches not so often. In the canteen these commodities had to be bought by the Somersets and then were not always obtainable. But still the Turks got theirs and in several instances flogged what they did not require to the troops on guard. Also, Turkish officers were supplied with what they required in such a manner that it would make the prudes of their country lift up their hands!

Most of the supplies for the Supply and Transport Corps were brought to a place called Khaukmyaung, a village on the Irrawaddy, by river steamer and then forwarded by bullock and mule tonga to Shwebo. The Supply and Treacle sergeant in charge often had to proceed to the river to take over the goods and as a rule he got a Somerset sergeant to accompany him. What an interesting ride this was through the jungle to the banks of the river, teak, tamarind and acacia, the flame of the forest. Trees seem to abound and in places the whole matted together by the immense climbing plants of the tropics, running from the smallest twine mesh until they appeared like giant manila hausers hanging from the highest points of the tree to the ground. The river at this point is 1,000 yards wide and fine mahseer fishing may be had by spinning from its banks.

One day, on a route march, the company was led by a young officer and no sooner had they got the order to march at ease when they started singing. After one or two marching choruses had been got off their chests, someone struck up, 'And a Little Child Shall Lead Them', which was immediately taken up by all. About five minutes of this and the youngster was getting angrier every minute and not knowing what to do, the sergeant major, seeing his dilemma whispered, "March them at attention, sir," which he did, and at once, so the incident ended; but many a laugh it caused afterwards.

When Christmas Day 1916 arrived the company quartermaster sergeant responsible for supplying the sergeants mess, was at his wit's end for something fresh outside the ordinary ration. The cold storage company in Rangoon had sent a few extras but not enough and it is not much like Christmas fare, rationed beef. But just before midday the Officer Commanding Company, who had been shooting at Wetlet returned and called on the quartermaster sergeant and asked for the number of sergeants in the mess. He was told 18 and then handed over 9 wild geese. The officers had had a good bag that morning. They were taken to the mess bobberjee without anyone being the wiser and later the geese were cooked, split in halves being the quickest way to carve, and each sergeant had a half placed in front of him on the table to his evident surprise. After dinner was over, it was the general opinion that this was the best meal we had received in the two years since leaving home.

On Boxing Day, Billy, one of our company officers (they were all known by nick-names which shows their popularity), went elephant hunting with the Burman before named. After a few hours trek they got downwind of a herd and approached, finally getting amongst them and selecting a bull, let go at it. The animal saw its agressors and at once charged. Billy took to his heels; 100 yards in even time was not in it and dodged behind a bamboo clump. Then, espying another, and better one, someways off at right angles, made for that one just as the beast dived headfirst into the first clump. The officer was never fated to reach the second bush as a deep nullah lay between, which he had not noticed in his headlong flight. He saw it too late, owing to the speed he was travelling and plunged headfirst or somehow to the bottom. Luckily he fell on soft sand but the breath was fairly knocked out of his body; he came to himself picked himself up and shook the sand out of his clothes, eyes, nose and mouth which all seemed full of it.

The elephant was trumpeting and Billy was at a loss to know why it hadn't followed him. He decided to investigate, reloading, and climbing back out of the nullah. Not far away he saw Mr. Jumbo; sat on his haunches, and some little way off, the Burman all the same. He approached the native, who seemed glad to see him again and still the animal did not move with the exception of waving its trunk in a sweeping circle, bellowing all the time. He asked the shikari what was the matter and the native answered, "Me give him Christmas Buckshis shot up backside". When the elephant charged at the bamboo his tusks became embedded in part of it for a short while, and the Burman, with commendable promptitude, had run behind and discharged his rifle at its hindquarters; completely disabling it in that region. It was soon despatched, but not before seven bullets had been put into it, one of which drilled a hole into its tusks. Later, the natives from the nearby village appeared, skinned it and were given the flesh by the killer. The skin, four feet and tusks being brought back to Shwebo. And one of the feet was a treasure in our mess until the battalion was leaving for India. Where it is now? Anyone know?

Night-time in certain seasons in Burma is not conducive to much sleep on account of the noises arising from the jungle. What with the dismal howl of the jackal, the peculiar laughing yelp of the hyena, the trumpeting of elephants, the snarls and snufflings of those big feline animals, the bellowing of the syne or wild buffalo, the screeching of the parrot, and last but by no means least, when a ramsammy is on, the infernal monotonous banging of the natives' tom-toms; they singly and combined turn the night into a hideous nightmare.

PTE B.G.L. RENDALL

If you wanted to go to the lavatory after dark, you had to go in twos for safety; no man dared refuse the request, whenever you wanted to go at night a man had to escort you. You had to sit on two planks and there was an earthenware pot in under which could be pulled out from the back. The smooth side of this planking was naturally towards us. One of the regimental drummers told us he wanted to go out. Now that was it, he went into the latrines and I stayed at the front, this was because several soldiers had been castrated by the natives in days gone by, in the Indian Mutiny. Which was quite easy; they could lift the pots and with plenty of clearance between you and the pot, the rest was easy. Cut and run. That was the reason for safety. Anyway, this drummer; there were no doors but you went into a tiny compartment. All of a sudden, without warning; "Christ, what's on me?" and he got up and as he did this scorpion was hung onto his backside. Well before I could turn him round and knock it off with a bayonet, it had stung him. By this time the bloke had started to get raving, we frogmarched him to the hospital, it was about 100 yards away and he went across, raving. Captain Ingston, the medical officer came down and said, "Catch him hold, this is desperate," and luckily we got him in the surgery door. Without anything else, he took the lump off and within seconds he was bandaged up. He recovered and pretty well got over it; it shows what quick action meant.

Funny thing about abroad; everything really poisonous like that was either brown or black. Back in our days nine out of ten of those bites, whether from a scorpion or a tarantula, was fatal; there wasn't enough medical development then to treat those things. There were few precautions we could take against insects. There was nothing we could do. Who in God's name would have thought that a thing like that would be stuck under the boards, who'd think of it? You see, you know what the country seats are like, we'll say no more. Who would suspect a damn great spider in England would be under a seat?

Occasionally the insects would come into the barrack room; not very often, but they were so large you either heard them or saw them. In the quiet of the barrack room, that was if half of them wasn't snoring, you had a reasonably quiet night. You could possibly have a tarantula crawl up the stairs from the ground, just like the inquisitive spider will.

We had trouble with mosquitoes, mainly at night. They were one of the biggest pests on God's earth. They would wake you up if they were in the nets; like a bugle. The noise really gets on your nerves and if you lit a match you may have caught the net alight, and then you'd had it; probably a court martial. When you went to catch the mosquito it had gone, you'd get nice and drowsy again and back it would be around your head and ears. It was hell of a heat, still in the 80's/90's and you'd have to pull sheeting right up round you. You sweat by the gallon. Occasionally you'd be lucky and clout one on your face, but in the dark you can't see. You're apprehensive when you go to sleep, not knowing whether you've killed it. They knew the most sensitive things to get at and it was hardly ever on the hands or arms, always on the face and neck. When they did bite it was like a sting and some were a fair size. Within half an hour they would bring up a rising on your face as big as a small boil, one bite on your eyes would close them, you couldn't open them, especially on the lids, that was another favourite spot.

There was an Earle Street boy, a pal who joined with me. We had so much illness one way or another, the guards were getting pretty frequent. This young fellow had come off guard, but he had dropped into a really deep sleep. He'd gone into one of the cells to lie down. I did that too; in one of those army prison cells, the doors were always open and you could lie down there when you'd finished your guard, pending dismissal of the guards later. They went in and the bugs were actually crawling on him. He was so deep in sleep that something had got into him. They cleaned these off him and took him to the hospital, by this time his mouth, eyes and nose were swollen up and closed. They'd even got under his shirt and vest. He was bit to pieces and died two days afterwards. They could do nothing for him.

Now when I talk about a bug, how can I describe the size of one of these? Well if you hadn't been to a place like that you hadn't seen a bug, they were about five times the size of an English bug, flat with six legs. They were flat as a pancake and they were hard.

So bad was this bug fever out there that once every week we had what they called 'Bug Parade'. This was after all ordinary parades, it was in your own time and your own interests. The bedding consisted of two iron trestles and three boards, eight inch boards. Now the bugs had eaten into these boards and nothing would get them out until the smell of your sweaty body brought them out after you'd been lying there for half an hour; they came out in troops, they knew where to go and what to do. So big were they that you seldom saw one trying to jump. On the 'Bug Parade' you worked in pairs, with the bloke on your right. We went across to the stores and drew about a pint of paraffin. When we were ready the mattresses were taken off the bed, these were coconut coir or the hair off the shell of the coconut. You took these off and put them on the barrack room floor, your bedboards were then right clear for you to run with. Outside was your partner making a complete paraffin ring on the floor, going round steadily and keeping it wet. You came outside and flung the boards into the ring and stepped back. You'd see the bugs fly out just like sand. The ring of paraffin was just right and it would catch them, a touch of paraffin and they would roll over. You'd get the next board and bang; you'd shake them out. Your partner was pouring the paraffin like an expert, and you were the expert with the boards. Eventually the paraffin would dry out and the native cleaners would come in. This was on the outer veranda on a level with the barrack floor because the barracks were on twenty feet of Burmese teak like a pier. The native cleaners would come and brush it up. It was sometimes surprising, between the whole length of the barrackroom, about 60 feet in all, you could pick up a good shovelful. But it wasn't all of them, some of the damn things were still in there.

Another favourite trick of ours was to roll a fine bit of paper into a cone shape, with the hole at one end no more than an eighth of an inch in diameter and you lit fags. (By the way, the cigarettes then were called Scissors, made by a firm called Bukkish Elahae, Basra; they had a pair of scissors and a captain engraved back and front on the packet. Ten Scissors cost 2 annas, which was about 2d. in English money.) We kneeled down beside the beds and we used to help out the blokes who didn't smoke, you'd take a fair mouthful of smoke and put this little cone affair to the bedboards and blow down it. The bugs stuck it and stuck it, but when they did come out, they came out drunk and fell down. You could pick them up by the score and we'd put them in a drum that was in the barrack room for it; it was just an airtight tin.

On one occasion some of our wits wanted something to do so they took apart a matchbox, and used the part that holds the matches and attached tiny pieces of rifle cord, like cotton, and by some way they struggled until they had eight bugs harnessed up to it. These bugs actually pulled this matchbox bottom across a kitbox top.

Relations with the natives were very good. Now Burma, well I could have cried when the Japs had it, the Burmese were one of the most docile, peace loving nations on God's earth. Nothing would perturb them, no malice, no murder, no anything. In fact such a thing was never even thought about. They once had a bit of an army, but don't forget we'd gone through Burma in earlier years. They gave us a damn good doing when we captured Burma. But Burma wasn't only for the Burmese, we had all types there of the Eastern World to deal with. We had several who, for all we knew would have taken part in the black hole of Calcutta. There were no Burmese servants in the barracks for some unknown reason; they were all Sikhs or Pathans, Hindus, from the durzai, which is the native tailor to the punka wallah boy that pulls the coolers in the ceiling in the roof.

This settlement was right against a jungle at Shwebo. You were free to go into the jungle any time whenever you liked, provided we notified. One day a barrack room pal of mine said, "Let's go into the jungle." A sergeant walking through the barracks said, "I hope you find some nice daisies out there, but *be careful and take a stick of chalk apiece and as you go in mark the tree trunk meeting and departing and put a nice white line on each trunk or God help you if we have to come and look for you." My job was to go to my section sergeant who was Colour Sergeant Ostler and to ask him if we could go for a walk in the jungle.*

This was in the Burmese evening, still with plenty of daylight and we wandered. The edge of the jungle wasn't more than 200 yards from the barracks and it wasn't long before we were in there. We were warned and made to strap on our side arms (bayonets) and we'd had to go to the CQMS's stores and draw a machette each. We went on, it was still daylight when we found a track, but we still marked up wherever we could – by this time we were as far in as safety decreed – almost half a mile into one of the densest jungles in the world. Occasionally there wasn't a tree to mark; we went on into a clearing. Here there was a couple of ricketty Burmese teak posts and on getting closer we realised it was a rope bridge. We had our heavy boots on, putties, long trousers because of jungle pests, resulting in our being fairly weighty. Also our heavy helmets, not the light pith helmet but the real service helmet with the regimental badge on it. We were on this ricketty turnout when we saw all this shining mass in under, and it appeared to be moving, glinting in the sunlight. There was a scream. This was from two Burmese, they didn't know a word of English and we didn't know a word of Burmese. But they made us understand that the bridge had been there a long time and it could break and for us to come off; one at a time. Realising the trouble we were in we crept off, damn lucky. That rope had been there for years and had never been used. These two natives showed us the way round and we came back on our track again. Later we went back and had another look over the edge and about twenty feet below was one of the biggest masses of slithering snakes that ever we did see. They had bred in there, all the water was gone and they were slithering in heaps like a load of mackerel, only black. No snakes in the barracks.

We went back to the barracks and the staff sergeant and officer came out and said there won't be many of them left when we've done with them. They brought out an old shell case and filled it with TNT. Between them they rigged up a safety line: and then a discharge line. They said go back 10–12 feet for safety and there was a muffled bang and this huge snake heap had been blown to pieces; they were everywhere, dead. I think that was one of my luckiest escapes. It was so funny and so weird, not having seen a jungle before, you'd heard about all kinds of weird flowers and butterflies with an 8in. wingspan.

But my troubles in Shwebo weren't finished. We were out on what was called infantry advance training, where you had to run forward 20 or 30 paces and go down. Then another section would advance, get in line with you and fall in with you. Then another section would advance and go another 30 paces again alternately. Unknown to me I'd caught my foot on a piece of jagged stone which had gone through my putties; or at least that is what we put it down to at the time. I didn't feel anything at the time until a day or two afterwards. It started to sting; on my leg was a nasty red spot, I took no notice, I wrapped my putties around the same. I couldn't be sure which leg I'd put the putty round the day before. They were identical and not left/right. A couple of days later I found a piece of skin had come away on my putties. I still tried not to feel sick or complain but this went on. I first

29

30

31

A REMOTE JUNGLE STATION

29
Wireless telegraphy
equipment.

30
On the Royal Lakes,
Dalhousie Park, Rangoon.

31
Cooking in the field,
Burma 1916.

32
CQMS Ewens.

discovered it on the Monday, by the Wednesday there were a dozen or so sores, with four or five on the other leg. It got worse but I didn't give in, all the time I was wrapping this muck around my legs in different places resulting in more arising. I was too big a fool to report sick.

Until one night I was on guard, and this had reached the stage where each time I pulled my putties off fresh skin came away. Then one night I came off sentry duty and laid in the guardroom on the bed, two on, four off, when at twelve o'clock there was a cry, "Guard turnout, grand rounds." There was a hurricane lamp coming towards us and this was Captain Ward-Jackson, who was chief of our company. Each company had a captain in command. I had to hurry out and one of my putties was dragging. The captain asked the sergeant why I was half dressed. The sergeant replied that he'd find out when he'd left, but the captain wanted to know why there and then. Everyone was at attention when he looked at my legs and commented what a fine bloody mess I was in and why was I on guard. I was told to go back to barracks and report to the hospital in the morning on the sick parade: and that was an order. If I delayed five minutes, I was told, I'd be slapped in the cells.

My legs were in an awful state and I needed medical care. The M.O. took one look and said I was beyond his repair. The M.O. said to the corporal on sick parade he was going to box me off to his brother in Maymyo, and thought that I'd lost my right leg already. Maymyo was only 40 miles away, but I had to go by train, specially on a stretcher, into the hills of Burma. It was one of the best medical stations in Burma, if not the best. There I was under the care of Colonel Ingston. He said I'd set him a problem. Now one of my legs had a red label, the other a yellow label. The red one denoted removal; the yellow one denoted doubt. He started on me the very hour I got there which was 9 o'clock. He told me the only thing he could do with the mess was to burn them singly with iodie, not iodine. Iodie is the neat mixture before being diluted into what we know as iodine. He told me my leg would be a mass of black holes, he could already see my shin bone quite easily. I was told what a fool I was to let this go on and he started the burning treatment.

The big black Sikhs' did the hospital work, good blokes they were, pretty awesome when they stood over your bed. It was like a kind of power they held over you. These two held me while the M.O. came, and he held a peculiar shaped dish. It was a kidney basin shaped like the legs about 9 or 10 inches long and as these Sikhs held me, gently but firmly, he pressed the kidney basin against my legs. On the end of the piece of sugar cane or bamboo was a big wad of cotton wool and then I saw the bottle, a screw capped, big mouthed bottle and he dabbed the wad into the bottle. I don't know where I went, I couldn't go far, and that was only the first one. They were now the size of a one pence piece, mucus filled holes of rotting flesh. He said that until he saw any alteration he was putting me off every morning and treating me.

I had to lie for as long as I could because the more I disturbed it the worse it would be. If anything was to touch it that would be the end and not to cover my legs. The next morning he came up and used what was called laudenum in those days, and put this wad under my nose. I was out like a light. When I woke up everything was gone, this went on for a fortnight. He walked in and said, "That's more like it, we've got a nice hard scab which is what we want."

Instead of losing my legs I've got them here. Even today my legs are like a machine gun caught me; there's 30 on one leg, 20 on the other just like a colander. Caused in my ignorance by those putties being full of infectious stuff known as frontier sores. It came from saltpetre in the ground and at some time I must have opened my putties when I went down on the infantry charges.

One day Captain Ward-Jackson came into the ward at Maymyo, there were four of us there. He was a very well liked bloke who could bite your head off with authority one minute but was very concerned underneath it all with everyone. There wasn't much any of us wouldn't do for him, he was so well respected. He told me that he'd heard from the M.O. that I'd soon be able to return to the regiment but to start with it would be very light and careful duties. Then he said, put this under your pillow and have a free month in Mandalay on me. He told me there were some very nice places in Mandalay to eat, and to look after myself.

About six weeks to two months after returning to Shwebo I got word that the Indian War Office wanted engineers for a new company they were forming on the North West Frontier. They wanted anyone they could get hold of for this company and I put my name down. I was the only one that applied from our company. It was about two months after this, a lance corporal walked into the barrack room and said, "What have you been up to, sonnie? You've got away with it, the orderly room want to see you. Do you know you're off from this regiment?" I said I didn't know. I went across to the orderly room and there it was; my railway warrant for five days time, to leave. The next day I went on parade as usual and when we were dismissed the RSM, a Yeovil bloke, said he wanted a word with me. He came up to me, putting his hand on my shoulder and said, "Oh my, oh my, what have you done? So you don't like the Somersets. It's been worked out with Captain Jackson and Captain Spurway and they reckon you're going to do 3,000 miles on your own, right down through Burma, back to Rangoon and if fortunes favour the brave you'll get a ship to Calcutta and then another 1,500 miles up the side of India, and you'll be passing Katmandhu, Nepal, Everest. I can do nothing in the matter, you'll leave here on Friday. In the meantime no more parades. You go over to Ed Ewens, the quartermaster sergeant. We want you to land at this company respectable and he'll have a look at you with some fresh kit, clothes, knicks, what have you, right down to army socks if it's required". It was. He gave me a few extras and into my kit bag they went.

Bert Rendall left the battalion in January 1917 and went to the North West Frontier of India where he joined the recently formed 2nd Mechanical Transport Company, an Indian Army unit. He never rejoined the 2/5th Somersets. Without him, the battalion continued with its training in preparation for its next move. In May 1917 the 2/5th were considered ready for active service. But it was not to be, their luck was holding and they were set to go to India for more garrison duties in and around Calcutta.

The battalion had acquitted itself with great credit in the 28 months it had spent in Burma. During which time it had been responsible for the various policing and guard duties considered necessary for the continued status of the country as a British Colony. In addition the men of the 2/5th had been responsible for guarding the prisoner of war camps at Thayetmayo, Meiktila and Shwebo. It had never been together as a complete unit since landing in Burma, being spread out between Rangoon, Shwebo, Meiktila and Bhamo with consequent difficulties of supply and organisation.

Many men had been lost to the battalion during these years, like Bert Rendall they had gone off to serve in other units of the British and Indian Armies. Several officers had been transferred away also, including 'C' Company's Commanding Officer, Captain C. Ward-Jackson who left on being appointed to the Burma Division Staff.

The battalion was drawn back together at Rangoon on 16 May 1917 in readiness to being transferred to India. It was relieved by two garrison battalions; the 3rd Garrison Battalion of the Bedfordshire Regiment and a battalion of the Royal Irish Fusiliers. Forty-three men were transferred into the Bedfordshires and were left at Meiktila, on medical grounds.

CQMS E.W. EWENS

Early in April in 1917 orders were once more received to mobilise. Everything was packed ready for the move, we understood it was to Palestine or Mesopotamia. By this date scores of our men had gone in drafts to Mesopotamia and three drafts from home had taken their place. A medical inspection was held by a travelling board of medical officers with the result that 43 men in the two companies were placed in Category 'B', which meant their transference to a garrison battalion. After being all packed up and nowhere to go for six weeks, orders were issued that the 3rd Bedford Garrison Battalion would relieve us in a day or so.

The well-to-do natives of Shwebo, together with the Government officials there, gave us a right royal to do in Shwebo Gardens as a farewell. There had been nothing but the best of feeling between us during our stay there. Tuesday May 14th 1917 saw the Bedfords march in, about 8.30 p.m. Soon the necessary formalities of handing over the bungalows, together with our forty-three 'B' men were gone through, and in doing so we lost our CSM, who was the senior sergeant major of the battalion.[17]

Next morning at 4 a.m. we marched to the station and entrained, (most of the baggage had been packed for weeks), and left Upper Burma, the land of palms and pagodas. The country we were leaving was by no means the worst in the east. During our stay here 'C' Company officers had won the Burma Polo Cup; is this not a record for officers of infantry? They beat a team in the final which had held the cup for several years. Our rugger 15 also won the Burma Rugby Cup. The other finalists being, 'First Line 4th Service Battalion of the Border Regiment' for so they styled themselves although only Terriers like ourselves.

Our cantonment appeared to be a patch of one square mile cut out of the jungle and scrub. In the north it was sparcely covered with prickly scrub and cactus and the ground in the clearing seemed to sparkle like hoar frost, especially in the early morning, caused no doubt by saltpetre. Woe betide the man who happened to bark his knees on it, the universal army salve iodine was soon brought into use.

To our east, stretching for 16 miles to the Irrawaddy, was all jungle, with the clearings of three villages in that space. The river at this point was 1000 yards

17. CSM A.W. Slocombe of Wellington.

wide and yet you were about 550 miles from its mouth. Behind it were high mountains towards the Chinese Frontier, in which were the ruby mines of Mogok. Through this jungle country, right across from the Irrawaddy to Chittagong on the Bay of Bengal runs a straight road like the old Roman roads of England. Local tradition says this was the road of Solomon's time to take the gems of Upper Burma to Tarshish, now Chittagong. South of us, scrub went to the road about one mile away and after that paddy fields and palms, and to the west a large nullah about 30 feet deep and 50 yards wide, separated us from the native barracks, behind again the old city of Shwebo. This nullah in the dry season was only a dried up water course, with a large number of quicksands; in one of which, 'Weal, Wed, Wust' got bogged down one day with his pony and it was with great difficulty and native help that the pony's life was saved. This place was out of bounds to the troops.

Our barracks was on a single rise in the ground and commanded extensive views which reminded one of a line in one of Bishops Heber's well known hymns; 'Where every prospect pleases and only man is vile', but he never said anything about all shrubs having thorns which sometimes on bush warfare training tore our khaki drill to pieces and it seemed impossible to get away from them.

We now return to our train journey down, which was very pleasant; we crossed the river again from Sagaing Shore to Amarapura. We joined up with our headquarters at Meiktila; here most of us received a shock. Our old RSM 'Chiko' Cayford, we were told, had left us and received a commission. A better liked or more tactful man had never been sent to a Territorial Battalion, and his place had been taken by a junior CSM who was one of the most unpopular of men it was possible to know. What qualifications he had, no one knew; it was only a short while ago that he had been sent on a musketry course to Pachmarlie and proved himself unfit for the job, according to other sergeants on the same, and when the exams were held, even the final, he was always ill and so came away with his certificate. He had served a few years in a cavalry regiment, was the yarn, and this qualified him to be a sergeant major in the infantry, so the authorities thought.

We arrived in Rangoon in the early morning of Thursday May 16th, 1917, were taken to the docks and detrained and started transhipping our baggage to the B.I. boat *Arankola* a fine two funnel steamer and quite new. We were pleased to meet here a few sergeants of the Royal Garrison Artillery and Rangoon Police whom we had known 18 months before. They had heard of our moving and came down to wish us a soldiers' farewell, bon voyage. They had also a bottle or two of Johnnie Walker with them which was very acceptable in the blazing heat, although the M.O.'s orders were not to touch it till sundown.

A military band was on the quay, possibly the RVR Band, and played 'Auld Lang Syne' and other appropriate tunes as we slowly left the pier. At midday we were well on our way down the river and Burma was a thing of the past: but to the majority of us it left very pleasant memories, and if our send off was a criteria the Somerset Terriers had created a good impression and enhanced the good name of the old 13th, whose name is often mentioned in connection with Burma.

One sad note was in recalling the many dear pals we had left behind, never to see their homes again; awaiting the 'Great Reveille' on Burmese soil. To return to mundane things, another fine sight over the stern; Syriam on our right, Dallas Dockyard and King's Road on our left and directly behind, the buildings of Rangoon, again topped by that golden pagoda the Shwe Dagon. If we had been going straight home no doubt this, to us, would have been the best night in all Burma. We knew though, that when we arrived in Calcutta, a thousand miles would have been knocked off the interval between us and our 'Little Grey Home in the West'. On leaving, the police sergeants informed us that there was a German sea raider in the bay, rumour said the 'Moewe' and as we rounded Elephant Point into the open sea we met our escort consisting of HMS *Diana*, *Psyche* and a destroyer. They immediately took post – the destroyer in the van and the two cruisers one off each bow, distance about 1 mile, and we proceeded on our journey, another 'Cook's Tour'.

To these sentiments the 2/5th Somerset Light Infantry left Burma. Despite not having seen active service they had lost a good few of their original number to disease, accidents and in the drafts which went to Mesopotamia. However, reinforcements had been sent out from England and the battalion's integrity was intact. Morely Chant was still with the battalion, promoted in 1916, as Bert Rendall recollects, to Lance Corporal Chant and, '. . .carrying all the weight of the world on his shoulders.' Thousands of miles away, on the Western Front, the Great War was struggling into its later stages.

7

SHWEBO TO RAWALPINDI

IN JANUARY 1917, Private Bert Rendall, then aged 20, left the 2/5th Somersets and travelled to the North West Frontier of India where he was set to join the 2nd Mechanical Transport Company, an Indian Army unit formed two years earlier. A notice, posted up in the barracks at the remote jungle station of Shwebo, had taken his eye and caught his imagination. The Indian Defence Office was seeking soldiers with engineering experience for a mechanical transport unit. Bert felt well suited for the situation, having done 18 months of his engineering apprenticeship with Petters Engines, and he wasted no time in volunteering to join No.2 MTC. No other Somersets volunteered from Shwebo and Bert was to make the journey on his own; to Rawalpindi in what is now Pakistan, a journey of over 3,000 miles.

PTE. B.G.L. RENDALL

At 4 o'clock that morning, one of the buglers who was on guard was good enough to say that he'd quietly crawl into the barracks and wake me up. By 4.30 I was stood in the barracks waiting for the gharry to turn up, a gharry is a tiny four wheel thing with a little horse. That drove me to Shwebo Station, from there I left for Rangoon. I can't determine the date but I got to Rangoon at 9 that night, 460 miles, as well as having to cross the Irrawaddy at a place called Sagaing which was just outside Mandalay. Now I had to go across because the Burmese Railway ran down the other side of the river so I had to cross, where it was a mile wide.

Eventually I landed in Rangoon, reported and was put in what they called the Attached Section of my own regiment; in every regiment there was part of the barracks set aside for those travelling. After another week in Rangoon, where another two or three times I went to the Shwe Dagon Pagoda and had my final views of that, I embarked on the BISN steamer the S.S. Bangala. I left there for Calcutta on January 18th 1917. The average trip across from Rangoon to Calcutta is 973 miles, which takes 3 days and 2

nights, I found. Within a few hours of boarding a young first officer came up
to me and said "I want to introduce you to a friend of ours, he travels
backwards and forwards on our boats. We get so many murderers, cut-throats
and what have you aboard these ships, and they are fully armed; so he wants
a word with you." Up walked a man with a white helmet that had a form of
a spike in the top, it turned out that he was one of the biggest detectives in
the Far East and his name was Anderson. He said, "I want you, Tommy, to
do a special favour for me, I shall feel a bloody sight safer with a rifle than
I shall with these revolvers. I want to go down in the depths of that mob,
I've got to look for two who are a mixture of Chinese-cum-Burmese that have
done a murder in Taiwan. They've raced across China and we know they've
boarded the Bangala, I want to find them before putting in at Calcutta.
Would you escort me down with your rifle?"

I asked what I could do with a rifle amongst a mob like that, it was one
of the most awkward things to have. "Never mind, it all helps with the sight
of a loaded rifle." I agreed and said lead the way. We got down into this
seething mass of humanity. Understand, not a white man amongst them! It
was one of the most awful gatherings of muck of the Far East ever seen on
God's Earth. We'd gone quite a little way through this mob, and we stuck to
our guns. Our luck was in, when this little boy said something in a foreign
language. The detective said, "Stay there soldier, I'm going ahead, put a
couple in." I put a few rounds in, a clip, which was five, with a rifle ready
to shove up to my shoulder and let go. Although to shoot that too would have
meant two dozen. What I had would have gone through all the rest stood
behind. He just walked up and took these two hold. One of them was just a
whimpering kid. We went along and I got the rifle, swung it upright, vertical,
after I'd made sure the safety catch was on because he said, "Don't unload
until we go up again, just make it safe." By this time we were up in the
foc'sle, getting to the front of the ship to go down to the cells in the bows. The
detective came back up and said, "By God I'm relieved, I think that rifle
saved me becuase with that bloody mob you'd be lost if they done you in. You
like your fags then? I'll see you in another hour." Apparently he went to the
ship's store and he got me a tin of 50 Capstans which were on a par with
Player's in those days, and to my astonishment out of a pretty full wallet he
gave me 10 rupees.

By the third night out we were within about 200 miles of Calcutta, we were
doing 20 knots which is roughly 25 miles per hour. In between all this I was
working on a woollen mat of all our Allies, around the Somerset badge. I
finished that as we came in sight of Calcutta; incidentally one of them was
Japan, and it was worked in wool on an army blanket. Now when I got in
the 2nd MTC I unfolded it one day and all the barracks made a crowd
around it and one or two couldn't recollect all our Allies; Rumania, France,
Italy, Russia, they are all still there, discernible, able to be read. I put the
last half dozen stitches in as Calcutta became clearer at 10 o'clock that
morning.

I was sitting on the skylight of the engine room. I was last off the ship and
an old lady from Basra (I'd given her my cabin as there had been a mix up
over her ticket booking) gave me another tin of 50 Players this time, and 20
rupees. I was one of the richest soldiers that ever got off a ship and I lost
the bloody lot!

I hung around and the Police Inspector came back and we shared a *gharry up to Fort William where we were both heading. Now Calcutta Police Station didn't have any cells and you had a place set aside against Fort William for prisoners. The gharry pulled up and he said; "You go another 150–200 yards, and you'll find the main gate of the barracks and someone will be there to ask you what you want."*

I got into Fort William. I'd been there about 10 minutes, stood up with the lance corporal of the guard, when the sergeant came up and I said to him, "2nd Lincolns." "Ah. Yes," he said, "all the bloody lot of us." My first night was alright, I wasn't on a bed it was on the barrack room floor of the Attached Section that looked after all the soldiers that were travelling all over Calcutta and back and forth from everywhere else. I had to stay there two or three days before the train left for Rawalpindi; right up on the North West Frontier, past Delhi, Agra, past Everest, Katmandhu and Nepal.

On the morning I had to catch my train for the North West from Howrah, a station in Calcutta; I got up from my bed and the belt around me fell in halves. Some louser had got in and cut it off me. I knew nothing. All the blasted lot I had on that ship; cleaned out. It was what was called an Indian Blow Belt; you could put money in a purse on the right hand side, take the belts off and it would be like a piece of tubing and all the money would run down away from the purse.

There were anything up to 20 or 30 soldiers sleeping in the barracks of the Attached Section, all on different journeys, some in pairs, some in threes, even half a platoon of another regiment. I told the first bloke I saw, a corporal, that I'd had my belt slipped. Belts were nicked so frequently that it was nicknamed 'belt-slip'. He asked what I had in there; "30 rupees in 10 rupee notes and 10 or 12 rupees in change." I had to go and see their Quartermaster Sergeant whose name was Mother, CQMS Mother, he advanced me 26 rupees. They'd gone in my kitbag too and had my fags away. This was all in the Attached Section at Fort William, Calcutta.

I went to Howrah Railway Station and got a reserved compartment. To my astonishment there were plenty of white people about on the station; including the station master who put me right as to which train to get on. Whilst we were there talking the train pulled up. Now I had a very nice set up: beds either side, it was a double compartment. On the window was an 'Army Reserve' placard so they were fully aware soldiers were about. I threw my kitbag inside.

Whilst waiting, a young Indian fellow came up and he turned out to be a stenographer working for the Viceroy of Imperial India: Lord Chelmsford. He asked if he could travel with me, he said he would feel safer with a British soldier in his company. So I agreed and it proved to be a Godsend.

We were on the Great Indian Peninsular Railway and we'd have to connect with the NWR at Delhi. There were a hell of a lot of railway companies. Eventually the platform started moving and we were on the go, when this young half-caste boy asked me if I'd eaten and that he'd wired ahead to the next station; 150 miles away for dinner. This was just as well as I'd been given no instructions about this sort of thing. We had our first meal at a place called Asansol. We had a fair meal there, cutlets, sausages, warmed up corned beef, baked potatoes and bananas in custard. Time went on and, though I can't remember the name of the place; we stopped for about six hours. As a Tommy I just rolled into bed and set my rifle alongside of me, it was chained to my wrist with handcuffs and I held the keys. For safety's sake it was locked up for any beautiful desperado who might chance his arm to get in there. I was going to the place where the whole of the universe was rifle mad. The North West Frontier tribes would pay God knows what for my Lee Enfield rifle. This was given to me automatically when I left Burma.

In the morning we pulled up at another place and my guide told me that we were on a line with Everest. He pointed to the big white one with the very dark cloud, "That's Everest, 50 miles away." We steamed on again, stopped, steamed on, stopped and we eventually go to Agra. Something was wrong with our engine and we were told there would be a delay of about 2 hours.

We left the train for a while to see the Taj Mahal. We went into this station and he had it all cut and dried; we went in there and two white girls, above all, served us with two lovely plates of food. The afters were sago and rice mixed. We then came out and, just like you'd find nowadays (all the taxis gathered outside the station), so were these tongas and gharries. Now a tonga was a two wheeled affair with horses; gharries had four wheels. And there were rickshaws with natives to pull you.

We had a splendid job; we had a four seater gharry, it cost half as much again as a tonga. As were getting out of the station I'd said on no account was I getting into a rickshaw. I wasn't having another human being dragging me through the streets like a horse; let those that have no faith or belief in anything do that. The gharry cost 8 rupees and he weaved in and out of the traffic, well paid you see.

Well, the wonders of the Taj Mahal just about made my day. But when we came out of there we'd certainly done some damage, and damage it was; our train had gone. It was a vile blow, the next was not until 9 o'clock the next morning. My kit bag, the lot, was gone. But my friend wired ahead to the next station and we were told we'd have it at the next pull up. We then went back to see the Taj again and we fixed up breakfast for 7 o'clock that morning. We saw the Taj by moonlight. He couldn't have suggested anything better. We went back to it by tonga. We saw more than we did on the first visit because he had a friend who was one of the keepers and he showed us into the jewel room.

What we saw in there; crowns, sceptres and the crown and staff of King Thebaw of Burma. Eventually we went back into the station at about 6 in the morning and walked into a little restaurant, or buffet bar. We enjoyed steaming hot mugs of tea and a meal. Our train chugged into the station. This train had a corridor and we had a complete compartment to ourselves. So we chugged on again, three days out from Calcutta, and pulled into Delhi which was a stopping place; all trains stopped there. My native friend went off and recovered my kitbag. He left me at Delhi and he gave me a tin of fifty fags, Capstans. It seemed a routine out there; fags. He also gave 10–15 rupees which he said was for travelling in the safety of a British soldier for so long.

After leaving Delhi my next move was to Rawalpindi, my destination; some 280 miles further on. I landed there at 4 o'clock in the morning, got a gharry up from the station and arrived at the guardroom of the 2 MTC. I went to the sentry, "My name is Rendall, I'm reporting to 2 MTC from the 2/5th Somersets, Burma. I've been transferred by Simla." He said, "Well, boy, bring your kitbag into the guardroom and there's a spare bed you can lie on until the barracks wakes up." The next I knew was that it was broad daylight, and the corporal of the guard sent a man, the orderly for the day,

*over to the barracks and he saw me into the barracks itself. I found it was a
very funny shambles of a lot.*

*Here I was handed over to a corporal, we were talking when up came the
dixie with the char; the morning tea, it was called gunfire in the army. My
cup was in my kitbag so the corporal, who was a Londoner, said, "Well,
have a wet out of mine when I've had one."*

*Next I reported at 9 o'clock after a lie down, to the CSM, disciplinary.
They had two sergeant majors; one was the CSM who was responsible for
drilling and looked after us for infantry training. The other looked out for the
mechanics side of things, he was the Mechanist Sergeant Major. He looked
after the workshop with its staff of twenty. Engineers, all sorts, from everywhere.*

*I soon found that I was yet another cap badge added to the regiment. You
could name any regiment you liked in the British Army, it seemed to be there
in 2 MTC; as an idea there were 16th/21st Lancers, the Welsh Regiment,
Hampshires, Kents, Wiltshires, Dorsets, two more Somersets, Surreys, DLI's,
HLI's and Seaforths.*

*All of these men from different regiments had been gathered from all over
India and Burma to form this new mechanical company. I'd undone my
kitbag and had been allotted space in the barracks, when this corporal came
up and gave me a real shock; I was promoted to full corporal! He took my
tunic down to the durzai and said, "I'll take your tunic and get the stripes
on, you're a full corporal now." I was just battered back, I didn't realise
how it worked; these stripes were only given you to be taken back on the least
pretext, if you proved incapable of doing certain work or you couldn't drive a
lorry, they then dug you out. They just took your stripes off and you went
back to your regiment wherever it was. I wasn't aware of it at the time but
I was on 'bloomer superior', a hell of a bloomer. However, someone elected
me and I'd done the travel.*

*I was there for a fortnight before the real test came. In the meantime
lorries were being sent out from England. I was only a boy when I left my
trade at Yeovil; I'd only done 18 months of my apprenticeship and when it
came down to it I couldn't time an engine properly so I was out of the
workshops. Simla hadn't checked my qualifications so it wasn't exactly my
fault. Now my stripes, everything looked set to go overboard and back to the
Somersets in Burma, 'Rendall, no good!'*

*I had everything packed ready to go back, after a month, when I was
called for at the Orderly Tent. Captain Bartlett, who was in charge of the
lorries, set me to work assembling these new lorries which had come out from
England, on a temporary basis. The lorries were beginning to pile up on
Rawalpindi Station. Captain Bartlett was Leyland's representative, he knew
his job damn well; believe me.*

*Now this is what sealed it for me to stay with the Company; there was a
thorough bunch of twerps putting these lorries together; only four of us knew
what nuts and bolts were. When we put the wheels on the lorries you had to
flop a great load of grease on the wheel bushes, yellow grease which resembled
margarine. You flopped your hands in it and you were stuck up mess. I
didn't know I was being watched when a youngster went to put a wheel on
without any grease. I said, "You bloody mug, that shaft's bone dry, where's
the grease?" I wasn't aware that Captain Bartlett and MSM Hutchins were
there watching. But it was a great feather in my cap. I fixed the wheel. As it*

Assembling new Leyland arrivals from England, at R. Pindi

33

34

Lorries and engine ready to leave station after assembly

pulling over workshop

35

SHWEBO TO RAWALPINDI

33,34,35
Assembling the Indian
Standard Leyland Lorries
at Rawalpindi, 1917.

36
Corporal B.G.L. Rendall,
Rawalpindi, 1917, on his
transfer to the 2nd
Mechanical Transport
Company.

was this kiddy was a carpenter who'd been mismatched somehow. That's why he made the bloomer, which is no different than an engineer drilling a chisel into a piece of wood and ruining it. Everyone to their trade.

We put together some 15–20 Thornycrofts and 8 Leylands. When the end came and all the assembling was done, there were 10 or 15 of us who were going to be discharged. What I did with the wheel was nothing really; it didn't fit me out to take a lorry and see the thing repaired inside out, from the Bosch magneto to the CAV lighting (although we had electricians for that). You had to know your engine or you weren't any damn good. Again I went up before Captain Bartlett, to go back to the regiment. Here Bartlett called in Hutchings, the MSM: 'Charlie', Bartlett said, (they used to chat with one another like that, you could call sergeants their Christian names except on the parade ground), "this is Rendall, who slashed Ramsden when he went to put that wheel on dry. Can't we do anything with him?"

With that Captain Bartlett got up and asked me to come with him and we went to where a great Leyland lorry was standing. It was 6ft. 3in. off the ground at the radiator cap. "Could you master that as a driver, Rendall?" I was honest, "I don't know" but he said, "Go back and undo your kitbag, you've got another fortnight here doing jobs."

I then went down to the barracks with another 15 blokes for driving tuition. I'd never driven before. I'd left an infantry regiment, the parade ground and the rifle, skirmishing and all the infantry boys, two on, four off. But that was all gone, I was now a corporal and I was going to learn to drive.

We went out along the Sohan Road which was a side road from 'pindi leading towards Nowshera. Each of us had a turn, sitting up, just running along, changing up. To our astonishment the corporal in charge, who was a good driver said, "You fellows have got 3/4 days of this." He taught us to change down through the gears, using the brakes as you changed down. You had to gauge it to the flat. God knows who was with me, either the Lord or the lorry, but I changed down three gears into first. We had one or two weeds, it would have been better to have given them crowbars instead of gear levers, Christ! Didn't they make a hash? We were lucky to make it back to the barracks with a sound lorry with one or two of them. We were sorted out once again and six of us were sent out on a test with the Mechanist Sergeant Major. We were reduced to five, one was put out. Now the final crack came.

The next morning, in the barracks, a Sergeant Taylor came up to me and told me to go the Orderly Room. Others had the same order. I knew what it was: we were the five who'd got through the first test. We had to go off with Captain Bartlett on a ten mile test drive. There was one fairly tough gradient in the run; one and a half miles, it was enough to try us out with the gearbox. One went, two went and as each one was nodded away, we watched from the back of the lorry.

The sing-out came, "Corporal Rendall," off I goes. Just before a wit had said to me to watch Bartlett making ticks and crosses on his clipboard. I started with the lorry in second gear, it was flat, when: "Pull up, corporal, what's the motive of starting in second?" I told him that it was flat and she'd take it quite easy in second and it would save petrol. "Yes, but I'm not taking it, corporal, pull her up, we'll have it from the start."

Off we went, 50 or 60 yards or so and we were soon in top gear. There were no speedometers on those lorries; you simply judged or gauged your speed according to the sound of the engine and gearbox; that was your salvation. I thought about the time and surged on forward for about a mile. "Pull up, corporal." Now I watched I didn't pull up too fast or too slow. I caught sight of Bartlett's book, I had three ticks; that really knocked my innards. We went over to do some reversing, the previous two had knocked their hubcaps here, but either the lorry or the Lord smiled on me and I went back perfectly, didn't touch anything.

Then we went back without using third gear, to teach me how to drive the lorry if it got crippled. I let her have it and found my second, I reckoned I was doing 10/15 mph and changed through the gear gate from second to fourth, click. Eventually we got back to barracks and pulled up outside. MSM Hutchins, anxious to get more drivers, asked, "How many did we get, Captain?" He said, "Four okay; one dud." "Back to your regiment, son," he had to go back to the Sussex, I never forgot; to Bangalore.

A couple of days after this the MSM came up to us, "You're out on a real test today, Corporal. You go up with Corporal Braxton and you're going up into the hills with a vengeance and there are six hairpins, two W's and one 8 bend, and you'll end up at a place called Murree." Now Braxton was a tall bloke and he was in the Cape Colony Police before the war. He made me drive. Now the convoy was all lined up; fifteen lorries had to go up there that day. We took tents, ice and all sorts of things for use by the civilians living up there.

I shall never forget my first hairpin, we went about 12 miles on the flat, out from Rawalpindi. Nearer and nearer these massive mountains loomed and at last we had our first pull up. Dick Braxton had been in the Company longer than me and he asked me what gear was I in? "Third". He told me to knock down a bit for my first hairpin I changed down into second on the little bit of flat that we had left and we went around the hairpin just fine and I looked at Dick Braxton, "What are you bloody well looking at me for? You did it alright or I'd have said something to you." He told me to look at the road or we'd go over the edge.

Eventually we got to a place called Tret, which was halfway up the Murree Hills, in the Himalayas, seven or eight thousand feet up. Our convoy pulled up. I was behind 3862, a bloke named Marshall. We'd left Rawalpindi at roughly 110 degrees, the sun was just warming up at 9 in the morning. We had to go into a place set aside for us, under guard where we had to change into English serge, thick driving gloves, overcoat, goggles and what have you. I wasn't aware of it, but we were going to finish in 3–4 feet of snow. I saw water running down the sides of the hills into the dust; this was the snow melt-line further up in the hills. Another couple of thousand feet and we were touching the snow line. We went round, did an 8 bend and came onto the flat and then a 1 in 10 gradient, one hell of a nap; you could have put steps in there. We did about 250 yards more, turned a bend and there was the snow, 1/4 inch of it, then more. As we went on the wheel tracks got deeper. The trees had snow stuck on the boughs just like in an Arctic winter. Finally we reached Murree, we were there.

We had to report to a Supply and Transport sergeant named Sorrell who was stationed up there to see to the lorries and their needs. There was a big depot there. This Sergeant Sorrell would unload us and tell us where to go. We drivers never actually unloaded the lorries, that was always done by whoever was on hand. That wasn't our job. We got rid of all the various stuff we'd brought up. We may have had a couple of hours free before we were set to go back down the hills again.

We were all ready, lorries reversed and we'd driven back down and pulled up in convoy ready to return to 'pindi. Now downhill is an ordeal, a hell of a sight worse than sitting in just keeping her in one gear on the flat at about 15 mph. You find that she gallops with the slopes so you had to watch your step. Dick Braxton was still with me, "Use your gearbox, use the compression and your gearlever but whatever you do don't miss a gear or we might go over the side and it's bloody deep over the side here. Some places are 9 thousand feet deep." We went so far down and we were last in the convoy, Dick had said to the convoy sergeant, "I'll come last if you don't mind sergeant, I've got a tutee here who needs finishing off. I don't want him to feel that he's being driven by the lorry behind him. I don't want his nerves upset by 10 lorries behind him, sounding their klaxons, telling him to get a bloody move on." There were plenty of times you were so close to the lorry behind that you could shout at the driver only 20 feet away, on an eight bend or a hairpin. We didn't want that, that's why we were last.

Now, we'd gone down four or five miles, that was about two or three thousand feet, when suddenly, it happened. The brakes went on, the lot. We stopped and Braxton said, "Get behind the wheel". So I did, and suggested that we went down in second gear. "You could do, but just watch it, mind, watch that switch on the dashboard. Now your engine will be running when you take the wheel. You'll shove her in second, come on down a little way, and just alter these regulators. Let the throttle be set for just ticking over, that way the engine won't race away and lose you your compression control. You'll need the compression to hold the lorry back when you're going down the steeper hills."

I put her in second, altered the ignition and stopped again, "Just trying it out, Dick." Put her back into second gear, touched the accelerator, slowly let off the handbrake and went on. Ahead of me, 35 to 40 yards was another damm, great, lovely 8 bend. Now all we had on board was a tent and a half, which was about 18 cwt to a ton, but that was enough. I eased her right down, round the bend. "Yeah, not much the matter with that," he said in his heavy voice, "Not a hell of a lot wrong with that, but let's have the next one a bit quicker. Do you realise the rest of the convoy is ten miles ahead of us, you'll have to put a bit of a gallop on, won't yer? We'll be back in the barracks after dark." I didn't think he'd fire like that.

However, I went down, swishing down this bit of a straight and that. I knew I could only hit the bank, if it came to that. On the next bend I used the footbrake, steady like, and came round okay. I was in third gear which was about 20/25 mph. So eventually we came down and around and we got to within two miles of the last bloke in the convoy ahead of us.

The further we went the faster I was getting, the more bends I took the worse the strain and a bloody sight worse my nerves got. We just whizzed round the bends without braking. There was this massive great radiator in front of you, you couldn't see the ground in front for a way. The wheels were pounding round beneath me, solid wheels and solid tyres, mind you. But oh, they were lovely strong things, and as we came out onto the flat we were about 300 yards away from the last lorry in the convoy. And these were all expert drivers. Dick Braxton said to me, "I shan't be up with you any more, nor you with me. I've some report for Charlie Hutchins when we get back. I barked at you but, by the Almighty, you have done well."

"There is one more thing we have to do and that's taking her from second to fourth gear." I upped and pushed on the accelerator, they were four cylinder

*engines, 36 horse power, Breeeoom. . . then he went like that (slap) on my knee
and I snicked her into top gear. "Keep your hand off the gearstick now, sonny,
you've got ten miles now without changing down. Ten miles down on a gentle
slope, we learnt that with experience," and we did. Now in between there was
always a slight rattle from the wheels, you know, they trattled against the bogies,
a sort of a metallic clank, clank. You could hear the engine going on under the
bonnet, whizz, whizz, whizz. We came all the way back in fourth gear. "Well,
we'll call you a 2 MTC driver now, I've finished with you and you have with
me."*

One of the leading figures responsible for the organization of Indian
mechanical transport during the early years of the Great War was John, 2nd
Lord Montagu of Beaulieu. He sailed for India on board the *Dunera* on 12
December 1914, in the same convoy as the *Ionian* and the 2/5th Somersets.
Colonel John Montagu had gained a great deal of military experience before
the war, having retired from the Hampshire Territorials in 1912 after 26 years
service. He returned to arms in 1914 to command the 2/7th Hants, another
Territorial Force battalion which had been raised in the same fashion as the
2/5th Somersets. The 2/7th Hants were similarly destined for garrison duties
in India.

On his arrival at Bombay, Colonel Lord Montagu accompanied his
battalion to its post at Secunderabad where it was to remain for the next 14
months. He did not relish the prospect of commanding a battalion faced with
garrison duties for the foreseeable future; he had long been an innovator, with
a particular interest in motor vehicles, and he took the opportunity of gaining
a more demanding position as early as he could. He was appointed to the
General Staff of the Indian Army at Simla on 7 April 1915 as Inspector of
Mechanical Transport. The job turned out to be more in the nature of
obtaining mechanical transport, for there was precious little to inspect in April
1915. It was shortly after this that numbers 1 and 2 Mechanical Transport
Companies were formed on the North West Frontier.

One of Lord Montagu's responsibilities was the preparation of periodic
reports on the state of mechanical transport. In the first of these reports, dated
1 March 1917 he gives a brief appraisal of the 2nd Mechanical Transport
Company and comments:

'British personnel seems here the chief difficulty. Many men posted to this
unit have been found inefficient as drivers and mechanics and taken a
considerable time to train before they become useful.'[18]

But Corporal B.G.L. Rendall had managed to weather the consequences of
his enthusiasm and he was to stay with his new unit as a Leyland lorry driver
for the rest of his time in India. He was spared an ignominious return to his
battalion.

18. *The Montague Papers.* VII/32.

8

LORRIES ON THE FRONTIER

LORD MONTAGU'S CRITICISM of the British soldiers posted to the 2nd Mechanical Transport Company might be considered somewhat harsh. Petrol-engined transport was at a relatively early stage in 1917 and progress was slow in the Indian Army. The majority of ordinary soldiers joining up for the war would have had little or no experience of cars and lorries: either of repairing or driving them. The recruitment of men for the mechanical transport companies seems to have been somewhat haphazard. Nobody at Simla had thought to check Private Rendall's qualifications. The shortage of men with relevant experience was to remain a pressing problem throughout the rest of the Great War in India. The mechanical transport companies were forced to look long and hard throughout the British and Indian Army units in India and Burma for men with engineering backgrounds. Hence Simla considered the expense involved in the transfer of a single British soldier, from Shwebo to Rawalpindi, to have been worthwhile.

Prior to the Great War, transport in the Indian Army was entirely comprised of animals, mainly mules and camels, which moved slowly, fed regularly and died frequently. These were under the control of the Supply and Transport Corps. There was virtually no mechanical transport in India. The subject had been well discussed, but nothing practical had been organised. As early as 1910 the subject was receiving serious consideration; the Indian Government had canvassed opinions from district officials in eighty of the country's districts as to the desirability of mechanical transport for civil duties. Despite receiving fifty-seven positive replies, nothing had been organised by the start of the war.

At the outbreak of war, India was seen by the British Government and the military establishment as a storehouse of men, materials and animals, ripe for raiding to assist the war effort. And well raided she was. In 1914, 'The troops sent to France were two infantry divisions, two cavalry divisions and four field artillery brigades; a mixed force was sent to East Africa and a brigade, after increased to a division, to the head of the Persian Gulf . . . the total was 23,000 British troops and 78,000 Indians.'[19] Much of the transport capability of the Indian Army went with them and, early in 1915, the authorities were beginning to wake up to the fact that too much had been taken. The Supply and Transport Corps was seriously short of animal transport.

Mechanical transport had yet to be accepted by all concerned as the answer to the transport problems in India. But by early 1915 there was enough acceptance by the military authorities at Simla for the setting up of two mechanical transport companies on the North West Frontier. No.1 Mechanical Transport Company was formed at Peshawar, No.2 at Rawalpindi. The exact dates and operational details of their formation are lost to us now, but it seems certain that they were fully organised by mid-1915. They started off with second hand lorries bought in Calcutta and Bombay by Majors' Nugent and Burgess of the Royal Engineers. The lorries, mainly three ton Fiats, were forwarded to Peshawar.

Personnel seems to have been taken initially from existing Indian and British units in the vicinity. Beadon records, 'Colonel Hodgkinson, an Indian Cavalry officer, obtained personnel by recruiting in his regimental area, and by this means two Indian mechanical transport companies were formed.'[20] To which Colonel Hodgkinson he is referring is unclear. There were two brothers and both were involved in mechanical transport on the North West Frontier; Lieutenant Colonel C. Hodgkinson (6th Cavalry) and Lieutenant Colonel J. Hodgkinson (5th Cavalry).

From the first tentative steps in 1915, to the end of the war there was to be continued expansion and progress in the field of mechanical transport. Colonel Lord Montagu was to provide much of the impetus by convincing the military authorities of the need for more petrol engined transport; in doing so he was having to overcome the natural British hostility towards anything new and mechanical. Many of the crusty old officers on the General Staff at Simla retained their cavalry and animals mentality. It is difficult today to imagine anybody seriously challenging the superiority of mechanical transport over mules and camels, even in 1915, but feasibility studies had to be carried out.

In July 1915 Lord Montagu prepared a report which compared animal transport to the newly purchased lorries, in the supplying of a division in the field with the 40 tons (excluding fodder or fuel) required daily. The report concluded that the lorries performed the job more efficiently in every respect. The lorries were more than capable of covering 60–100 miles per day in comparison to the average 10 miles a day covered by a mule and camel train. Lorries needed fewer personnel and running costs were much lower than with animals. Necessary animals amounted to 672 pack mules with 267 men in attendance; or with mule carts 1,242 draught mules with 139 men. Camels could do somewhat better than the mules; the job could be done with 246 camels ridden or chased by 89 men.

19. *A Matter of Honour* by Philip Mason (Jonathan Cape, 1974).
20. *RASC History of Transport and Supply in the British Army* Vol.II (Beadon).

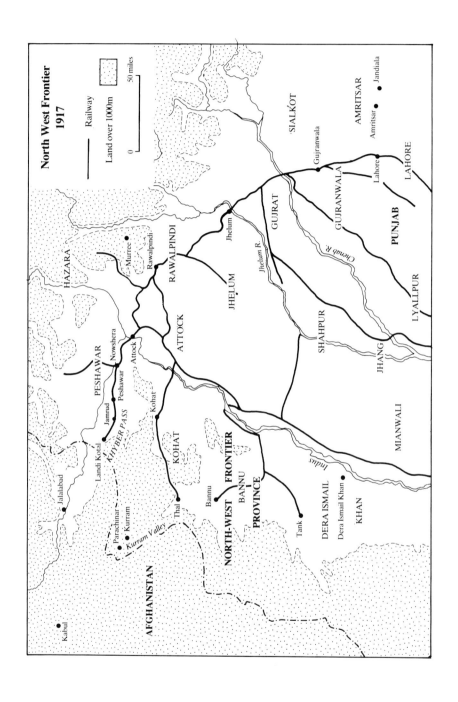

The same task could be performed with 21 two-ton lorries (42 drivers) or with 13 three-ton lorries (30 drivers). The study concludes; 'Mechanical transport, (average of both 2- and 3-ton lorries) is therefore much cheaper than animal transport, besides being faster and less liable to attack. . . .Transport animals even when not working entail a heavy daily cost for feed. Mechanical transport when not working merely requires superintendance. On these grounds I suggest that the Government of India should consider before long the extension of Mechanical transport all over India for Army purposes.'[21]

Further drawbacks to animal transport were seen to be the insanitariness of large numbers of animals using the roads and the very high death rate amongst pack animals in the Indian heat. Montagu highlights this aspect in a further report on The Mechanical Equipment of the Army in India, drawn up in April 1916; 'One of the most important lessons of the present war has been that mechanical equipment counts more than ever before in battle. . .Motor Transport. This should be used generally throughout the forces in India not only on account of the great mortality in the case of camels and mules from disease which reaches sometimes a figure as high as 100 per cent in a three months campaign, but also on account of superior mobility, the reduction of the number of personnel required and the lessening of tonnage to be carried.'[22]

Roads were vital, of course; it was quite pointless spending money buying lorries and organising mechanical transport in India if there were no adequate roads. Unfortunately, road building had been badly neglected in the years before the Great War. Simple reasons existed for this; there were no mechanical vehicles in India in any number hence few good roads. The railways carried most traffic and animal transport the rest.

The roads therefore needed much attention in 1915 and 1916. Large and heavy military lorries, running on solid tyres were going to cause much wear and tear. Roads were categorised into either pukka, meaning well made up with tarmacadam, and katcha, which were not and consisted mostly of dusty tracks. These were very susceptible to damage in the rainy season, during which they became impassible to military lorries. Lord Montagu's sphere of influence necessarily took in the state of the roads and they were the subject of numerous reports and memoranda between the various authorities involved. One such report came from Lord Montagu on 15 July 1915:

'It is very desirable that the Government of India should possess in mechanical traction an alternative means of transport to railways in times of internal disturbance, the Grand Trunk Road should be made continuous and able to stand heavy traffic and the more important of the roads connected with it should be put into a proper state of repair. . .The provision of mechanical transport and of armoured motor cars for the army in India will entail more attention being paid to roads, in fact it is putting the cart before the horse to

21. *The Montagu Papers* VII/7.
22. *The Montagu Papers* VII/16(b).

CPL. TAYLOR

...96(?) ... after her arrival from England.

37

On Instruction on
Murree Rd
1916

38

Going on test after erection

39

40

41

42

LORRIES ON THE FRONTIER

37
Corporal Rendall (on the left) at the garages, Cambridge Barracks, Rawalpindi.

38
Corporal Rendall and other trainee drivers of 2 MTC, on the Murree Road, North West Frontier.

39
Testing a Leyland, with a 1 ton box of sand, prior to the body being fitted.

40, 41, 42
Corporal Rendall, with his Leyland lorry No.3861.

embark on a scheme of motor transport before the roads over which this transport will have to be used are in a fit state to carry it.'[23]

Montagu's recommendations included the tightening up of administrative policy regarding road building and repairing; roads were under a variety of authoritative bodies and a cohesive approach simply did not exist. Roads in the sensitive areas where the use of military mechanical transport would be vital, such as the North West Frontier, needed to be strengthened. A uniform system of repair and depths of metalling needed to be adopted.

The years 1915 and 1916 saw the consolidation and expansion of mechanical transport in India; the early lorries purchased secondhand were being replaced by the Indian Standard Leyland and Thornycrofts which were being shipped out from England. The lorry, which was shortly to be given to the newly trained Corporal Rendall was a remarkable success story. The Leyland lorry, generally to become known as the RAF Type, owing to the large numbers supplied to the RFC/RAF, was perhaps the most successful lorry of the First World War. They were manufactured by Leyland in their factory at Preston and some 6,000 were commissioned by the War Office between August 1914 and November 1918. The Indian Standard Leylands, of which only 127 were made, were lighter than the RAF version, with a carrying capacity of 2-tons rather than 3. They differed in other respects; having larger diameter pressed disc wheels and a fully enclosed wooden cab with an extendable canvas awning which covered the bonnet, protection from the Indian sun.

The lorries were powered by a four cylinder unit which produced 36 horsepower; it had two pairs of cylinder blocks with screwed plugs over each of the valves to facilitate the removal of the valves without disturbing the cylinders. A skew gear driven camshaft ensured quiet running and the carburettor was a Claudel-Hobson. Sparks were provided by Simms, Bosch or BT-H, (in the case of Corporal Rendall's Indian Standard, a Bosch). It had four gears and a low oil pressure lubrication system. Oil pressure could be checked using a spring-loaded plunger on the dash board and oil level was ascertained by a float level on the crankcase. The clutch was a leather lined external cone type with a brake which decelerated flywheel speed when changing up the gears. Front and rear suspension was by semi-elliptic leaf springs attached to a channel section chassis.

When Private Rendall arrived in Rawalpindi he was initially set to work assembling the last batch of the 1916 Indian Standards. Ninety-seven of these were sent out in 1916; they were the last to go to India.

CPL B.G.L. RENDALL

Well, the next day I got sent for by Charlie Hutchins the MSM, he said,
"You'd like your own lorry, Randall?" Always called me Randall instead of
Rendall. "Like your own lorry, Randall?" "Yeah, at least I won't say no."
"Right, go down there, the third one in, there's no number plates on 'em yet.
That third one is yours, Corporal Stafford, the petrol minder will bring your

___
23. *The Montagu Papers* VII/9.

number plates down." I was there about 10 minutes with the lorry and there's a shout, "Corp, are you there? Got your number plates for you." So what you did was push your little block in, you had your round head screws straight through all the little lightening holes in the strengthened piece, and you screwed your number plate to the blocks, back and front. My plate was 3861; that was my lorry.

British personnel attached to Indian Army units retained their regimental cap badges and everything else that went with it. They were permanently attached to the Indian units they joined, but were nevertheless still soldiers of their parent regiment. This was all quite confusing to the ordinary British soldier who did not know much of the administrative workings of the British and Indian Armies. During the compilation of this book it took some time to explain the status of the 2nd Mechanical Transport Company to Bert Rendall. The proliferation of the different cap badges displayed by the various British soldiers in the company had led him to think of the unit as a maverick formation, not a pukka regiment at all. During his time on the North West Frontier Bert was to amass a large collection of the different cap badges on view.

CPL B.G.L. RENDALL

We weren't the only ones in the hills, mind, there was 693 ASC and 694 ASC. We used to call them the 'Star Badge Boys'. They were a proper Corps with their own badge. Now all of us lot – all of us lot in 2 MTC had no Indian cap badges and it was a sight to see, when they cleaned up and tidied up and one thing and another, all the different British Army cap badges they had there. It was a sight; and that's what made up my mind for my collection of cap badges.

Now we also had the Ambulance corps and they possessed Vulcan ambulances. And there were small Fords, we used to call them tin lizzies, they were up and down there like flies. And besides all this to contend with, we had the Mule Corps with their mule carts, we had the Camel Corps and there was more than one mule there, and more than one camel.

The Army Service Corps units referred to came to India in May 1916 together with 630 ASC Company which was an ambulance unit and 692 which was a supply column unit; the same as 693 and 694. They were to lose ten of their men in the lamentable Sind Desert Affair of June 1916. By mid-1916 the strength of mechanical transport in India was beginning to look respectable. Lord Montagu records the numbers;

'There are now about 670 Mechanical Vehicles of all kinds employed by the Government of India worth about £500,000. There are about 1,000 British rank and file and 410 Indian personnel. The number of vehicles is increasing very rapidly, and in a few months time will approximate to 1,000 vehicles with corresponding increase in personnel. The ordinary Mechanical Transport duties with existing Divisions will entail not only those connected with war, but before long with supplies of all kinds in every large Cantonment, provision of Staff Cars, demands from Medical and Hospital Authorities, as well as store keeping and repairs not only for Mechanical Transport but also

LORRIES ON THE FRONTIER

43
Colonel Lord Montagu of
Beaulieu, North West
Frontier, 1917.

44
Corporal Boniface with
second driver Grayson and
lorry.

45
A Vulcan ambulance.

46
A Thornycroft.

Cpl standing and vulcan ambulance

Transport which gives a complete picture of the state of the art in India on 1 the next few years.'[24] The strength of 2 MTC was as follows;

The unit is shown as having 47 lorries, makes not specified, 8 unit cars and in respect of personnel; 6 British officers, 64 British rank and file and 68 Indian rank and file, complemented by 31 followers and cleaners. In addition to the mechanical transport units mentioned so far there were also units at Bombay, Nushki, Karachi and Aden.

Not long after Private Rendall received his corporal's stripes and his brand new Leyland lorry, Lord Montagu prepared his first overall report on Mechanical Transport which gives a complete picture of the state of the art in India on 1 March 1917.[25] It is worth quoting extensively from this report, one of three that he wrote, giving a thorough appraisal of the situation:

'The period now under review is from September 1st, 1916 to March 1st, 1917. There has been, however, a large increase of mechanical transport both in personnel and lorries. In the spring of 1915 there was only one company of mechanical transport, with lorries of many types, and of varying carrying capacity. Three- and-a-half Indian transport companies are now practically complete. . .No. 2 Company had. . .47 Indian Standard lorries of homogeneous design and standardised as far as control, tyre sizes, carrying capacity and engine power are concerned. Additional standard lorries are constantly arriving which will soon make this company quite complete.

The results shown by both the Leyland and Thornycroft lorries of the Indian Standard type during the Khyber Road trials on December 19th 1916, showed that this type is the most suitable for work on the frontier and in India generally, especially during the hot season.'

The Khyber Road trials Lord Montagu refers to here were carried out in order to establish convoy speeds in the Khyber Pass, travelling from Peshawar to Landi Kotal and back, a journey with which Corporal Rendall would later become very familiar; Peshawar, Jamrud, Ali Musjid and Landi Kotal. The Indian Standard Leyland, with 2nd Lieutenant Bartlett in attendance, proved to be the best lorry on the day, with the Thornycroft performing very creditably.[26]

Returning to the report of 1 March 1917, the advantages of standardization in the design of the lorries was heavily emphasised.

'The general policy in regard to vehicles should be to equip generally all mechanical transport units in India with the standard type on the grounds of efficiency, economy and simplification. . .In regard to the personnel of Nos.1, 2, and 3 Mechanical Transport Indian Companies, some of the officers and most of the men are drawn from either the Territorial forces in India, or from outside industrial or commercial sources and a proportion only will remain after the war. The problem therefore of providing in future officers and men for regular Indian mechanical transport units is not an easy one and needs immediate attention. The best solution in my opinion will be to

---

24. *The Montagu Papers* VII/10.
25. *The Montagu Papers* VII/32.
26. *The Montagu Papers* VII/28.

establish without delay a training school for both officers and men and to invite all ranks in the Indian Army, Territorial Army and qualified civilians, both British and Indian, to volunteer for permanent service in the Indian Mechanical transport, which will be eventually a branch of the Supply and Transport Corps, when the mechanical transport is taken over by the Quartermaster General's Branch. . .As regards the use of mechanical transport in India. . .military operations demand nowadays a continually increasing amount of transport of a faster, more reliable and more sanitary type than animal transport. But this change connotes more and better roads and therefore the requirements of supply and military road policy should go hand in hand with mechanical transport policy. In addition the animals needed in India for transport purposes whether horses, camels, mules or donkeys are not only increasing in cost but diminishing in quality and numbers as well, and the continued prevalence of fatal animal diseases such as surra makes the rate of wastage of animals engaged in transport work very high.

In the 1915 campaign in the Swat Valley 100 per cent of transport animals died in the first six weeks. There are other important reasons also why animal transport on roads should as far as possible be replaced by mechanical transport, namely the amount and weight of fodder needed to keep the animals compared with the amount of petrol used by lorries, and the attractions to flies and other noxious insects which animal refuse provides, tending to spread disease among the troops.'

Lord Montagu concludes the report with his usual well reasoned and argued requests for increases in mechanical transport and further road building programmes. The following chart gives the strength of 2 MTC on 1 March 1917;

No.2 Mechanical Transport Company, Rawalpindi.
Commandant – Major Hall, I.A., S & T.

Vehicles:–

46 Indian Standard 2-ton lorries. Leyland and Thornycroft. 4 Napier 30 cwt.	The lorries, most of which are of the new Indian type, and comparatively new, were in good condition when last inspected on February 6th, 1917.
Cars:– 7 unit cars 8 motorcycles	The unit cars and motorcycles were in fair condition considering the inferior workshop facilities and personnel. The unit cars are frequently ordered out as staff cars as well. This practice should cease.
Workshop	No. 2 company has a stationary workshop in addition to 2 Indian Standard mobile workshops, the whole being under the supervision of 2nd Lieut. Bartlett whose former experience at Messrs Leylands of Preston enables him to make the best use of the means at his disposal. Petrol tank on Bowser system being installed.

Quarters	British NCOs complained of insufficient accommodation.	
Deficiencies on	British Personnel	33.
December 6th 1916	Indian Drivers	19.
	Vehicles	16.

It is to be hoped that this unit, when the remainder of its vehicles arrive, and consisting as it does, of nearly all new standard type vehicles, will shortly be one of the most efficient on the North West Frontier.

9

THE LUCK OF THE 2/5TH

'They also serve who only stand and wait'
MILTON. Sonnet 19, (1655).

THE 2/5TH SAILED from Rangoon to Calcutta on the *Arankola* with an escort, amidst rumours of German warships patrolling the Bay of Bengal, they arrived at their destination on 20 May 1917. Battalion Headquarters was set up at Dinapore where 'A' and 'B' Companies remained. 'C' Company, with CQMS Ewens and Lance Corporal Chant went on to Barrackpore, 15 miles north of Calcutta. The remaining company was posted on to Dum Dum, renowned for its firing ranges where the first testing of flat-nosed bullets had been carried out many years earlier.

Britain had been ruling the Indian sub-continent since the middle of the 18th century. In the year the 2/5th Somersets arrived the British were in the early stages of losing their grip on that vast country. The loss was to be a slow process, it would be another 30 years before that hold was relinquished completely, but the early signs that Britannia would lose her 'Brightest Jewel' were becoming apparent. Change, accelerated by all wars, was in the air in India during the First World War.

The demands of the war inevitably depleted troop strengths throughout the Empire as the regular battalions were sent to the Western Front and other active theatres. Many of the newly raised Territorial battalions, such as the 2/5th, were sent out to replace the recalled Regulars. The difficulties and dangers of transferring troops between Europe and the far flung parts of the Empire meant that usually units stayed in the Colonies; once sent there. India was no exception to the steady withdrawal of British soldiers, the number dwindled from the pre-war strength of 75,000 to as few as 15,000 at its lowest ebb.

This gave the various revolutionary factions in India the confidence to attempt some insurrectionary activities. These, most notably the actions of the Ghadrites, never came close to being effective rebellions, but they caused the authorities many headaches, with so few British soldiers to call upon in times of crisis. Even before the war, the number of British soldiers in India meant that they were thinly spread across that vast country. India had a population of just over 400 million in 1914 and in 1917 the 800 volunteers from Somerset were responsible for the policing of a province of 30 million Hindus and Moslems.

The battalion was to remain split up between Dinapore, Barrackpore and Dum Dum and was never together as a complete unit except at annual winter camps. Principal tasks at Barrackpore and Dum Dum included guarding a rifle factory at Ishapore, an arsenal at Dum Dum and a further gun factory at Cossipore. The battalion was part of the Presidency Brigade of the Lucknow Division and its Headquarters at Dinapore was quite near the City of Patna where the Government of Bihar and Orissa was situated.

CQMS E.W. EWENS

We had a lovely trip across the Bay on the *Arankola*, nothing exciting or untoward happened and we arrived in the Hooghly late on Saturday 18th May. It was getting quite dark as we anchored in the river off the low lying, swampy shore of the Sunderbuns. Our escort left us outside the mouth near the guard boat and proceeded south in quest of the German, all three of them at full speed. The sea was like a mill pond and that night in the river everyone was sleeping on the upper deck. Everything seemed to be steaming; this Bengal climate is very oppressive for a few weeks before the monsoon breaks.

The next morning we weighed anchor and proceeded upstream to Calcutta, arriving at the Kidderpore Docks at midday; 100 miles from the sea, and not a picturesque journey by any means. As we were docking we recognised a Yeovilian on the side of the quay. The greetings were mutual, as this was the first we had met from the town since leaving home $2\frac{1}{2}$ years before. We were all surprised to see him as we pictured him still working at the *Western Gazette*. How this paper was looked for when the Blighty Mail arrived. It did the round of all South Somersets with us, and was well thumbed when finished.

We received orders here; A & B Coys to Dinapore, C to Barrackpore, and D to Dum Dum. We relieved 2/4th Somersets in all stations who then proceeded to the Punjab. After disembarking and entraining with the usual fuss and bustle, cursing etc from a few executive officers, (we always did better when the men were left to their own NCOs) left for our destinations at 5.30 p.m. Dropped D Company at their station and reached Barrackpore 16 miles from Calcutta at 7. p.m. and marched into cantonments. Here again we were welcomed by several old townies, whom we left behind at Taunton and had meanwhile been sent out to the 2/4th on draft; they were of the opinion that it would have been better for them if they had come out with us at the start.

We took over early the next morning, the 2/4th Somersets marched out and we settled down once more to our duties, thankful to be in some sort of civilisation after so long in Upper Burma. At Barrackpore there was a large Attached Section of men from different regiments working at the Ishapore Guns and Ammunition factory about 3 miles away. A CQMS of the 6th Hants from this section kindly offered to pilot two or three sergeants around Calcutta on the following Saturday if we were available. This was arranged, for after nearly two years in the Shan States we were glad to get to a large city for a change. We left accordingly for Sealdah Station, Calcutta, on the Saturday noon and it took about $\frac{1}{2}$ an hour to get there. Our start was inauspicious, taking a taxi at the station we proceeded through Dhurrumtollah to the Hotel Bristol. (How many Hotel Bristols are there in the world? It speaks well for the old merchant adventurers from the busines centre of the West of England.) In Dhurrumtollah Street we unfortunately collided with a native carrying a large truss of hay on his neck and head, this appeared to over-balance him and he fell right in front of our car, the truss of hay was on the bonnet and the poor man, when we pulled up, was about 10 yards behind. We at once placed the man in the car and gave the taxi wallah instructions to take him to hospital, the native died and after giving our version to an inspector of police we heard nothing further.

Our pal of the Hants evidently knew Calcutta and proved an exceptional guide. Calcutta is no longer the capital of India, but it is the second largest in population in the British Empire: only the Hub of the Empire beating it. At Barrackpore there is an old English house built to suit the Indian climate, over the door of which and built into the wall in coloured tiles, is the name 'Charnock's Post'. This is supposed to be the outpost built by Job Charnock, the first pioneer of the old 'John Company' who landed an expeditionary force in 1686. The foundations of modern Calcutta were laid in 1690 under Charnock. The exceptional situation of the site was the reason for this, being at the highest point, ocean going boats could safely reach the river and it was also a position which tapped the fertile plains of Bengal and the valley of the Ganges. It was supposed to have been selected by chance as Rudyard Kipling writes in his Departmental Ditties;

'Thus the midday halt of Charnock more's the pity
Grew a city;
As the fungus sprouts chaotic from its bed
So it spread –
Chance directed, chance erected, laid and built,
On the silt.
Palace, mire hovel – poverty and pride,
Side by side;
And above the packed and pestilential town,
Death looked down.'

The first real set-back was in the days of the Siraj-ud-Dowlah, the notorious Nawab who thrust the captured garrison into a small room 18 by 14 feet known as the Black Hole of Calcutta. In the intense heat the 146 human beings in this closely packed place were overcome and in the morning only 23 were found alive. A tablet now marks the site near the Central Post Office, which is an exceedingly fine building.

The architect of modern Calcutta appears to have copied other fine buildings, in parts of the town, such as the fine Government House built in 1797 when the Marquis Wellesley was governor. This is based on Kedleston Hall, how prophetic this appeared when about a century later the owner of Kedleston Hall was appointed Viceroy of India.

The High Court is suggestive of the Town Hall at Ypres, before Jerry got at it, of course. Another fine sight which catches the eye on entering Chowringhee, one of the main streets, is the Ochterlory Column standing 165 feet high on the Maidan. Several other fine statues are to be found around Calcutta erected to the memory of past viceroys and generals. One extremely fine one is to be found in Park Street of Sir James Outram, cheering his troops onwards.

The Cathedral Church of St. Paul's is also well worth a visit and not far away

47

48

THE LUCK OF THE 2/5TH

47
Life in the Indian barrack room.

48
CQMS Ewens and other 2/5th NCOs in a river boat on the Hooghly, Calcutta, 1917.

49
Calcutta, 1918. Seasoned soldiers now.

is Bhowanipore Cemetery where one of our party a twelve month later was laid to rest. Charnock's remains rest in the old church of St. John's (which is supposed to be the oldest piece of English masonry in the town) covered by a mausoleum. The Maidan is a large open space given over to recreation and many a game of cricket and football the Somersets played there later.

The Bathing Ghats on the Hooghly are also well worth a visit, hundreds of natives bathing and all covered by a piece of cloth, they evidently believe in mixed bathing in India. On the opposite bank of the Hooghly lies Sibpur with the Botanical gardens; to the botanist a visit here affords a rare treat, one of the great objects is the acclimatisation of foreign plants, the greatest success being the China tea plant. Here grows the gigantic Banyan tree, over 90 feet in circumference, and is very often mentioned when tropical plants are being spoken or written about. The renowned Bishop Heber visited here at one time and referred to it as Milton's idea of Paradise only he (Bishop Heber) complained that it was flat and not a hill as per Milton.

Our visit ended here and after a peg or two at the Bristol we returned to our cantonment at Barrackpore. Barrackpore (in spite of fact that history books give Meerut as such) was the first place at which the Indian Mutiny broke out; a European sergeant major of a native regiment was here shot on the parade ground by discontented sepoys and so spread the flames of revolt through the Ganges Valley. His tombstone recording the fact may be seen in the old cantonment cemetery here.

Our cantonment is placed near a fine park attached to the Governor's country house, which is like a large country house park at home. Here may be seen the oak in company with the deodar of India, the mahogany tree of Australia and the maple of Canada, another immense squat tree about 20 feet high with very few and small branches but the trunk took 18 paces around it, over 50 feet, roughly a diameter of 18 feet.

The country around is very flat and largely given to the cultivation of jute, oilseeds, sugar cane and produce, clarified butter or ghee and food grain, amongst which is the universal food of the East, rice.

A small wireless station was attached to us here, for use possibly by the military in the Internal Security Scheme of India. Our duties were fairly light consisting of Quarter Guard and a weekly guard for the Ishapore Gun Factory. The Company, to the regret of many, was gradually losing its county and district character. Several men had been sent away from us to the different fronts and others drafted to us from home to take their place. Also Category A men from garrison battalions; amongst these others were a few rotters who caused us no end of trouble, having none of the usual esprit de corps manifested by the county men. One day one of these latter was brought up before the C.O. for being 'absent without leave' and he wore two conduct stripes on his forearm, however he got them goodness alone knows. The C.O. says, "What, absent without leave and a corporal too?" "No, sir", says the man. "Then what are you wearing those stripes for then?" responds the C.O. "Good conduct stripes, sir," answers the culprit to the discomfort of two other officers and the CSM in attendance, through causing them to bite their tongues to keep from laughing. It was not long after this occurence that Lieut. Jaspar (nickname) and our CSM were walking across the cantonment going to the Sergeants Mess for a lemon (sic) and a dog that had attached itself to No.11 Platoon, of which the above named Lt. was in charge. Several men wanting the dog to go for a stroll with, shouted, "Jaspar, Jaspar", the animal at once obeyed. The Lieutenant turned to the CSM and said, "What do they call that ruddy dog Jaspar for S.M.?", the CSM answers, "Don't know, sir." Officer; "I think they named the blighter after me." CSM; "It's quite possible, sir." And so it was.

At Barrackpore there is a first class race course and on race days the Coy is asked to supply men to act similar to policemen around the course. These men were placed under the charge of a sergeant who claimed to know everything there was to be known about a good horse undoubtedly because he looked after the Colonel's horse whilst in England. One of our younger officers, 'Weal Wed Wust' had a horse running that day and the troops backed it, to their detriment notwithstanding the advice of the owner, which was to leave it alone; but the sergeant put his shirt on his own fancy and it came up.

When he arrived back in the mess after racing was over, there was very little money about and faces looked long as the chit system had about reached the limit for that month. The NCO had a pocketful and always being free-hearted many thirsty souls drank his health as long as the money lasted. All the while he was extolling his knowledge of horseflesh and pointing out to the rest their ignorance of same; of course he was allowed to go on, because he was paying the piper so was allowed to call the tune. Afterwards, at another race meeting, the same officer entered another horse. This horse had run a secret trial with its opponents and they simply couldn't light a candle to it, we were given orders to put our last anna on it if money was wanted. We did, except the sergeant mentioned before who claimed the young officer didn't know a horse from a mule, and said he would back his own fancy as before. This time it won 5 to 1 against, bags of chips that night in the mess and no one was thirsty when the horsey man walked in looking glum, at once the leg pulling started but he was supplied with the necessary lubrication; all night, for his previous kindness, we heard little about horses afterwards.

The summer of 1917 was the third the men of the battalion had suffered; they were unaccustomed to the intense tropical heat and their health was beginning to reflect the fact. In traditional 'British in India' fashion many of the men were sent off to hill stations to give them some respite from the Indian sun. They were to spend short periods at Lebong, near Darjeeling and Jalapahar where the battalion's C.O. Lieutenant Colonel J.R. Paul was Acting Commandant.

CQMS E.W. EWENS

Late that summer the first batch of our fellows were sent to Lebong in the Himalayas past Darjeeling, and a wonderful journey it was too. A few of us left by the Darjeeling Mail at 5 p.m. one day and proceeded to Santahar. Before reaching this place we crossed the wonderful Sara Bridge. This bridge is erected to cross the lower Ganges instead of having to take steamer and join up by train again on the other side; it is a wonderful engineering feat, guide banks having to be built first to keep the river within its proper bounds. The immense strength of the banks will be understood when it is explained that in flood the river rises more than 30 feet above its normal level; the bridge consists of 15 spans of 352 feet and two land spans of 75 feet, total length of 5,430 feet, built to carry a double line broad gauge railway. The approach to the bridge is four miles long and at places 50 feet above the surrounding plain, on the right bank the approach is about 3 miles. Its cost was five million rupees.

At Santahar we changed into a metre gauge railway with the usual Indian sleepers, expecting to reach Siliguri at 8 a.m. the next morning. We reached there to time having a glimpse of the plain of the Eternal Snows on route; here the Eastern Bengal Railway ends.

We partook of breakfast in the dining room and joined the Mountain Railway for Darjeeling. According to the *Darjeeling Gazetteer* this railway did not take the engineering skill it was expected to, as it was built on the hard road from Siliguri to Darjeeling which was made many years before by the Public Works Department. The first view of the engines and coaches on this mountain railway strikes one as an elaborate model, they are so small, the coaches are about six feet high from the rails to the top and the wheels cannot be more than a foot in diameter. The seats carry three a side and then it is a tight squeeze. As you rise up the mountain railway with its many curves and gradients one realises that this small affair is just the train for the job.

From where we entrained, which is only 400 feet above sea level, to the terminus nearly 7,000 feet up is a distance of 51 miles, the gradient after the first few miles is always steep. The steepness in different places is overcome by different means; reverses, zig-zags and spirals, a peculiar one of which is the figure 8 bend, it looks exactly when sat in the rear coach, where we were, that the engine is coming round to meet you. The views going up are wonderful; neat tea plantations, forest clearings and fine waterfalls and one also experiences the cooler mountain air, after three years on the torrid plains.

One of the finest views is seen from the peculiar station of Kurseong; the mountains appear to drop away suddenly from your feet and in the clear air you see the plains of India stretching away into the misty distance, we were here about 5,000 feet up in the Himalayas. Fruit in abundance was passed on route; oranges, lemons, limes, mangoes, bananas etc. We did not go short of what we needed and there is nothing better to slake your thirst than these semi-tropical fruits.

On reaching Darjeeling we were struck by the motley and miscellaneous crowd of natives; Bhutanese, Thibetans, Nepalese, Marwaris, Punjabis and the ever present Bengalee babu. We made our way by the mountain road to Lebong, not knowing of the shorter cut throught the forest, with magnificent views of Kinchinjinga over 28,000 feet and the Sikkim range. Finally arriving at Lebong we found the bungalows well built of stone, they are built on a spur of a hill which has immense valleys both sides and in front and backed by the range on which Darjeeling is built.

In the early morning on walking to the door of your quarters these valleys are enshrouded in mist, and to you, being above it, it appears like a foam-flecked sea or lake, the shores on the other side rising up to the roof shaped and gable ended Kinchinjinga 50 miles distant. The rising sun's rays may be seen sparkling on the snows of the mountain, a long while before it touches the place on which you stand. As the mists roll away, dispelled by the sun, they assume fantastic shapes in the morning air and as it clears, it gives one a view at the bottom of the valleys of the rivers Rungeet and Teesta which are only 600 feet above sea level and you are nearly 6,000; the distance covered in the drop about four miles and covered with forest and trees. The rivers at that distance are quite discernible: their course may be traced for some considerable distance by the white plume by which they are covered, in the rapid course of the rock and boulders with which they are strewn. There is no more wonderful sight than the view from the top of Tiger Hill; a few of us left at midnight so as to enable us to reach the top before sunrise. It must take an artist's pen to describe the glory of that scene. We rode up on ponies and arrived at the top before the sun was over the edge of the eastern horizon. This spot is 8,500 feet up, not far from the barracks at Jalapahar and as King Sol arose above the earth we had one of the finest sights the Himalayas or the earth could produce. Away to the north-west was the cone-shaped Everest and the eternal snows seen to connect it with Kinchinjinga to our north. On the north-east was the Sikkim range and well above the snow line and running easterly nearly as far as the eye could see; this appeared like the teeth of a saw with no outstanding pinnacle.

One may better realise the immensity of the Himalayas when you are told that the whole of the Alps in Switzerland could be placed in the valley between Mounts Everest and Kinchinjinga and this comprises only a small part of the Himalayan Range. These snowy peaks seem to touch the sky as they rise up past tropical forests where the palms and plantations quiver in the sun's heat, through the temperate zone with trees which remind us of home and as they get higher the pine, fir and larch show themselves before the snow line is reached.

Practically all the valleys around here have been cleared of trees and are now flourishing tea plantations and it is quite an everyday sight to see a long line of coolies with tea chests, with familiar marks as seen at home, slung on their backs, steadied by a strap round their foreheads. Our stay at Lebong came to an end, but not before the Autumn races were held on a miniature course near our barracks, in fact it was our parade ground. These races were graced by the Governor of Bengal Lord Ronaldshay, and everyone appeared to have a flutter on the 'tote' which is in use here; no bookies to be seen.

It was at the end of September 1917, when many of the battalion's soldiers were resting at the hill stations, that the Islamic festival of Bakhr'Id led to the inevitable internecine rioting between Hindu and Muslim Indians. Serious rioting broke out at the beginning of October in Arrah, fifty miles from Dinapore. The local police had opened fire on the rioters. In response to the situation the 2/5th sent a force of two officers and seventy men from Dinapore, which left by rail within a few hours of receiving news of the disturbances. The detachment reached Arrah after dark and set up its headquarters at Jagdispur. They remained at Arrah for the next three weeks and helped to contain the situation. Generally the Indians kept well clear of the troops except on one occasion when a mob of about 5,000 Hindus were fired upon by the command of 2nd Lieutenant Revell in order to protect his soldiers. The small force of Somersets were reinforced by cavalry and military police and by 307 2/5th men who were recalled from the hill stations. Further disturbances were contained by the Somersets under Major Speke, in Gaya, south of Arrah. After some five weeks the 2/5th were recalled to Dinapore, having contained the situation.

Some minor rioting was to occur later in the year in Calcutta, shortly after CQMS Ewens returned from Lebong;

CQMS E.W. EWENS

Returning to Barrackpore we felt much better for our stay in the hills. During this football season which runs in the monsoon weather, our Battn soccer team was successful in getting to the final of the All India Challenge Shield. The rugger team went one better, winning the Calcutta Cup, open to all India and thus establishing a record, we understand, for the Army of winning the Burma and Indian Challenge Trophies in consecutive seasons.

It may be as well to mention here that while the battalion team was in Calcutta with their attendant men on leave, a few natives of Somerset who were domiciled in the city, took a great interest in their old county Regiment's doings. Particularly, was a brother of the late Colonel Marsh, an old 5th Battalion Commander and also a lady from Wiveliscombe who was so pleased with the result that she invited 10 of our sergeants for a trip by private launch on the Hooghly; this was readily accepted and a right royal time she gave them.

We understood that her husband was M.O. to the Bengal Nagpur Railway so possibly someone in West Somerset may know the generous lady. Three of us who were there, again thank her for the kindness.even after a lapse of 11 years.[27] Previously we had not been treated as though we were human beings by civilians, but rather as a nuisance that must be endured for want of a cure.   We wondered if this was the way the Regulars were treated in India.

We decided one day for the want of something better to do, to try and entrap a jackal and have a course the next day on the Maidan. A carpenter by trade who was with us fixed up a box much like a mousetrap; a lovely smelly piece of meat was put inside as bait and next morning there was the jackal all serene. Being a Thursday and a buckshee day all the dogs that could be got from the cantonment, Artillery, Attached Section and Somersets were taken together with the cage and its inhabitant on to the Maidan. Tommies held the dogs about five feet from the cage, the tykes had already been shown the animal and the excitement of both men and dogs was great as the word was given to open the door. As the jackal emerged the dogs were let go and at once turned in and had a great scrap amongst themselves, while Mr. Jackal sauntered off to safety and the jungle.

December 1917 the Viceroy paid his annual visit lasting one month to Calcutta and the battalion was honoured in having to supply the Viceregal Guard at Government House, although a Garrison Battalion of the Lincolns was in Fort William. This led to much heart burning and a scrap happened in this way. One Thursday, while the Guard was on duty there; as many as possible of our non-duty men would take a ½ day in Calcutta and at eventide would repair to the 'Temple Bar' in Dhurrumtollah. On this occasion about as many of the Lincolns were there at the same time and it was not long before the Viceregal Guard was mentioned. This caused a tremendous amount of leg pulling and they, then and there, decided to fight out the question in the street. Tunics off they were soon pummelling each other for all they were worth. A native policeman at the Chowringhee end blew his whistle as he spotted the melee and in about five minutes there were close on 200 policemen armed with batons charging the fighting Tommies. As soon as the latter spotted this, they forgot their grievances and like one man turned to meet the police whom they drove and completely broke up with their fists, then returned laughing to finish their drinks together at the saloon.

The men on guard won praise for their smart guard mounting and general carriage from several officers in high command, another feather in the Somerset cap. About this time rioting broke out in Calcutta between the rival factions of Hindus and Mohammedans. After it was quelled by the calling out of the troops, the 'sets among them were given to understand that the blarney started

---

27. The only indication in Ed Ewens' account which dates it as being written up in 1928.

through the Islamites killing a cow in the precincts of a Hindu temple somewhere in the Chitpore Road area. The followers of Krishna, Vishnu etc at once drove a herd of swine through a Moslem mosque and so desecrated and polluted it; therefore the row. After a few shots and a bayonet charge the riot was quelled but always after, should you be walking through Calcutta in uniform and the youngsters noticed the Somerset Badge they would at once cry, "Somerset barbary wallahs" and scoot away as fast as they could go, possibly chary of the walking out cane.

1917, Xmas Day was about our most miserable in the Sergeants' Mess. At that time we were mucking in with the Artillery in a so called station mess. A lot of extras for dinner were sent to the Mess by our Somerset pals in the district. It should have been enough for all. Upon our CSM, who was the senior in the Mess, taking his chair, the viands were brought in. Nothing was issued to us Somersets but army rations and to the Artillery who had charge of the arrangements, the good comestibles. The CSM saw through the move, protested and withdrew from the Mess. We all followed and for the rest of the time in Barrackpore never entered the Artillery Mess again. We fixed up our own mess in the SM's bungalow and we had, for the rest of our stay here, as comfortable and cosy a home as it is possible to have in the army.

In January 1918 the battalion was to train together at the Brigade Camp at Madhapur which was on the Bihar and Bengal borders. In all 520 officers and men were to attend the Camp which was under the command of the Brigade Commander, Brigadier General Strange. General infantry training was carried out, including the Kitchener Test, and the Brigade Commander was to congratulate the 2/5th for their efficiency.

CQMS E.W. EWENS

January 1918 we went under canvas for 6 weeks at Madhapur with the rest of the battalion and the food that we then received in the Regimental Mess did not compare with how we fared when responsible for ourselves. We noticed this at different times, why was it?

Orders were issued at Madhapur for us to transfer 7 Category B men to Mesopotamia. A bit of a wangle here, the last Medical Board had placed 7 of the worst, dirtiest and laziest in the Company on B1, us Sergeants were strongly of the opinion that our M.O. had something to do with this, for as soon as these men were for any extra duty they swung the lead and went sick and so got known. It was with the greatest of pleasure we saw them pack up and shove off. By their acts they had been detrimental to the rest of the men. One was supposed to be a penal servitude man let out to join the army and he was simply impossible in every way; yet in his manner to officers and NCOs very inoffensive, yet so cute, just one of those men it was hard to get at. We were also of the opinion that our OC knew as much as the M.O. about this send off. You will understand by now that this is not given to you as it possibly appeared to others, but only as it appeared to us.

Whilst at camp we were supposed to have a night march by compass, what a farce judged by what we learnt afterwards; the officer who was supposed to lead us actually went over every bit of the route by daylight, the same day as we marched by night. After the march he was congratulated by the GOC when as a matter of fact he was entirely ignorant of what marching on a compass bearing was.

We returned after the training to our old station and the first item of interest was an invitation to the sergeants to spend an evening with the Cossipore Artillery Volunteers I.D.F. at their camp near a place called Joffarpore. This corps is made up of civilians, like ourselves and are known to the Tommy as 'Jute Wallahs' being fellows employed in the jute mills which abound along both banks of the Hooghly between Naihati and Calcutta, and especially thick near Barrackpore. A very fine evening we had; everything was 'freemans' and they laid themselves out to entertain us properly, which they did.

There are a few old ruins hereabouts – possibly the remains of an old palace or something of that sort, for by its name it gives one the impression that it was once the home of Mir Jafar who was made Nawab of Bengal by Lord Clive after his victory at Plassey. We experienced here at Barrackpore a plague of flying ants. We were taking our places for dinner when in a few seconds the whole of the mess was a mass of these insects. As they alighted their wings dropped off and covered everything – foodstuffs, tables, floors and by the time the invasion finished, although this may appear unbelievable, we swept up three baskets full of these fine gossamer wings from the floor. There must have been millions, besides those that we swept out of the doors.

In June 1918 the companies were turned around, 'D' and 'C' Companies were sent up to Battalion H.Q. at Dinapore and the two companies previously at Dinapore relieved them at Barrackpore and Dum Dum. By this time the 2/5th Battalion (Prince Albert's) Somerset Light Infantry had lost many of its original county volunteers. The battalions in India and Burma were to constantly supply men for other units in need of personnel, in the more active theatres of the war, such as Mesopotamia and German East Africa. Many Somerset men, such as Bert Rendall, had left the battalion. Signalling and machine gun sections had further depleted the ranks of the county volunteers. In July 1917 the battalion became more cosmopolitan with the arrival of 250 reinforcements from England, not all of them from Somerset. Some men left on duties at Army and Divisional Headquarters, others went to the Ordnance Department and to the Supply and Transport Corps. The Indian Defence Force and the various newly formed Indian Army units absorbed more of the soldiers of the 2/5th. The Book of Remembrance records, 'A marked feature was the number of NCOs sent to the newly raised units of Indian Infantry for duty as sergeant instructors. On 7 November 1918 no less than 11 Sergeants and Acting Sergeants of the battalion left Calcutta for Mesopotamia attached to the 3/9th Bhopal Infantry.'

One of the few mementoes left by Morely Chant records his having joined the Bhopals shortly before this. A card with a bible quotation from St.Matthew, Ch.11, Verse 28, which was secured in the frame of the photograph of him taken in Calcutta, had written on the back; 'Joined Bhopals at Calcutta 23.9.18. Left Bombay 10.11.18. Arrived Basra 16.11.18. Left Basra 2.2.19. Sailed to the bar on H.S.Bandra.' It is not known when he was made up to sergeant. Bert Rendall remembers him as a Lance Corporal, and was most surprised when shown the photograph of him as a full sergeant, 'So Morely got three up, well I'm damned!' When the Armistice came the newly formed units of Indian Infantry such as the 3/9th Bhopals were no longer needed and the Somersets who had joined the Indian battalion were probably the first of the 2/5th to be sent home from Mesopotamia.

CQMS E.W. EWENS

In June 1918, we exchanged places with 'B' Coy and proceeded to our H.Q. at Dinapore, a journey of 350 miles. We arrived at Khargoul; the station for Dinapore, in the morning after travelling all night and proceeded to cantonments. The country around was much the same as in Bengal; flat and with very little to relieve the monotony. The River Sone, a tributary of the Ganges, ran alongside the northern side of our barracks. These barracks were brick-built bungalows, but not such imposing affairs as at Barrackpore. The Sone is not a large river by any means in the dry season, but when the monsoons are on it compares very favourably with, and is larger than, the Thames at Windsor. Many a pleasant hour and day we spent on this river on Thursdays in a boat provided by the Government for the troops as on the lakes, Rangoon.

A Battery of Artillery was stationed here and they turned out to be Terriers from Kent. Needless to say we were pals from the start, quite the reverse to the unpleasantness at Barrackpore. Several native battalions were also stationed here; but we had very little to do with them, outside some vey strenuously fought hockey matches.

It was in our early days at Dinapore, when we were under a kind, but soldierly – every inch of him, Acting C.O. and a rotten Acting Adjutant, the two gentlemen whose place they took being away on some duty or leave, that C Coy was told off to build a double trestle bridge over a swollen stream. Up to now not one in the Coy had any experience of actual bridge building although well versed in the art of knotting and lashing and fairly well theoretically trained in the other.

After a struggle the bridge was erected by the NCOs and men themselves under the CSM when the Acting Adjutant rode upon the scene, and at once started criticising. Now this man was in training as a civil engineer at home and didn't forget to let everyone know it;

Adjutant;	"Sergeant-Major you have got that damned bridge higher in the centre than at the sides."
CSM;	"Yes Sir, about a foot."
Adjutant;	"What the devil is that for?"
CSM;	"Camber sir."
Adjutant;	"What ruddy well is camber?"
CSM;	"Well sir, if you are a civil engineer and don't know it's not my place to tell you."

This officer had make a mark of our CSM two or three times before, who awaited his chance and got one home, the Acting Adjutant was very chary after this but his nickname was very appropriate;. . .*(Here the next line in the account has been rubbed out.)*

Our RSM was not noted for his learning or knowledge of Hindustani. One mealtime in the mess a sergeant called one the the bearers and said, "Boy curry lao monta hai." Boy; "Ah cha, Sahib." The RSM; "What, bring I some too, boy. Mountains high. I can eat as much as he." And even then he couldn't 'savvy' why some of us had to leave the table with our sides aching; it was impossible to carry on eating. He tried to be very regimental at times and didn't know how.

Whilst at Dinapore the Sergeants' Mess was asked to play football against a

50

51

52

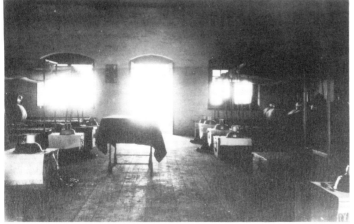

53

THE LUCK OF
THE 2/5TH

50
The origin of much of the
souvenir brass-ware which
found its way into
Somerset homes after the
2/5th returned.

51
In the native quarter,
Calcutta.

52
The napi (native barber).

53
The barrack-room,
Calcutta.

school at Digha Gleat named St. Xavier's (could this be Kim's old school), some went by gharry and five by boat. It was about two miles to 2½ down stream on the Ganges, at eventide just as it was getting dark they started to row back to Dinapore, but the river was in spate and after two hours in pitch darkness, and properly rowed out, they again made the bank and had not the slightest idea of where they were. Imagine their surprise when they found they had landed within 10 yards of where they left 2 hours before and still in the school grounds! They returned later, by gharry, after another meal at the school.

Early one morning all were awakened by a peculiar rushing and rumbling noise and presently the doors and windows swayed to and fro banging and slamming. Nearly all jumped out of kip and made for the outside. Just another earthquake experience but they are not pleasant, especially when things rock a bit and you don't know whether you are on land or sea.

'C' Company missed the major rioting which was dealt with in their absence by the other companies. Again, in September 1918, serious rioting broke out in Calcutta. A large group of Muslims attempted to gather in the city, in which demonstrations had earlier been banned by the Governor of Bengal. 2/5th soldiers from Barrackpore and Dum Dum were rushed to Fort William and a small party under Lieutenant J. Bell was forced to fire on the rioters after the natives had repeatedly rushed the soldiers with bamboo lathis. *The Statesman* said of the riots; 'There can be no question as to the justification of the action of the troops. If a mob, fired by fanaticism, had swarmed across Calcutta Maidan and forced their way into the city, a situation of the utmost gravity would have arisen.' The British were beginning to lose their grip on the Indian subcontinent.

CQMS E.W. EWENS

July 1918 our fellows were again doing well in the Calcutta Cup and riots broke out in Calcutta on the same night as we won the final against the Duke of Wellington's, this was one of the regular battalions left behind when war broke out and they suffered from swelled head a bit. They had only to walk on the field to frighten the Terriers but did they? We beat them by more than we beat the Calcutta team in the semi-final.

The 'chipping' and 'leg pulling' between the partisan onlookers who could get leave was unmerciful, whilst the match was in progress, but those who laugh last laugh best when the final score was 15 pts to 3.

That night and for some little time we were on outpost and picket duty in Calcutta streets, all our men at Lebong also being brought down for the blarney and a collision occurred between a few of our 'B' Coy men and the natives trying to rush the Tollygunge Bridge; to the detriment of the natives, but this incident stopped the row in Calcutta and it gradually died away once more.

We occasionally visited Patna, one of the sacred cities of the Ganges and about seven miles from us; nothing unusual was here except sedition and several enormous dome shaped structures, with no apparent doors or windows and which we were given to understand were granaries to store grain from the surrounding country, when plentiful, to enable it to be kept against the time when famine stalks the land. Our RSM was sent up to the hills in July for a fortnight's leave, but he was kept there at least for another four months as an instructor to the I.D.F. What a relief for us. How very stupid some of our WO NCO's made themselves, they had only joined for the duration and seemed to forget that the very men they bullied at times would be their townies again when the war was over. And now some of these same NCO s are full of remorse, when a little tact would have made it pleasanter for everyone concerned and yet it would not have been 'conduct to the prejudice of good order and military discipline.'

10

AN UNSUNG TASK

THE NORTH WEST FRONTIER of India, for so long the hot spot of the British Empire, ran from Chitral in the north down to Baluchistan. It consisted of a belt of administered territory adjacent to areas of unadministered tribal lands which separated India from Afghanistan. The terrain was spectacular and harsh, inhabited by the fierce, proud Pathan tribesmen. The Frontier tribes, of which there were many, varied in the degree of loyalty, or hostility, they showed toward the British Empire.

The political make up and composition of the North West Frontier area meant inevitable and frequent hostilities with the Pathans, fuelled by Afghan and British intrigue with the occasional jihad (holy war) to add to the general unrest in the area. The Frontier gave the British and Indian Armies a good deal of fighting experience. The Indian Government always maintained a sizeable military presence on the Frontier, using both regular forces and the Frontier Scouts, who were a militia force largely recruited from amongst the more friendly Pathan tribes.

The 2nd Mechanical Transport Company was employed in supplying the various army units throughout the North West Frontier; an unsung task but one vital to the establishment of the British presence on the Frontier. The climate was, at all times, exceedingly hot, with some areas in summer registering temperatures of up to 120 °F. The terrain presented spectacular gradients with which the lorries had to cope. They were aided by many varieties of specially constructed bends; hairpins and eight bends, W-bends, all designed to minimise the steepness of the incline. Corporal Rendall was to spend two years and nine months at Rawalpindi, driving some 38,000 miles in all, hauling all manner of stores, equipment, ammunition, tents, ice to remote outposts, to the hill stations, up through the Khyber Pass; all over the North West Frontier region.

CPL B.G.L. RENDALL

We weren't the only ones at Rawalpindi, we had one or two more corps at Cambridge Barracks. There was the 28 Motor Ambulance Corps and they had Vulcan ambulances; they were up and down there like flies and they did the work of bringing down the wounded, two at a time, that was all they could carry.

Then we had 693 Army Service Corps, their lorries had small wheels. The front wheels had five spokes and the rear ones six. Now a Thornycroft had six spoked wheels front and back. Thornycrofts were mixed in with our Leylands. The ASC Companies had Albions, I think; much more in the front than our Leylands. We used to have a lot of friendly banter you know, at times we passed each other so close on the bends that we could shout to each other, and I must admit that I did it myself: "Get your bloody Thorny off the road, get your Albion off, there isn't a lot of room with you here." It was just plain daftness you know, and of course they would bang back with their retorts. Something on the same standard as two sailors from different ships meeting ashore might, "We'll take the Newcastle out and sink her." Something like that. 'Twas friendly enough, well, regiments used to be like that. It went too far sometimes, I saw it happen once, two damned fools fighting over a cap badge; there were some fools about mind.

We occasionally had some unpleasant skirmishes with the drivers of 693 & 694 ASC; there wasn't much humour in some of them and one day it happend in our Corporal's mess. They used to come across to our mess sometimes for a change of venue, and put a drink or two down. We often went to their mess. There was a very poor standard of joking about their Albions, and our Leylands, they got funnier and funnier. Then it got beyond a joke, I was sitting with this Devon corporal; Alf and I were having a drink. Suddenly a table near us went over and I heard the words "I ain't scrapping for bloody cap badges but I will fight over the lorries." The bloke they took apart was, as luck would have it, a big mouthed aggressive cove from our Company, so we didn't get too involved. But it damn soon got around the barracks and it enlarged so that the officers on both sides threatened to call us together and line us up face to face for two hours. Either the hate that was creeping in would disappear or it would get worse, in which case it would be "ASC confined to barracks, 2 MTC confined to barracks."

A lot of the tension was caused by us laughing at their bloody small wheels, we used to call their lorries platform trollies. We used to say to one another in our barracks, "Bugger off then son and join 694 ASC, then you can drive a platform trolley." Some of our blokes had too much wallop and big mouths. And we saw some fights over cap badges as well, that was one thing you would stand up for. All you had to do was look at the bloke and say that his cap badge wasn't much good, that was all.

But most of the time things were alright, the ASC weren't all sour you know, it wouldn't do; you couldn't have sour next door to each other all the time. All the regiments had their trouble makers though, all through life there's those that will put up their fists for the looking at.

Shortly after Corporal Rendall gained his brand new Leyland lorry Colonel Lord Montagu gave a brief appraisal of the situation in India regarding Mechanical Transport in a confidential document.[28] At that time there were

28. Montagu Papers VII/30.

some 700 vehicles in India, comprising lorries, ambulances and staff cars. A third mechanical transport company was being formed at Karachi. In addition there were the three ASC Companies making a total of five mechanical transport companies in all, with a total carrying capacity of 450 tons per day, enough to supply $2\frac{1}{2}$ divisions in the field.

Mechanical Transport was by then regarded as the answer to India's transport problems by all the authorities concerned. The number of vehicles was still small though and it was seen as important to conserve existing vehicle carefully, 'M.T. cannot achieve the impossible. . .During this war we must nurse our Mechanical Transport in India.' There was still a pressing shortage of trained British drivers and no solution to the problem in sight. A driving school had been mooted for the training of native drivers; 80% of drivers were British Territorials and it was realised that the majority of those men would return home as soon as the war was over. The drivers worked a six day week, five days driving and one day cleaning and looking after their vehicles.

Despite, 'Increasing difficulties and cost of obtaining satisfactory animals for transport purposes and prevalence of animal diseases,' rough and heavy work was still allocated to the animal transport units, especially where considerations of time and speed allowed of the use of pack animals. The Mechanical Transport units were reserved for the more important transport tasks. Railways were still to be used wherever possible with the lorries carrying supplies from the railheads.

The Indian Standard Leylands and Thornycrofts were continuing to impress. The Indian Standard lorries were specially designed to cope with the exigencies of the Indian climate. They differed in several respects from the lorries of similar make sent out to France; 'Much larger radiator: higher fan speed: more cover for driver: increased clearance from ground: greater engine power compared with total gross weight – tare and load.'

Standardization had many advantages, '. . .interchangeability of drivers: store keeping: suitability for running on rails. Already wheels: tyres: control: weight carrying capacity: tare weight: are the same in vehicles of Indian Standard type'. Lord Montagu continued in his role as innovator with many other suggestions for the future improved efficiency of the Mechanical Transport capability in India, there was a 'Need of close touch with European mechanical developments: India Office and Mechanical Transport supplies.'

Corporal Rendall knew little of the overall scheme for mechanical transport in India, he continued with his job of driving the lorries. Life in Rawalpindi, as at every other military cantonment, was insular and isolated for the British soldier, they had little or no contact with civilians. Rawalpindi was a large garrison town with several other infantry barracks in addition to Cambridge Barracks, which was comprised of transport units and other specialist arms.

CPL B.G.L. RENDALL

Also in the barracks at 'pindi there was the 22nd Motor Machine Guns, they had a bright idea of carrying a machine gun in battle. They had Norton motor bikes with a second bloke sat in the sidecar with a machine gun attached to a bracket. He sat comfortable like back in a seat and rattled away at the enemy. You have never seen such a carnival in all your life, talk about half cocked! Well for all this they were a nice bunch of blokes and once, just once, we saw them in action. It was a Sunday morning and all the other men had been taunting them and one of their sergeants got permission for them to put on a display for us. They put six of these motorbikes through their paces for the benefit of the motor corps. I don't think there was a man who stayed in the barracks that morning, it was bloody wonderful, the shapes they turned those motorbikes round; they nearly turned them inside out, upside down. They wound up with two targets and they blew those targets to pieces from 200 yards. So the ribbing died out and they became our pals.

Further over in the barracks was a wireless section, near the 22nd MMG's. They were wireless telegraphists. These were all well made brick barracks, they weren't bungalows by any means. They had stone and concrete floors and gas lights (some difference that from the oil lamps in Burma, hanging from the roof.)

Cambridge Barracks, Rawalpindi were some 60 miles from Peshawar which is nearer to the Khyber. The East Yorks barracks were about $1\frac{1}{2}$ miles from us and the Gordon Highlanders were down the other side of us. 'Pindi was a really big army depot. I'd first heard of Rawalpindi when I was in Burma and two of our lance corporals had gone there on a platoon drill course. They shortened the name to 'pindi so I only had half of it then. There were two lovely great railway stations there.

There were also picture palaces, we could go into town on our days off. The soldiers had a bad time with the civvies generally. The civilians lived in their own areas of 'pindi. It was like that in any town or city in India; they had their own streets, one of which was the Mall. One of our lorries went down the Mall one day and that same night a notice was posted that this corporal and his lorry down the Mall would be dealt with pretty severely if he ever did it again. We had to keep off the civvies' precincts; they had some lovely brick built buildings, they had the lot. Now you can understand the damn stinking snobbery; there were retired colonels, retired generals, all the medical chiefs, you name it they were there. Oh yes, there was very little below the rank of major up there, and the bloody tommy had to wipe his boots before he could even walk down the street. That occurred, it's written all over the British Raj, they used to love their chukkas you know and their games of polo on their polo ponies. Each officer had to have a couple of polo ponies; he wasn't much of an officer if he didn't.

We got friendly with a section of the public, hence we could borrow some civvy clothes and get taken in, we'd get a high collar, what was called a butterfly collar. We could look smart. Or we used to go out in what were termed blue patrols. That means we were all dressed in blue. My regimental colours were blue with white piping and a red stripe down the legs, gold and red lined stripes on the arms and gold and red epaulettes on the shoulders. Other than that the various different uniforms we could wear were many. It was quite relaxed. The variation of clothes we had was anything from a pair of knicks like footballers wear, pair of long socks and a singlet to your proper tunic with leggings and breeches or puttees. It seemed that anything went; we had four or five different uniforms.

The other units I've mentioned, such as 693 and 694 ASC, had pretty much the same duties as us. We were transport drivers and we carried

The Broken Road and lorry.

54

55

In the Indus.

56

57

58

59

AN UNSUNG
TASK

54
A Thornycroft having run
out of road!

55
The over-turned
Thornycroft.

56
Another Thornycroft, in the
River Indus.

57

Men of the 2nd Mechanical
Transport Company view
Calcutta by gharry.

58
Cambridge Barracks,
Rawalpindi.

59
Tank, Baluchistan, 1917.

Cpl. Thompson driver to General Dobel

60

61

View of Leyland Workshop with sideflaps down
this one contain, a lathe, bench and vice,
double wheel grinder, and small forge, all worked
from engine when lorry is stationary, as well
as its own lighting plant and has accomodation
for 3 workmen at the same
time. Basla 1918

M.T.6 Repair dep? Sunnybank
Murree. 1917

62

Snow and frost at Murree, but down at R Pindi 38 miles away was a temperature of 125°

63

64

65

anything and everything on the NWF. We were part of the Supply and Transport network. They had great depots which contained everything you could think of, you name it they had it, down to a food service, tents, suits of clothes, army socks, hats, cap badges and grey shirts, lovely things.

The roads were just like a lovely old country road in England. There wasn't much tarmac, for a start off; nothing like that. And so often did we go up and down these dusty mud roads that in some parts they were wore so smooth that you could almost play a hand of cards driving on them. The wheels bedded the roads down where we had cut it away so and it powdered away into dust, you see. The same applied in the Khyber, we'd ploughed it out so, we drove in darned great wheel ruts. There weren't too many potholes around, it was very good for that. We'd worn such a lovely smooth track all up and through the bends, we cut our own track. We had what we called the 'wheel wobbles' but nothing whatever serious. The front wheel would jump a bit, but there was nothing to be alarmed about. We'd go off in convoys, the number of lorries varied on each occasion. We had regular runs, like up the Khyber to Landi Kotal or from Rawalpindi up to the hill station of Murree, that's where a lot of soldiers had their rest periods. We never had much warning of where we were going off next. The sergeant would wake us up in the morning, pull up the mosquito net and would say, "Your orders, Corp, out on the road at 9 a.m., report to Sergeant so and so, S & T Corps. Report down there and take a load of tents to Burhan Camp."

There were quite a few natives attched to the barracks; we had boot boys and what have you. We had a punka wallah who sat all day long from daylight till dark pulling the punka. This was worked by a series of ropes hanging from the ceiling with a pole holding a square of canvas maybe 18 inches square. This lot rocked backwards and forwards, connected to the punka wallah who sat outside pulling the rope; this left the barracks nice and cool.

Another thing out there in Rawalpindi was a damned thing trying to keep the barracks awake and with all my trying I never managed to see one; they were clapper frogs. The din that they kept up was just like rattling about 10,000 glass jars and always after a monsoon rain. God knows where they came from but they always came out after the heavy monsoon rains.

On the convoys in the hot weather there was always a load of dust flying about. If you were 20 yards behind the next bloke in the convoy you couldn't see his number plate owing to the dust. Well, you can just imagine that. It was so hot when we stopped at the changing rooms at Tret half way up the Murree Hills, that the ignition would backfire and the engines would run backwards with the sheer boiling heat in the radiator. Everything was red hot, that's why the radiators were so big on the Leylands, they stood 6ft. 3in. off the ground.

Now, in 2 MTC, the corporals and sergeants went into Rawalpindi and bought all the different cameras they could find. They could afford it, being NCOs we got paid more than the privates. But I was no photographer so I didn't try it. Every so often in the barracks they'd come up to me and say, "Here, corp I've got a few more; have you seen these?" And I'd buy all the best photographs from these six or so cameras and ended up with the best collection of pictures in the Company. I have about 720 of the NWF and another 100 or so of the action in the Khyber.

All through 1917 and 1918, while the Great War raged on and on in the fields of France and Flanders, Corporal Rendall and the other drivers continued to ferry supplies around the various army units and civilian establishments on the North West Frontier. The 2nd Mechanical Transport Company was almost complete in early 1917, all its Leyland lorries had been sent out in 1916, but the other M.T. units in India were still expanding at a rapid pace. The numbers had more than doubled upon the writing of Colonel Lord Montagu's second Report on Mechanical Transport at Simla on 10 April 1918.[29]

'The period under review is from March 1st, 1917 to April 1st 1918. There has been a further increase in Mechanical Transport both in personnel and vehicles. . .there are altogether five complete Mechanical Transport Companies in India. . .this comparatively meagre provision of Mechanical transport cannot be said to be excessive.

The road trials held in July 1917 under Lieutenant Colonel W.P. Robinson, DSO, showed the suitability of the Indian Standard type, especially that of the Leyland lorry. . ...Since last year, my recommendation in favour of establishing a school for Anglo-Indian and Indian drivers has been adopted, and the school at Sohan near Rawalpindi has been turning out 300 to 400 drivers a month, most of whom have been sent to Mesopotamia. As there is little chance of obtaining European drivers in sufficient numbers at present, this school will be of increasing assistance to the M.T. Services both in India and in areas supplied from India.

The bodies for motor vehicles now being built in various railway shops in India for M.T., though rather crude in workmanship, are serving their purpose well, and in course of time, with proper skilled European supervision it may be possible to build all bodies for M.T. units in India.

A further study of the conditions both in peace and war of the three frontier brigades at Kohat, Bannu, and Dera Ismail Khan, has convinced me of the desirability of forming a Frontier Brigade M.T. Company.

I put on record. . .that the present state of the M.T. units in India is as follows:–

Officers	70
British personnel	1196 (including 258 artificers)
Indian personnel	596 (including 89 artificers)
Indians under training	1388
Total	3,250

These figures do not include drivers of –
Armoured Motor Batteries.
Machine Gun Batteries.
Signal Unit
Indian Civilian Staff and Central M.T. Stores Depot at Rawalpindi.

There are 1,620 mechanical transport vehicles now comprised of lorries, ambulances, armoured cars units, staff cars and motorcycles.'

Colonel Lord Montagu, with his usual thoroughness of planning and his

29. Montagu Papers VII/41.

66

67

One of the hairpin bends on the Murree Rd - 1917

68

2 MT Convoy waiting to leave Sunnybank for Rawalpindi

69

On the road to Dera Ismail Khan

70

AN UNSUNG TASK

66
The Soldiers Home, Rawalpindi.

67
Colonel Lord Montagu dismounting from one of the Indian Standard Leylands which had been converted for use on rails.

68
A hair-pin on the Murree Road, 1917.

69
A 2 MTC convoy waiting to leave Sunnybank for Rawalpindi.

70
On the road to Dera Ismail Khan.

keen anticipation of the future needs of India, was contemplating the end of the Great War and all the problems that would entail. In particular he had organised the Sohan driving school to alleviate the difficulties which would be caused on general demobilisation. India was to lose many of her British drivers who would be only too glad to leave India when the war ended.

DEAD ENDS IN THE DESERT

*'The East was an incongruous place to toast the
victory of the West, which seemed to have happened in a different world at a different time.'*

STANLEY WEINTRAUB. A Stillness Heard Round the World.

THE WORLD RELAXED ON 11 November 1918, the Great War had finally been fought and negotiated to a standstill. Most of the Western World went ecstatic with relief and celebrations without parallel spontaneously erupted throughout the Allied countries. Things were somewhat quieter in the East, the war had been predominately fought out on the Western Front. It had not been a global war in the same manner as the Second World War and apart from the various sideshows, such as Mesopotamia and German East Africa, very little fighting had occurred away from Europe.

CQMS Ewens was at Dinapore with 'C' Company of the 2/5th and despite the remoteness of their contribution to the war the soldiers from Somerset seem to have enjoyed the news of the Armistice. Perhaps a little too much.

CQMS E.W. EWENS

You have not been told of the Armistice scenes at Dinapore, it is better for the good name of the battalion to pass over these with just a hint of the scene outside the Colonel's bungalow, which to say the least was disgraceful. Then there was the scrapping between ourselves at our Armistice celebration at Patna. But the majority of the men looked at it in this light; the war was over and their agreement was finished and they were entitled to be sent home.

Sergeant Chant was aboard ship, a day's sailing out from Bombay, on his way to Mesopotamia when the end of the war was announced, and Corporal Rendall was at an even more remote place; Juzzak, near Persia. The end of the war was celebrated by Corporal Rendall and the rest of the men of the 2nd Mechanical Transport Company in an almost surreal atmosphere. The company, with most of its lorries, had been sent by rail from Rawalpindi, through the Bolan Pass and across the Sind Desert down to the remote rail head of Juzzak. It is not known for certain exactly what they were doing there but one of the papers of Lord Montagu provides a clue;

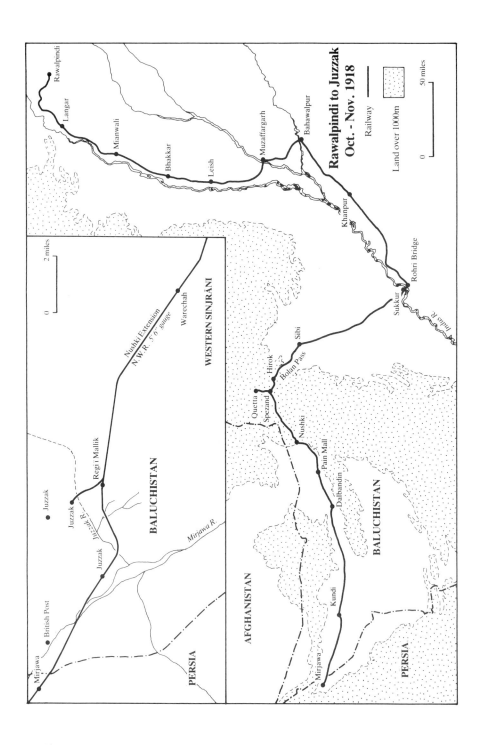

Rawalpindi to Juzzak
Oct. - Nov. 1918

Railway

Land over 1000m

50 miles

2 miles

Rawalpindi
Langar
Mianwali
Bhakkar
Leiah
Muzaffargarh
Bahawalpur
Khanpur
Rohri Bridge
Sukkur
Indus R.
Sibi
Hirok
Bolan Pass
Quetta
Spezand
Nushki
Pain Mall
Dalbandin
Kundi
Mirjawa
PERSIA
BALUCHISTAN
AFGHANISTAN

Warechah
Nushki Extension
N.W.R. 5' 6" guage
Regi i Mallik
WESTERN SINJRÁNI
Juzzak
Juzzak R.
Juzzak
Mirjawa R.
British Post
Mirjawa
PERSIA
BALUCHISTAN

MEMORANDUM ON THE NEED FOR MORE MECHANICAL TRANSPORT IN INDIA[30]

2. There is also. . .the need for an increased number of British and Indian troops on the North West Frontier, both on account of the unrest among local tribes stirred up by German influence, and the risk of Persian or Turkish troops led by German organisers coming towards India through Northern Persia, and also the possibility of hostile forces crossing the Caspian, or north of it, and coming through Afghanistan or Northern Baluchistan.' 18.9.18.

Whether it was for the purpose of an exercise or for real is unknown, but the company was encamped at Juzzak when the news of the Armistice reached the men. With the war ended, presumably there was no longer any need for 2 MTC to remain there and the company came back to Rawalpindi.

CPL B.G.L. RENDALL

Towards the end of 1918 we had orders for Rawalpindi Station and rumours were rife in the barracks, "Christ knows where we're going boys but we're going there." We had no idea now, but this would be an unrepeatable train journey. Well, we got to hear that we were off down into the Sind Desert and why we didn't know. That meant off up through the Bolan Pass by rail.

We had to load our lorries onto the railway trucks and a lot of us were milling around on Rawalpindi Station when a sergeant came up and spoke to the corporal next to me, "We'll start with you, Jepson." And he said to me, "You next, Rendall, get on board." This was onto the railway trucks, ordinary steel trucks with the ends let down. And we had to drive onto that train, we only had 2in. to spare either side from the hub caps to the sides of the railway trucks, and woe betide the man who hit the side and had his wheel pulled over; poor devil. There was no room on those trucks for reversing. It meant straight on and you had to get it right first time.

Well, Jepson did his satisfactorily and I was next. Jepson was first, next to the railway engine. I had a tap on the shoulder, "You're next, corp" And I was. Off I went, now you went up a ramp, 10ft. wide by 7ft. high lined up with the truck. As soon as you were on the ends were pulled up to lock you in there. I got up okay and I was stood up there on 'pindi Station, a terrible, proud, happy man, I got my bloody lorry up; mine hadn't caused any trouble. Neither had Jep's. When I felt a tap on the arm, yes, I well remember, being stood on 'pindi station surveying my handiwork in having got my lorry on the train, and I was stood like this, a stance I couldn't bear myself, but I didn't know I was doing it. Another tap on my arm, and this convoy sergeant pointed to my stripes and said,
"Have you used 'em corp?"
"No."
"Not in anger?"
"No."
"Not in authority?"
"No."
"Well, you've got some authority now, that's your train!"
And we were going to end up in the Bolan, with three engines and I'd be king of the lot. I was in charge of that train, the sergeant winked at me and

28" M.A.C. vans going to Persia with 2 M.T. Cos 1918

Taking workshop off chassis to allow it to go under bridges "Dalbandin", Sind Desert 1918

71   72

73

DEAD ENDS IN
THE DESERT

71
28th Motor Ambulance
Corps vans, going to Persia
with 2 MTC 1918.

72
The workshop body came
off to allow the vehicle to
go under low bridges.
Dalbandin, Sind Desert
1918.

73
Entering one of the tunnels
in the Bolan Pass.

74
The desolate emptiness of
the desert.

75
Brewing up the tea, Persia,
1918.

76
Unloading the Leylands
from the railway trucks.

said, "We're working it nicely, the sergeants are coming up in the last one, with the bloody officers."

Well, the next I knew was that the last lorry went on and the end was snapped up. We then had a snack meal on 'pindi station. We had our kitbags packed in our own lorries and we had bed and bedding so that first and second drivers could sleep in the lorries. There was no need to worry about the weather because there was no fear of any rain. This was about 9 a.m. and the convoy sergeant came up to me again, "Meet your driver," and he was a white bloke (he had a native stoker) and his name was Charles Griffin, and the sergeant rapped it into him in no uncertain terms, "He's only got two stripes, driver but if he sounds that whistle you've got to stop."

Well, the railway engine got well and truly steamed up, it was a massive great engine; one of the big Garratts. Off we went, we steamed on and on and on, for two days, when eventually we came down to the nearside of the River Jhelum to a place called Rhori, this was the first interesting thing I'd noticed on the trip. We were now some 400 miles from 'pindi, we'd been going days and nights, mind. They then changed engines at Rhori. The driver was changed here and the same sergeant gave the new driver orders in no uncertain terms that I was in charge of the train.

Right, now at this place called Rhori there was a huge bridge. One of the most interesting bridges I've ever seen, over the Jhelum. A massive great steel construction. There was a railway and footpath over this bridge. Cars weren't thought about up there, you see. Now we ploughed along steadily, and pounded over this bridge. We went on another two days, when we finally landed at a place called Spezand. Spezand is the first station in the Bolan Pass. Now and then we stopped for food and water of course, here and there on the way.

Now, we were at Spezand and I then saw what a sloping railway was; it was just damned uphill. We needed another two engines, Garratts, attaching to the train to pull it up the hill. The driver said, "We are having another engine at the back and another one attached to mine at the front for safety, Corporal." So we were going to do it with three engines. Well, we had a little rest at Spezand for about an hour, an hour and a half. All three engines were blowing steam out damn near everywhere, at full power. And we started. There was a hooter and whoosh, whoosh, whoosh, it was like gunfire.

Now, with me were eight men, their lorries and the drivers. And I was in charge of the lot, well, I couldn't see anything the matter with it; in fact I was quite beginning to enjoy myself. Here's a list of the stations we went through in the Bolan Pass; from Spezand to a place called Reti, then the next was Hirok. Then came Doctor Cha and Quetta. I didn't know until afterwards that the Bolan is about the same length as the Khyber; about 32 miles. Now we went through 36 tunnels on the way through the Bolan, and many's the time when the front of the engine was going through one tunnel as the last part of it was coming out the previous one. Half the journey was under tunnels. Just sheerly cut through the mountains, you never saw a railway like it. It was a weird sight.

We went through Quetta and Nushki, another station, I believe that was at the top of the Bolan. Now we were on the borders of the Sind Desert. We pulled up and had another meal, whenever we pulled into a station the army authorities had wired ahead and they were expecting us. The natives had prepared meals for us as we went along. Now we left two of the engines *behind, now that we'd got up the Bolan. They went off back to Spezand.*

While we were having this meal one of the drivers came up to me, "Corp, we're in for the worst trip of the lot, no sightseeing, son, nothing to look at but sand for another 800 miles." I wanted to know where we were going, "We're going to Jazzak, well down near Persia." We got going again and the next real place of any size was Dalbandin, well into the Sind.

We'd gone through another station called Painmal and entered the Sind on a wide half circle route. The Sind Desert is quite deceptive, the nearer you get to Persia the more hills there are; hill mountains in the middle of the desert. You can't travel an inch over 15 mph on sand in the desert for safety. The lines were fixed into the hard sand by a series of welded metal cups, into which the rails are dropped.

We had a few sandstorms on the way, there was a fair amount of wind, you get these in all deserts; wherever there's sand and heat. Some of them are very violent. Now we were trotting along at 15 mph, I suppose we were some 30 or 40 miles into the desert when, to my astonishment, instead of me and my whistle stopping the train, the train stopped me and the whistle. The next I saw was the white coated driver along side the truck and he said, "Come here, Corp, have a look at this lot, this will be a three hour delay." Quite.

Well, out I jumped, young and agile, a young soldier then, I just put my hand on the side of the truck and, waaing, I jumped down on the line, beside the truck. Some of the line had collapsed and the engine was on a good 25 degree cant. We shunted it back and with the aid of some form of telephone they summoned up some native workmen. Now the Sind Railway, at that time kept batches of natives under a super native and they tended to the line. Mended any breaks. So they arrived and got to work. But not with picks and shovels; they used in the main large wooden levers to get the line back into place. They dug up the cups and put the line back into place.

When the gang had finished they jumped onto our train to go back to their desert habitue where they stayed and we continued at the same slow pace as before. We were now two days into the Sind and stopped at Dalbandin. This was the only place in the Sind where we could get water and fuel. The carriages were attended to and various things. At the end of about two hours we had a fair meal of bananas and what nots. Everyone was satisfied, the engines were given a nice drink and plenty to eat and the throttle was touched again and I was invited up on the footplate for a change.

It was a thing I'll never forget. I then saw the weariness of the damn great railway engine going across the Sind, that seemed to be doing nothing but pulling a hell of a lot. This massive great Garratt, there was no effort whatever. I wouldn't say the Sind was a flat place, we had our run downs when the brakes were off, and there were the pulls up small hills. Slowly but surely we were getting to our destination and God knows where that was. We knew we were going there but when and how and what?

Well, at the end of one day, it was getting dark and I saw a party of my boys getting together for a hand of cards which, strictly was unlawful but I didn't say anything; I couldn't. I couldn't say "Just stand on the train and look at the sand." We continued through the night and for some unknown reason we were all sound asleep, which was wrong, strictly, but it had happened and we were awakened by a jolt. A bloke next to me shouted, "By Christ, we're home." We were pulled up at our destination – smack into a

2 MT Camp Kazzuah Persia. 1918 Where news of armistice arrived

Hauling lorry over sand dune in sind desert 1918

77

78

One of the few beaten by the Desert sand. Persia 1918

79

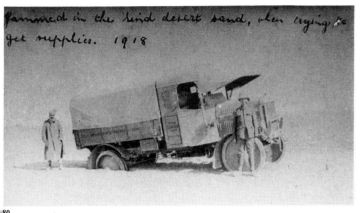

Jammed in the Sind desert sand, when trying to get supplies. 1918

The stopped engine. Persia 1918

Moving out to entrain for Rawalpindi Jazzach. Persia. 1918

77
2nd Mechanical Transport Camp, Juzzak 1918. News of the Armistice was received here.

78
Attempting to extricate one of the Leylands bogged down in the sand.

79
One of the few beaten by the desert sand. Persia, 1918.

80
Jammed in the Sind Desert sand, when trying to get supplies, 1918.

81
The stopped engine.

82
Moving out to entrain for the return journey to Rawalpindi. Juzzak, 1918.

railway stop at a place called Jazzak.

This was at the extreme end of the Rawalpindi to Sind Railway. This was actually on the Persian borders, now Iran. Well, we didn't know, never did and never will know the purpose we were there, why we were there or ought. All we know is that our train was unloaded and we were formed up on the sand. The train was slowly dismantled and towed away to a massive long siding. This was a big railway town with a water tower; things that looked quite natural to us. Now all this lot was based on a damned great load of sand, just stuck on the Sind.

The heat was hellish; at times up to 125 degrees, as much as we could stand in our lorries. Later the second train pulled in with more lorries and then the third with the rest of them. We were all assembled in a great square, with the lorries on the outside and tents pitched on the inside. A great oblong of tents and lorries. What we were doing there God only knows, I'll never. The first and second days came. We were neither infantry nor cavalry, neither hussars nor lancers so there was no infantry parades. It was a funny set up.

Suddenly, one morning, five lorries set out, no one knew the destination. One was Bill Marshal, a pal, and Dick Braxton, from my learning days. I'm not quite sure where they went but when the whole fiasco was over they came back on foot; four of the five lorries had got bogged down in the sand, up to their wheel hubs, stuck solid. They'd only gone eight miles. No one seemed to have charge, except a sergeant. There wasn't an iota of sense to it, they were just trying to see if the lorries could get through the sand. 100 men, fifty to each side, pulling on ropes; only managed to get one out. It was such an effort. Captain Bartlett stopped it, it was too much. And the lorries could be there today, mounds of sand. And think of it; 67 years ago! The drivers just had to leave them.

We lost our monkey mascot; the drivers didn't think to give it a drink. She went in the heat. After that episode we were generally poking around in loose order clothes for nine or ten days, in heavy boots, grey socks, singlets.

When suddenly it was out, "Christ, Armistice, boys. War's over! It's official from Simla." And so it was, we first heard the war was over at Jazzak. We'd been hearing very, very little of the war until then; practically nothing. We had nothing to celebrate on, we were just on army rations. We were in the sand, just dead ends in the sand. Nothing to celebrate with except a few hoorays and shouts.

At the end of about ten or fifteen days we were back aboard the train. Loaded the lorries again. We'd done nothing only looked at the sand. We still didn't know what it was about, whether it was a forlorn thing which turned out a fiasco God only knows. Nobody will ever know the mystery.

During this time we'd left a skeleton crew at Rawalpindi Barracks, they were the lucky ones. After tussling back, the same old drudge across the Sind, back to Painmal, back down the Bolan, across Rhori Bridge, Sukkur right back to 'pindi. We got back in late 1918.

12

RIOTS IN THE PUNJAB

IN THE SPRING OF 1919 *came the rioting in the Punjab. First we heard was waking up one morning, I pushed my mosquito net up, and the four convoy sergeants detailed us to assemble out on the road. I was ordered out with my lorry, from the garage, onto the road where there were quite a few other lorries with their drivers. One of the convoy sergeants walked up and down the line of lorries and he was shouting,*

"Amritsar, boys, Amritsar and Lahore, that's where you're off now. Sergeant Wilson and Corporal Braxton will be in the lead lorry to show you the way, see you don't get lost."

So we pulled on down, on down, on down through towards the Punjab. We crossed a couple of rivers on the way. We had 14 hours journey and most of this was done through the night to avoid the full heat of the Indian sun. When we approached our destination we saw a few things in our headlights that we wouldn't forget. At a place called Gudrunwallah, about 20 miles from Amritsar we saw a railway engine over on it's side, still blowing steam, totally upended. We then learnt that the job we were going to do was going to be a bad one.

Already one white woman and two little kids in a pram had been killed. On arriving at Lahore four of us were ordered to Lahore Arsenal, or the barracks. There we had a machine gun fitted to each of the four lorries, on the second driver's side. This was fixed by a metal bracket which was put onto the wooden board with bolts. Now our job was going to be to patrol through the streets ensuring that no bunches of natives gathered together; up to no good. With the lorries being able to move around quickly we could do as much as a regiment of foot soldiers could. We were on the go, round and round. When one four was finished the other drivers took over, so that there were always lorries going round. We did it in reliefs, night and day. We went at random through any of the streets. Most ticklish time was midday when the natives thought that the British soldiers would be flattened out with the heat. And we had orders that if we saw any more than four natives getting together we were to pull the lorry up and warn the crowd to disperse, then to move the machine gun muzzle up and down and again over their heads. A young officer told us all this, and then he said if they didn't move after all the warnings we were to shoot into them; someone else would be along to pick up the 'rubbish'.

We encountered two groups of natives, but we didn't use the gun, we didn't want to if we could help it. That was our first lesson in the army; only to kill if it was really necessary. We took any street at random, there were a lot of streets to cover. Eventually we began to learn the streets, saying, "Hello, we've seen this street before." Then we'd bump into one of the other lorries in which case we'd turn tail and go the other way. We weren't allowed to join up and go the same way together. The idea was to show our faces everywhere we could, warning the natives that what we had on these lorries could kick. In other words it was a warning to the natives not to start parties.

In the full heat of the Punjab sun on Sunday 13 April 1919, Brigadier General Reginald Dyer led a small party of armed soldiers into the Jallianwala Bagh, a piece of enclosed waste ground in Amritsar. There was a large meeting in progress and Dyer had earlier banned such seditious meetings as unrest was spreading throughout the Punjab. The large assembled crowd was unarmed and peaceful. Without warning, in his own admission, Dyer ordered the troops to open fire on the crowd; which they did, and they continued firing for some ten minutes. Exits from the Bagh were limited and inevitably the large crowd suffered high casualties. At the end of the day 379 people had been killed and a further 1200 were wounded. The party had fired 1,650 rounds of ammunition and Dyer ordered them to stop firing only when the bullets were beginning to run out. With the firing over Dyer withdrew his soldiers leaving the Indians to their own devices. Dyer was unrepentant; he considered that a show of force had been necessary in order that Martial Law would no longer be flouted, as in the earlier days. He felt it was his duty to disperse the meeting promptly with rifle fire, although he later agreed that the crowd had been unarmed; even with sticks.

The massacre at Amritsar was the culmination of a series of largely spontaneous demonstrations and incidents of unrest throughout the Punjab. India had suffered a great deal in the Great War, sending thousands of men to the Western Front and enduring higher taxation, rises in food prices and famine in the wake of the failure of the 1918 monsoon. The country further suffered a very high mortality rate in the influenza epidemic which stalked the country in that year.

The victory of the Allied Forces in 1918 had stirred a nationalistic vigour for freedom. Freedom which had been much curtailed during the war. The people felt ready for some form of recompense for their suffering. The troubles were sparked off in the capital, Delhi, on 30 March. Gandhi had organised a hartal, a widespread shutting down of shops and commerce, for the 6 April but it was mistakenly started earlier in Delhi on 30 March. It led to some arrests and caused incidents which led to a small party of British soldiers opening fire on a crowd. A few Indians were killed.

The hartal was widely recognised all over India on 6 April. All the shops in Lahore and Amritsar were shut down for the day. Crowds gathered in both places. Things quietened down until 10 April, when Ghandi was banned from visiting the Punjab as he had planned. More disturbances followed in Lahore, Amritsar and Ahmedabad, Gandhi's home town. Further riots and trouble occurred in the three towns, most seriously in Ahmedabad where several Europeans were killed. General Dyer was ordered to Amritsar and given powers to take whatever measures were necessary to restore order.

In defence of Dyer's actions it can be said that there was widespread panic and cut off in the Punjab, the European population really did think that there was the chance of a repeat of the events of 1857. The spectre of the horrors of the Indian Mutiny haunted the perceptions of most Europeans in India. Britain only ever had a consensual rule over the Indian sub-continent and the number of British soldiers in India had never been large enough to prevent an Indian rebellion; had one ever been organised effectively.

Whatever the rights and wrongs were of the threat to British Rule in the Punjab in 1919; two schools of thought emerged as to the validity of General Dyer's actions in the Jallianwala Bagh. The first, supported by much of the European community in India, was that there really had been a threat of a second Indian Mutiny and that Dyer's actions nipped it in the bud. Corporal Rendall's view of the business came from second hand sources; he was in Lahore at the time of the massacre, and the story had been sufficiently tailored to fit the second mutiny theory by the time it was related to Bert. The second view, widely supported by the majority of Indians, was that Dyer's actions had been heavy-handed, unnecessary and served only to increase nationalist support in the country. Quite simply that Dyer, reflecting European fears, had panicked.

CPL B.G.L. RENDALL

And I'll explain about General Dyer; why he got sent home in disgrace and cashiered. And I still believe today that he saved one hell of a big North West mutiny; it could have been a mutiny all over again. Now as far as I'm concerned (I didn't see a great deal of the matter as I wasn't there, but according to a second hand account of it), the Sussex Regiment and a mixture of others were formed in a quadrant and they were facing thousands of real bad, rioting murderers. They were holding them in a square. Now a captain was in charge of these troops. The rioters had found plenty of stones and one soldier after another was wounded, clouted. At last this young captain gave the order to fire over their heads, a couple of volleys to frighten and warn them.

Well, they fired over their heads and still the stones came flying. In three, distinct languages he warned these rioters what would happen if they went on with the stoning. Men were still getting hit by stones. He said the orders in Hindi and two other languages so that all could understand. But after another five minutes he said, "Lower your rifles, men and fire into them." And of course, as you know there was havoc. Now this is the awful side of it; in command of the lot was Dyer and that man unquestionably did the right thing. He settled a mob of hooligans that could have turned from a couple of

EXTRACT FROM MR. CHURCHILL'S SPEECH
("Times" Report.)

"AT the Jallianwalla Bagh the crowd was not armed, except with bludgeons, and it was not attacking anybody or anything. It was penned up in a space smaller than Trafalgar Square. The people ran madly this way and that, and the firing was only stopped when the ammunition was on the point of exhaustion. When 379 persons had been killed, the troops, at whom not even a stone had been thrown, marched away. He did not think it was in the interests of the British Empire or Army for us to take a load of that sort for all time upon our back. We had to make it absolutely clear that that was not the British way of doing things. . . . His personal opinion was that the conduct of General Dyer deserved to be marked by a definite disciplinary act. It was quite true that his conduct had been approved by superiors and that events had taken place which amounted to virtual condonation. General Dyer might have done wrong, but he had his rights, and he did not see how, in face of such virtual condonation, it would have been possible or right to take disciplinary action against him."

EXTRACT FROM GEN. DYER'S STATEMENT
("Times" Report.)

"I TOOK the small force at my disposal . . . and . . . arrived about 5 p.m. in the Jallianwalla Bagh. . . . I found a large meeting, afterwards ascertained to be from 15,000 to 20,000 in number, being addressed by a speaker engaged in violent exhortations . . . There were no women and children. . . . Hesitation I felt would be dangerous and futile, and as soon as my fifty riflemen had deployed I ordered fire to be opened. . . . When 1650 rounds or thereabouts had been fired . . . the whole crowd had dispersed. . . . I cannot understand how it can be suggested that the objects of crushing the rebellion, of diminishing the dangers in Lahore by 60 per cent., were not proper objects upon which to employ a military force. . . . I knew that, if I shirked . . . there would infallibly follow a general mob movement which would have destroyed all the European population. . . . I knew that I could produce no sufficient effect except by continuous firing."

EXTRACT FROM SIR W. JOYNSON-HICKS' SPEECH
("Times" Report.)

"HE (Sir W. Joynson-Hicks) had just returned from a visit to India and to Amritsar, and the opinions he was expressing were held by at least 80 per cent. of the Indian Civil Service throughout India and by 90 per cent. of the European people. . . . The General in charge at Lahore considered the quieting of Lahore was due as to 60 per cent. to the action of General Dyer at Amritsar. . . . General Dyer was faced with a rebellion. . . . He had talked to men on the spot, both native and English, and native officials supported General Dyer to the utmost, and they all testified that the inhabitants knew of the proclamations and the danger they would incur if they did not heed them. . . . When it was all over, was General Dyer assailed by the people? Not at all; they came in their thousands and thanked him. He was made a Sikh, and was employed to march round the whole district, and to pacify it this bloodthirsty man! And let there be no mistake about it General Dyer was beloved by the whole of the Sikh nation. . . . He (the speaker) insisted that the right thing to do was to trust the men on the spot."

84

RIOTS IN THE PUNJAB

83
Brigadier General
Reginald Dyer.

84
A private soldier of the
2/6th Royal Sussex
Regiment, which was
involved in Martial Law in
Lahore, April 1919. It
went on to become the first
Territorial battalion to see
active service on the North
West Frontier of India, in
the Third Afghan War.

thousand to twenty thousand. The population of India is so thick, even in our day, that there would have been no difficulty in getting together enough men to swamp the British regiments. But Dyer killed that rising at birth. And the poor devil was sent home and cashiered for it. This was by our government, yes, our government. And they cashiered him and ruined him. And well known to all our soldiers he saved the day by sudden action. There was no damn silly hesitancy; when he gave them orders that was it. It could have been the flint which started a massive fire.

Whether or not Dyer was right I wouldn't question, but he certainly doused the flames before the house burned down, if you get my meaning.

I had a second driver, a Lancashire kiddy, a fella named Private Shiel. It was on that Sunday morning that I did rather a foolish, daredevil act. We were going throught the streets of Lahore when we suddenly saw a Martial Law Order pinned up on a lamp post. I saw afterwards that it was issued by Colonel F. Johnson of the Sussex Regiment. He was in charge of Martial Law at Lahore and Amritsar. I said to my second driver, "I'm going to have that bloody order." He replied, "You're a bloody fool, corp. Come on stop the lingering." I told him to stay behind the wheel, and he did.

I stuck with him on the driver's side of the cab, with my back to the front wheel for the biggest part of $\frac{1}{2}$ hour, Shiel was reaching out of the cab, patting me on the helmet saying, "You blasted fool, they'll have you." But at last I screwed up my courage and by the time he'd spoken I'd slipped my sheath knife under the order. I knew I had to be careful; I knew the risk. I was a determined bloke, though soldiers were standing about everywhere. I was pretending to shout at the second driver, "This is murder, Bill, this is murder, son, we'll have to do something to right this lot." As I was talking I just gently cut the corners of the Martial Law Order away, cutting the sticky plasters and broke it away. I shoved it under my tunic and was off, three bounds and I was back in the lorry. And that Martial Law Order is here in one of my photograph albums; I've still got it.

Certainly the British had reacted with savage punishments; whippings were the order of the day and it was a punishment carried out widely and indiscriminately in the Punjab. A total of 270 floggings had been carried out. More serious crimes had been punished by sentences of death and imprisonment. Twenty-three executions were carried out; many others were pardoned at the end of 1919.

Lieutenant Colonel Frank Johnson of the 2/6th Sussex Regiment was particularly criticised for being high-handed and severe in his administration of Martial Law in Lahore. His belligerent attitude can be gauged by reading the terms of the Martial Law Order posted in Lahore on 15 April. Martial Law Orders had been posted on specific Indians' houses with the intention of making them responsible for the guarding of them, from defacement or removal. When Johnson learned of an Order being torn down at the Dharam College, 65 students and professors were ordered to march for three miles in the midday sun and to stand out in the open for the rest of the day. One wonders how he would have reacted had he learned that one of his own soldiers had torn one down for a souvenir. Martial Law in the Punjab lasted until 6 June 1919, by which time the situation had been totally contained by the British.

Shortly before the riots occurred, Colonel Lord Montagu had prepared his third report on Mechanical transport.[31] By this time there were five Indian Mechanical Transport Companies in addition to the four RASC MT Companies. The period under review was from 1 April 1918 to 31 March 1919. The Leyland and Thornycroft lorries had proved themselves to be ideal for Indian conditions, the Thornycrofts having been converted to four speed gearboxes. The Leyland was the superior of the two lorries, 'The Leyland Indian Standard lorry is capable of taking $2\frac{1}{2}$ tons on any military road now existing in India, and the Thornycroft lorry can safely be rated at 2 tons.' Despite the war having ended, Lord Montagu was still pressing for expansion. The North West Frontier was to vindicate his prescience in the next few months; 'The same need for the use of Mechanical Transport in India, especially on the Frontier, exists today as during the war and in view of the havoc recently caused by surra and other diseases among ponies, mules and camels in the North West Frontier districts, the use of Mechanical Transport should be extended there.'

Summary of Mechanical Transport Formations administered from India.
Personnel

Officers	139
British other ranks	1,807
Indian	1,009
Indians under training	1,082
Total	4,037

Indian Formations.
No.2 Mechanical Transport Company, Rawalpindi
6 Motorcycles
5 Cars
1 Thornycroft Store lorry
13 Thornycroft Supply lorries
2 Leyland Store lorries
3 Leyland workshop lorries
64 Leyland supply lorries

31. Montagu Papers VII/51.

NOTICE.

No. I.

Whereas the Government of India has for good reasons proclaimed Martial Law in the districts of Lahore and Amritsar : and

Whereas superior Military authority has appointed me to command troops and administer Martial Law in a portion of the Lahore District, now known as the "Lahore, Civil" command whose boundaries may be ~~~~~ ~~~~~

    The Civil Lines ;

    The Municipality and City of Lahore ;

    The Fort ;

    The Mogulpura Works ;

    and any other area not included in the above between the Ravi River and Lahore Branch of the Bari Doab Canal inclusive within three miles of the Central Telegraph Office, Lahore,

and whereas Martial Law may be briefly described as the will of the Military Commander in enforcing law, order and public safety :

I make known to all concerned that until further orders by me the following will be strictly carried out : —

1. At 20·00 hours each evening a gun will be fired from the Fort, and from that signal till 05·00 hours on the following morning no person other than a European or a person in possession of a military permit signed by me or on my behalf will be permitted to leave his or her house or compound or the building in which he or she may be at 20 hours. During these prohibited hours no person other than those excepted above will be permitted to use the streets or roads, and any person found disobeying this order will be arrested, and if any attempt is made to evade or resist arrest that person will be liable to be shot.

This and all other orders which from time to time I may deem necessary to make will be issued on my behalf from the Water-works Station in the City, whither every Ward will keep at least four representatives from 6 A.M. till 17·00 hours daily to learn what orders, if any, are issued and to convey such orders to the inhabitants of their respective Wards. The onus of ascertaining the orders issued by me will rest on the people through their representatives.

2. Loyal and law-abiding persons have nothing to fear from the exercise of Martial Law.

3. In order to protect the lives of His Majesty's Soldiers and Police under my command, I make known that if any firearm is discharged or bombs thrown at them the most drastic reprisals will instantly be made against property surrounding the scene of the outrage. Therefore it behoves all loyal inhabitants to see to it that no evil-disposed agitator is allowed on his premises.

4. During the period of Martial Law I prohibit all processions, meetings or other gatherings of more than 10 persons without my written authority, and any such meetings, gatherings or processions held in disobedience of this order will be broken up by force without warning.

5. I forbid any person to offer violence or cause obstruction to any person desirous of opening his shop or conducting his business or proceeding to his work or business. Any person contravening this order will be arrested, tried by a Summary Court and be liable to be shot.

6. At present the City of Lahore enjoys the advantage of electric lights and a water-supply ; but the continuance of these supplies will depend on the good behaviour of the inhabitants and their prompt obedience to my orders.

FRANK JOHNSON, Lieut.-Colonel,

Head-Quarters, Punjab Club ;   2/6 Battalion, Royal Sussex Regiment,

Lahore, 15th April 1919.   Commanding Lahore Civil Area.

No. 2.

All tongas and tum-tums whether licensed for hire or otherwise will be delivered up to the Military Officer appointed for that purpose at the Punjab Light Horse ground by 17·00 to-day —Tuesday, 15th April. Drivers will receive pay and horses be rationed.

FRANK JOHNSON, ~~~~~

Commanding Lahore Civil Area.

No. 3.

All motor cars or vehicles of any description will be delivered to the Military Officer appointed for that purpose at the Punjab Club by 17·00 this day.

FRANK JOHNSON, Lieut.-Col.,

Commanding Lahore Civil Area.

13

WAR ON THE FRONTIER

'When you're wounded and left on Afghanistan's plains,
And the women come out to cut up what remains,
Jest roll to your rifle and blow out your brains
An' go to your Gawd like a soldier.'

RUDYARD KIPLING, *The Young British Soldier.*

THE AFGHANS, UNDER Amir Amanulla, encouraged by the unrest which was spreading throughout the Punjab, made their first move into the western end of the Khyber Pass on 6 May 1919. The Third Afghan War was a short lived affair; by the end of two weeks the Indian Government had mobilised a Frontier Force of some 140,000 men, despite the difficulties posed by the general demobilisation which was then in process in India. The Afghan Armies were beaten off without too much trouble.

The nearest they came to any success at all was in Thal, at the southern end of the Kurrum Valley; the Afghan General, Nadir Khan, moved swiftly on 22 May and surrounded the town with its garrison fort. The Afghans laid siege to the town and for four days the garrison was desultorily shelled. A relief force under Brigadier General Dyer came down from Kohat and relieved the garrison; chasing Nadir Khan's army to the west on 1 June. Corporal Rendall and his Leyland lorry formed a small part of the relief force, towing a gun down from Peshawar. Further Afghan assults in the north and the south were repulsed relatively easily. By 3 June the Afghans were requesting peace terms and the war was over.

CPL B.G.L. RENDALL

Now, after the Lahore/Punjab Riots we were ordered back to 'pindi. And we'd seen through the riots, we were back in 'pindi Barracks again when practically all of us were ordered up to Peshawar, roughly 60 miles from Rawalpindi. The next place up towards the Khyber is a place called Jamrud, that is the key to the Khyber Pass. We weren't told what was going on at first, all we knew was that we had to take a whole load of new beds to Peshawar for the natives and white men stationed at Peshawar. What they were, actually, was a new type of bed made with steel slats to replace the old string mattressed charpoys, which were awful for gathering bugs which were rife as I told you before. Some of these bugs were horrible great things, about the biggest bugs I have ever seen. They were lousy in the woodwork. These new steel charpoys were to cure the problem; steel frames which stood on steel stands. But here and there the bugs could not be avoided.

They were in all kinds of woodwork in the barrackroom. But our barracks up at 'pindi were all brickwork so therefore we were fairly free from bugs, but we caught a few now and then. God knows how but they'd get under the stone floor or you'd put your cap down and then feel a nasty biting sting.

I will first say that we were in Peshawar assembling for two or three days and we'd left five or six lorries in 'pindi for any necessary work left there. The 693 and 694 ASC boys went up with us and the 22nd MMG's with their motorbikes and machine guns. Now all this lot as well as camels and mules were in the Khyber action. And, to my astonishment there were, unknown to me some Somerset soldiers up there, off the beaten track, I had no idea that any Somersets were up there. It was the 2nd Regulars.

Well there was a lot of running about to be done, we were the boys for that, our lorries went everywhere. We had to carry ice around, huge blocks of ice, 1 ton blocks which would fit our two ton lorries nicely. It would melt on the way, no matter how well covered it was, I remember following one lorry and water was pouring out of the back of the lorry. Often we would arrive, say at Burhan, with only 15 cwt of ice left out of the ton we started with. Now tents were taken up, all sorts of stuff.

Now the main object was Landi Kotal at the top of the Khyber. Now I never knew what half my journeys were for, I just did my duty and drove where I was told to go. Now halfway up the Khyber was another encampment called Ali Musjid and that was ten miles from the entrance to the Khyber at Jamrud. Then it was up to Landi Kotal at the top. When we got to Landi Kotal four lorries, mine included, were sent up to the place where all the fighting was going on; a place called Thal. Thal is well back in Pakistan. We learnt that one of two of our regiments had got stuck in Thal and that we had to get through somehow and relieve them. They were surrounded by the Afghans and Afridis. And with all the strange things we were told; we didn't really know what was going on or what was expected of us.

Well, off we went and it was well away from the Khyber: another sphere of the fighting on the Frontier. Now when we got there we found it very strange. with all the different regiments posted along the roads, everyone was on the move, the roads were very busy. There were Sikh Regiments and they were all formed up on the roads, like you would see at a ceremonial parade in London. These were all part of the Thal relief force. They were to ensure that we got back into Thal. Now I never knew who was in charge at Thal but when we got near there we had another order to go right back to Peshawar to bring four guns up. We picked up four 18 pounders each with 80 shells, now we had to tow these guns the 60 miles back to Thal. We got to Peshawar at five in the morning, it was four hours back to Thal. I can't remember going through any towns or villages on the way, I don't think there was much in between Thal and Peshawar.

We were joined in Peshawar by a section of Artillery and another section of artillery was taken up to Thal by the ASC. Now it was doubtful whether we could get through to Thal with these guns, as the place was surrounded to all intents and purposes. When I tell you what was surrounding the place you'll have a good idea how many, together with some Afghans, had closed Thal in. Here is a little list of the tribesmen involved; there was the Wazaries, the Zaka Khels, the Mahsuds, the Mohmonds and the chief tribe, the biggest of the lot and the most formidable, the Afridis. Then there were the Khurds and the Chinwaris. Now all these were helping the Afghans to try to regain the Khyber and other parts of the Frontier such as Thal. There were thousands of them. Now we couldn't raise a defence force of much more than six to eight thousand men, so it could have been a very prolonged job.

Anyway let's get back to these guns; a Major at Peshawar simply gave us two commands and said, "A gun each for your four lorries". Now we had to take the limbers as well and it just worked out wonderful really. We towed them using their tow pins which were only used in emergencies as they were normally horse drawn guns, six horses to a gun, but there was a great shortage of horses at that time. We didn't leave Peshawar Fort until about midday but when we did go we travelled as fast and furious as we could go. Besides a second driver we now had a gunnery sergeant each with us. Occasionally we would pull up for a rest and a dixie of tea.

Now I don't know how the wooden wheels of those guns stood up to it in the boiling heat of the afternoon sun. We were trundling on quite nicely when we were stopped by a young lieutenant of Artillery and he said, "Well take it a bit easy, on wooden wheels you know." Oh, God, right! Well we'd been doing a constant 20 mph and we went a few more miles on. We pulled up again and inspected the wheels which had been creaking a bit, one of the Artillery sergeants looked at them; "Christ, the wheels are falling to bits, we've got to water them." And I don't know where they dug it up from, but it was the most foul smelling water, stinking, stagnant stuff, even the dying animals wouldn't drink it. We got canvas buckets full of it, we had to grin and bear it and slosh it over the wheels of the guns. Within minutes the wheels took up the slack as the wood expanded. This had all been caused by the horrible heat of the midday sun, this was one of the hottest places on the NWF; between 9 and 10 in the morning it was 100 degrees and at midday anything up to 120. In fact we used to worry about our petrol tanks expanding and blowing up.

The engines were affected by the heat a bit; there seemed less pull in them than when we were in cooler air. Now going up in the Murree Hills you could notice the difference between the heat and the cool in the effect it had on the engine. We had Zenith Carburettors and you could literally hear these carbs suck in the air as each cylinder went round, and as the carbs drew in the cooler mountain air you could feel each cylinder jerk back into more life than they'd had in the hellish heat. Those Leylands were the most wonderful lorries I ever set my hands on. We had the precise number of 16 in dock the whole time I was there, out of 60 nearly. That's not bad in nearly three years is it? I only knew 16 of them pulled to pieces, minor little things really, bolts loose, mudguards loose, petty things, like that.

To a certain extent we had to maintain our lorries; one day a week we did that, Sundays I think, but they were such lovely machines you didn't need to do much to them. They were your pals, they were your life, they would get you into some scrapes and they had to get you out again. I had a nasty

Clearing Thall Sunday Morning June 1st 1919. Taken showing guns in tow of 2 M.T. Lorries just before the order "Action Left". Each lorry had besides loads of ammunition and a gun each 10 fully armed men and kits so that I can assure reader that the drivers had a good time in the hills with a 30 cwt gun hung banging along behind.

85

The first shot at the Afghans on arrival of relief force from Peshawar after a month's siege it was relieved in two days June the first to June the third though some of us scrambled in to our hard pressed mates on the first day with water and food and relieved some of the firing and defenders.

Afghanistan 1919

86

The relief guns from Peshawar Sunday June 1st 1919 preparing for another salvo at Afghans 200 yds away on another hill, with lorries standing by with ammunition and ready to move to fresh position which was constantly being done that day to relieve the enemy fire on fort Thall.

Afghanistan 1919

3861

my gun which I had to move 00 aegd

87

88

89

90

WAR ON THE FRONTIER

85, 86, 87, 88, 89 & 90
Action in the Third Afghan
War of May 1919.

escape in the Khyber once, we were caught out on the road with four or five Afghans, me and my second driver. The Khyber was a damned dangerous place after dark and a fool sergeant kept us hanging about too long. It was really dusking down before he let us off back to Jamrud. He should have known better. We were lucky that it was only a small party that caught us, the second driver had two with his revolver and I clobbered one with my rifle, more in fright than anything else. His face disappeared down below the cab and the other one scarpered. He dropped his Jezail on the ground and I retrieved the bullet which he had fired at us but had failed to go off. I've still got that very bullet, a lot of their bullets were crude and would misfire like that. Another bullet had smashed one of my headlights, CAV lights. That was the only time I ever came into contact with the tribesmen. There was very little fighting near the roads.

Occasionally we saw British soldiers marching up the road and then fanning out into the hills to tackle the tribesmen. When it came to action it was all on a small scale; companies and platoons or even smaller groups of men. You had to fight the tribesmen at their own game, which was hard. It was never a pitched battle ending in a bayonet charge or anything like that. It was all fighting amongst the rocks. Solid granite.

You had young officers and they would take small parties into the rocks to root out the natives, he'd have to use his wits. The Afghan War was a funny lot, you would suddenly see a native in his white nightgown miles above you, say 3,000 feet further up. You'd never know how many might be up there, the officer had to use his discretion as to how best tackle things. You had to first send out a few scouts. And then the tribesmen would fire down on you sporadically, they were sinking a lot of lead into us from a great height. They used to split up during the day and group together more at night. It was a peculiar kind of war. The infantry regiments were trained for fighting on the Frontier while they were at Peshawar, they did a couple of months training in mountain warfare.

The heat was always our biggest problem, I know that whenever I had to get out of my lorry, for some reason, you had to be careful at midday or in the afternoon. I've known a rock at midday to blister my hand, or if you put a tool down, a spanner or something, you then had your troubles; you couldn't pick it up after it had been there for more than five minutes. What you had to do was to kick it into the shade, under the lorry and leave it to cool down a bit before handling it. We often had to do a few minor adjustments at the side of the road, a wheel loose or getting a bit dry, needing a spot of grease, things like that. These things all slowed you down.

Ice was carried a lot, we could get two 1 ton blocks of ice on our lorries, it was needed mainly for the wounded; they'd break a chunk off to hold on a soldier's brow. Or if the poor devils were dying for a drink. The ice was made in a factory, it was wonderfully organised. I remember one corporal, Marshall was his name and he was a bit of a pansy boy and he'd taken exception to carrying ice for some reason. He thought the weight would damage his lorry and one day when they'd loaded a good couple of blocks onto his lorry he said to me, "Somerset", (my name was always Somerset in 2 MTC, because of my regiment, they never called me Rendall), "They are going to stop my lorry, Somerset, don't let them put any more on!"

The lorries were covered by heavy canvas sheets which were supported by large 'U' shaped steel bands which went from side to side and the canvas was held down by adjustable leather straps. These were fitted to the wooden base of the lorry and you could tighten them up. I used the word sheet to describe the coverings because the word 'tarpaulin' wants so much dragging out. So the army would say, "Get sheeted up corporal and you're off." And off you would go.

We carried everything you could think of in those lorries, occasionally we had army baths full of grapes; round tubs. These were for the wounded again, we thought. The wounded were tended to in a very well engineered tent set up. A big batch of tents. Now and then there were arguments with the medics who preferred these tents as they said they would let the air circulate more than in a brick built place.

Dust was always a nuisance and whenever you had a chance you had to dust up your lorry and oil the ticklish parts. The dust got caked on in great lumps and you had to pick it and scrape it off. That was after just one run up the Khyber, which was about 32 to 36 miles roughly. Now I remember one good escape for one of our drivers. The driver was a real wit, a likeable bloke. He should never have been in the army, he had a habit of putting a cigar act on: he should have been an officer. We were coming down the Khyber one day and his lorry got stopped, wallop. It had been hit in the bonnet by an Afridi bullet and the bullet had gone right through into the magneto, walloped the magneto mechanism and stopped the engine dead. Wyles stopped with his second driver and assessed the damage. Suddenly he had the answer and he stripped one of the bamboo handles on the canvas buckets we carried and used a piece of bamboo as a temporary make and break lever mechanism on the Bosch magneto. A tiny spring had been broken and the bamboo replaced it, off went this lorry with the bamboo part. And he cut back and did the last 13 miles into camp. Bloody clever really.

We had massive workshops at 'pindi and they looked after the lorries in the barracks. And for repairs out on the road we had two Leyland mobile workshop lorries. These were great big affairs on the back of the lorries. They were 7ft. from floor to ceiling and contained a lathe, grinding machine, drill and a workbench. We always had one at our destination and one where we started off, this was for big convoys. So that you had repairs when you got there and repairs when you struggled back, for instance one might be at 'pindi and the other would be at Landi Kotal if you were going up the Khyber.

Let's get back to these guns that we were taking up to the action in Thal. When we finally got the guns to Thal they were delivered into the charge of the Artillery and this young Artillery lieutenant and a couple of sergeants came up and commandeered us. The guns were still attached to the lorries. The lieutenant said to me, "Corporal, you are now in my charge, and this lorry does everything I tell it to do bar turn upside down with those guns." He pointed up the mountain where he reckoned there were a number of sniper Afridis who had been causing some casualties. They'd lost nine men that day. He said, "Action rear, corporal, that means get your tailboards down with the guns pointing that way."

When we got out of the lorries six native gunners came up and took over each gun and they were Maharatas. This was the first I'd seen of the action. They started firing upwards at an angle of 45 degrees and we couldn't reach them with our rifles. On the other hand the tribesmen were in clover, they were always firing downwards at us. The weight of the bullet falling 4,000 feet alone could kill you. They were dropping their bullets in our camp.

Some of them had the old seven feet long *Jezails*. They were a homemade business made somewhere near Kabul and they made them out of unrifled tubing, exactly the same as a piece of gas pipe and had a bore of about ½ an inch. The barrels were 6ft. long. They fired huge bullets which would flatten out on impact if they caught a bone. Horrible things. Often they made them into dum dums. They didn't all have these ancient things though, many of them had modern rifles which they'd stolen from the British or copied from our rifles. They really valued those rifles and would go to extraordinary lengths to get them. Now and again we would lose a rifle on the Frontier and the penalty could be severe. They would give their lives for a good Lee Enfield. And every rifle lost on the Frontier meant some of your mates got killed. Oh yes, they came back to us all right! That's why I had to be so careful with mine when I was going from Shwebo to Rawalpindi.

Now these Artillery boys had been firing into the hills for a while when the officer said to me, "You'd like a view driver?" I went down to an Artillery telescope about two feet long; they were damned powerful. Gradually I focussed up and came to a dark spot which was a hole in the mountain top where these natives were supposed to be. In a moment it happened and I saw a man in a white sheet appear and disappear quickly. They were well concealed, knew what they were doing, had good cover if you know what I mean. Occasionally I could see a "phut, phut" as they fired at us.

It was like trying to hit a single wasp in a wasp's nest but the Artillery officer was a determined man. He asked if I wanted a few potshots at them and told me to get my rifle out; it was like being at a fairground. He gave me ten rounds and I put the rifle sights at 3,000 yards like I did in infantry training and let fly with a few. I can't have hit anything.

By this time the gunners were unloading more shells from the limbers; each limber carried 80 shells. It was a marvel to watch them, they were shouting things about the elevation and the native sergeant was giving his orders and they'd move the gun this way and that, reading their instruments, correcting their aim. The gunners were sat on tiny seats on the guns, but got off as soon as it was loaded, these were the gun layers. They fired six shells at a very rapid rate of fire; wallop, wallop, wallop, one behind the other. This bloody place where I'd seen the natives lit up with the flashes. All of us, eight drivers, and the gun crews thought that had done the trick. These were shrapnel shells and we were quite happy that we'd blown these buggers to pieces, when the young officer was shouting that they were back up there firing again. We hadn't touched them at all. He was really worked up.

They fired another six or so shells and then the officer called it off and he ordered us to take the guns to another spot. Now this time they were more successful and caught of load of the tribesmen coming down the hillside. There were forty or fifty of them. You never heard such rapid orders in your life, "Wheel round right, wheel around left, action front, action left, action right, go, fire. Get a bloody move on." Then there were instructions like set detonator, move shell cap, things like that. These gunners were experts, the officer was down on his belly, "Fire." and all four guns let fly together, there was a blasted row, bloody smoke, you've never seen anything like it in all your life. The smoke drifted away slowly in the mountain heat and we could see the bodies on the hillside, strewn there like dead flowers. I don't know whether any got away, but they were caught napping in the open. The officer swore,

"That'll settle you for your bloody snipers earlier." Well, we really caned the lot, it was just like shutting flies in a box. They were hoist by their own petard you see, they loved their mountain warfare and they died on the bloody mountain.

I'm not quite sure what I thought of my first action, it's hard to say. Now this was nothing like the action in France of course. Nothing like that. Ours was more, how can I put it, a spasmodic little war. It consisted of a lot of tribes organised by the Amir of Afghanistan and he was mad keen to take the Khyber back for some reason. Some say he was never satisfied with the monetary upkeep he received from the British Government. Either that or he wanted more money from the Khyber to build a new palace or something.

We saw quite a few tribesmen who had been taken prisoners, we saw them in batches. Some were wounded. And the tribesmen took our men prisoner sometimes and they committed some hellish barbarous acts on them. Some of them had to crawl away, horribly mutilated. Don't forget we were dealing with some of the biggest heathen on God's earth. We were dealing with wild-brained men. If you found a more gun happy bloke than a bloody tribesman you have done well to find him. They would fire at anything moving and it was actually known that, for no damn reason whatever, they would attack one another just for someone to fire at. They were actually noted for that; the different tribesmen, they were forever wrangling with one another, there was never any end to it.

Going back to the forty or fifty we'd killed; they then moved the guns further off in another direction to find fresh targets to attack.

We were well armed personally when we were driving around the Khyber, we had our ammunition in the bottom of our lorries, under the seats which had a special cut out. We carried a fair amount of it you know; .303 for our rifles which were locked into carriers in the cab between the two seats, and .45 for the hellish heavy service revolvers that we also carried; unlike the infantrymen who only had their rifles.

This young Artillery lieutenant made us stay with the lorries for a while longer. He then ordered just one gun to be taken about a mile off where they had another target and this was some old church or something like that, which was far away on another hill in the distance, some mile or so from the spot where the natives had been killed. And it had to be my lorry which went. The gunners, native gunners, came with us and they set the gun up again and let fly at this old church. A young officer came up and said, "You see that bloody tower there? When we bring that down it'll break their bloody backs." Now the shells could be set for percussion when they'd explode on impact or they can be set with a time fuse. The young officer said to me in a sort of a half mumble as the gunners were setting the gun and, "Bloody natives, they'll never hit that tower in a hundred shots, if they do it'll all be over." But they did hit it, beautiful shot! The young officer turned to me and said, "By Christ, they did get it." With the next few shots the whole thing disappeared in a cloud of black smoke.

Two days after this we heard that the Afghans had cracked up, that was the end of it and we came back to Rawalpindi. But there was still a lot of trouble ahead with the tribesmen. Apparently they wanted to go on fighting despite the fact that the Afghans had given up. So there was still a lot fighting the rest of that year, though I saw none of it, of course. And I still don't really know what we were doing up at Thal; never will.

14

PIANOS OVERBOARD

*'He came out of the army last year, less than a year ago.
From India, I rather think. He may have picked up
certain tricks out there. . .and improved on his position.
Some of the men were like that. But it does them no
good, they have to fall back into their old places when
they get home again.'*

D.H. LAWRENCE. *Lady Chatterley's Lover*

MANY OF THE British troops in India at the end of the Great War had their return to England delayed by the Third Afghan War in May 1919. The majority of the 2/5th were still there in October 1919. On 18th October a group of some 200 men, all of whom had been on the *Ionian* in 1914, were sent to Deolali in preparation for their return home. A change of orders meant that the remainder of the battalion overtook the 1914 men; 13 officers and 132 men were put aboard the 'Nevasa' and they arrived back in England on 16th November. The 1914 men followed soon behind. 'Cook's Tour' does not make it clear when CQMS Ewens returned but it seems probable that he was with the 1914 men. It was almost five years since they had sailed for Burma.

CQMS E.W. EWENS

In January 1919 we were returning from camp when a breeze blew up concerning the coaches we were to be put into. This passed by but not before hard things were said once more. Men were now being sent home continually and the battalion was only a shadow of its former self and removed to Fort William, Calcutta, in the spring. What a place this is; standing about a mile across the Maidan from Chowringhee it is only discernible as a rise in the ground, surmounted by the Union Jack. With the entrances through deep cuttings, when one gets inside one marvels at its size: immensely large, three storey stone bungalows, a beautiful old garrison church, very much like a village church at home, stores, magazines, bazaars, football and other athletics grounds. In fact it is a small town quite contained within itself, and a wide sweep or maidan slopes away from its ramparts on three sides and on the other, fairly close to the river. This place, up to the time of the modern high explosive shell and long range gun, must have been absolutely impregnable.

In the days of the mutiny several thousand could have lived within its walls without any discomfort, and it is possible and even rumoured that all the civilian

European population of this part were inside at the time.

It would have been better if the whole battalion had been sent home together, the continual dribbling of a few going home every week or so only made the unfortunates, as they considered themselves, who were left behind more discontented. Those who were sent home were first put into a concentration camp at Deolali, about 100 miles from Bombay. What reunions took place here; men of the battalion met again from Mesopotamia and the North West Frontier together with those from Calcutta. Whilst here the Australian Light Horse arrived from Mesopotamia and were placed in No.1 Coy tents, No.6 Rest Camp. After two nights in tents they soon made a complaint about same and were shifted and English Tommies were put in their place. They soon found out what was wrong; tents, ground and everything there was crummy, complaints were made to the Camp Commandant but the men got choked off; that night every tent rope was cut. The men then had to be moved and the place fumigated, but the poor devils lost two drafts home through it.

It was here, whilst some of our later fellows were waiting for a draft, that the cadre passed through on their way home consisting of the Colonel and about 25 other ranks. They were given a Civic Reception on arriving at Taunton. Coming home in so many drafts, it is impossible to give a description of the journey home, but with what delight was the Bishop's Rock Lighthouse off Land's End hailed. Gone was the Bengal Blanket, the blue skies and bluer seas of the Mediterranean and the steely blue sky and sea of the tropics. All one could see was the grey-green sea and grey sky of old England.

It was with mixed feelings that we heard reveille go on the troopship, an hour too soon in our opinion after a night's farewell bust in the saloon and turning in at 4 a.m., to be awoken again at 5, and to find that it was really 6 a.m. summer time. When we got on deck we found we were abreast of the Skerries Lightship off Anglesea. The pilot had come aboard and he altered the time and we lost an hour.

Now after ten years as we arise in the morning our thoughts are apt to stray to other early morning scenes of the past, which constituted our first view of the new born day in the Golden Pagoda of Rangoon, the serrated tops of the hills towards China at Shwebo, the immense roof like peak of Kinchinjinga at Lebong and the plains of the Ganges from the train, but the finest sight of all India was the view of Bombay on leaving for home.

Corporal Rendall was to leave India later still, he was not to return until early December 1919 and he was demobilised at Fovant on 9 December. An incident occurred on board the *China* coming home which involved the officers cordoning off a large area of deck for their own use. It is interesting to note the reaction of the soldiers of 1919; compared to the grumbling but impotent acquiescence of the men on the *Ionian* in 1914, when the officers took similar steps to provide for their own comforts. A great deal had changed in those five years.

CPL B.G.L. RENDALL

After the action in the Third Afghan War we were sent back to 'pindi and we were back on regular duties running backwards and forwards over the NWF. I do remember going to Parachinar, I drove my lorry there though I can't remember exactly when that was, it was off the beaten track though. I remember a village or two on the way, one was a place called Adazai. That was halfway between Thal and the Kurrum Valley. That was a celebrated place, mind, Roberts met part of his trouble in the Kurrum Valley before he ever got to Kandahar. Miles and miles of dead road was all I saw.

Now it was getting to the end of my time in India, we had been kept back specifically for the action in the Khyber, you see, or we would already have been on our way home. War broke out when they were thinking of putting us aboard ship for home. So without a word or anything we were soldiering on well after the Great War had finished. But I wasn't sorry, we just soldiered on. This was late 1919 now, autumn.

We were paraded one day, Lieut. Hambly came out and said to us, "News, boys, you'll all be aboard ship at Bombay inside another week or so." But we didn't go crackers, by that time we were all fairly hard-nosed soldiers; philosophical about things.

On the night before we entrained for Bombay from 'pindi station Rendall had to make a bloody fool of himself. Unknown to me there had been a Yeovil bloke in Cambridge Barracks almost the whole time I'd been out there though we didn't know it. But we suddenly twigged this: we were together in apprenticeships. We met up that day and, as he was only a private I got him sanctioned to come into our corporal's mess. We had a damned good wet together and I got horrible blind drunk and I was still in a real state the next morning when we were paraded to go to the station.

So, the next day we were leaving our lorries behind and I suppose it was silly but I damn near cried when I left 3861 in the garages at Rawalpindi. She'd been so bloody faithful, I'd never had her in dock once you see. And that despite seeing some of the most hellish hills and the worst conditions imaginable. I never saw lorries like them; those Leylands. The Thornycrofts were quite good as well but not so reliable, they were always in dock. But our Leylands, they were hellish powerful; 36 h.p. works tested, and we could get up to 40 mph out of them. There wasn't much that they wouldn't go up, bar the side of a house.

Those old engines used to whistle in through the carburettors the nearer you got to the snowline in the hills, the thing would jerk a bit and you could feel each individual cylinder, chug, chug, chug, you could feel the life coming back into them, when you got in the real snow, look out.

By mid-1919 there were two driving schools busily training native drivers to handle the Indian Standard lorries. Lord Montagu refers to them in his third report on M.T. in India,[32] 'The school for training Indian Mechanical Transport Drivers at Sohan near Rawalpindi under Lieutenant Colonel C. Hodgkinson (6th Cavalry) has been most successful in turning out a great number of drivers, until recently up to 300 or 400 a month, for Mesopotamia, India, Persia and other theatres of war. In consequence of the need for more drivers, a second school was formed in the autumn of 1918 at Meerut under Lieutenant Colonel J. Hodgkinson (5th Cavalry), who was originally responsible for the establishment and excellent system of the school at Sohan. . .The Indian Standard lorries have cost the Government of India £1000 a piece delivered at their stations in India and it would be false economy and bad policy to hand over the driving of them to half-trained Indian Mechanical Transport drivers.'

32. The Montagu Papers, VII/51.

PIANOS OVERBOARD **123**

CPL B.G.L. RENDALL

*Not everyone from the Company went home though, there were some who'd
volunteered to stay in India to teach the new drivers, to teach some natives
to drive their lorries. It came through the barracks, "Anyone want three up
and another 18 months service?" And I had volunteered myself, I still had
the instinct of a kid in me and I wouldn't have objected to the sash down my
right side. And there would have been extra money, I'd already saved £90
in my years in India and I saw a future in this lark. But I changed my
mind after putting my name down, I don't really know why I did it, it was
no more silly changing my mind that it was in volunteering for it in the first
place.*

*But I really regretted it afterwards and I was determined to do something
to avoid it if I could. Luckily the forms that I'd signed didn't go to Simla
immediately. I levelled with the Sergeant Major saying to him, "Major, I
believe I've buggered things up somewhat and volunteered to stay on. I've
changed my mind. Can I halt things?" He told me that the only thing to be
done was a bit risky and that I'd have to go into the Orderly Room at night
and remove the form I'd signed.*

*I did that and rummaged around in there, quietly so not to disturb the
sentries, I had a small oil lamp with me and that gave me enough light to
find the tray with the forms in it. At last I found my form: 'Rendall. B.G.L.
Rendall. Corporal. 2nd Mechanical Transport Company, Rawalpindi Barracks hereby undertakes a further 18 months service in the interests of
teaching native drivers to drive lorries.' I had it and I'd saved the day.
Luckily the duty officer hadn't kept a separate register of who'd volunteered so
I got away with it.*

*Anyway on the day we were to leave for Bombay we were taken down to
'pindi Station in some of our own lorries; in batches of thirty. Well, about 4.30
in the afternoon we were on the train in 'pindi station and a shout went
through all the train, "We're off boys, we're on our bloody way," and that
was it.*

*The train journey to Bombay took getting on for three days and two nights
and then suddenly we were going over the Bombay Ghats, a little known
range of mountains just outside Bombay. There were some wits on the train
and they seemed to know every inch of the journey, when to get out, when to
stay put and all that palaver. We went straight to Bombay Docks where the
ship was waiting for us.*

She turned out to be the China. *We were there about 10 in the morning to
catch the right tide. We were a mixed bag on that trooper, there were men
from all regiments all over India going back home. A lot of us had been out
there five years like myself. There were quite a few officers about and they
had their own area of the ship and they quite took to this area. So much so
that they tried to cordon off a great area of it, just like they did on the* Ionian
*in '14. Well, this time were having none of it. As I said there were men from
all regiments around and they'd all given years of their lives. And this was a
year after the bloody war finished! Anything could happen: there were some
determined blokes on that ship.*

*One day it did, we woke up and they were cleaning and swabbing the
decks at 6 in the morning and there were some ropes across where we were
not allowed to go. Oh, yes, all the promenade decks were roped off for the use*

of about half a dozen officers! The first rumblings I heard were some twenty or thirty Artillery men who were there aboard and one of them drew himself up to his full height on the corner of a rail and he said, "Will we stand for this boys? We're all on the way home now and anything can happen now." A young officer looked out of a nearby window and he looked nervous. Who the hell had sanctioned roping the ship off on the way home anyway?

The rumblings went on and then the Artillery men, with their great sheath knives, began cutting the ropes which divided the ship; they had these great knives for their gun horse's hooves, for removing stones and the like. This young bombardier was the ring-leader, and he cut a few of the ropes. A Captain came out and challenged him, "Bombardier, what are you doing here?" "The same as you are, sir, claiming my bloody deck. Have a care sir, we're all on our way home."

Now what happened after that was a real mystery; as to why the ship was not quarantined. It was about a fortnight getting home, you see, and it was in the Suez Canal that the ropes were cut, near Port Said. Worse was to come.

One of these officers, fool like, walked out and gathered the other officers together and they all had a stand up hamjam with the soldiers. They were all getting on the same level and the day of an officer's authority was gone, you see. There were a lot more rumblings and the next piece of trouble occurred when a bunch of men went through into the well deck and they started pulling out the musical instruments of the ship's orchestra. I was just looking out to sea and there was a hell of a splash and the spray came back up. This was a piano overboard into the ocean and we could just see it keys and all before the water enveloped it. Next were the rest of the instruments, clarinets, oboes and trombones, the bloody lot. All overboard. There was a near riot.

The Captain came up on deck and addressed the crowd, "There'll be trouble when I wireless this back to Plymouth, you'll all be kept on board for a month." But the ropes were taken off. The Captain should have known better than to have allowed a ship going home to be cordoned off for the use of officers. Going out was different, the officers had their say then. Those in charge were threatening us all with being clapped in irons, etc, what have you, in the ship's cells.

Well, everything blew over after a while but everyone was wondering what was going to happen at Plymouth. We went through Alexandria, past Malta and Gib, back through the bay of Biscay and into Plymouth.

I saw another thing on board that ship that I'll never forget, despite the fact that there were Red Caps on the ship to try and keep gambling down, and that was the old Crown and Anchor board. They called it the 'old lucky dice' you would throw three dice, the clubs, diamonds, spades etc. Well, I ended up with £94 after playing for a while, but the amazing thing was watching a regular sergeant who'd put a huge wad of money on. He was quivering with nervousness, I don't think he'd played before. Anyway he'd put £930 down on the board and he won and ended up with £1300.

We pulled into Plymouth and they lost no time in bundling us into two trains and we went hell for leather up to Fovant on the Plain. And what do you think happened? On the way we pulled round a bend and passed Yeovil Junction and we could see into Yeovil, from a distance. We were put into a large tent at Fovant and there was a huge bowl of soup for each of us, my God we could do with it too.

We were then split up into small 'demob' sections awaiting our turn at the little demobilisation post. There we handed in our bayonets and Christ knows what else. I'd already thrown my helmet overboard when we were on the ship. As I was going through the post the sergeant that was in charge offered me the chance to buy my greatcoat. Well I saw a future for this coat, it was a well made thing you know, army stuff was. 'What do you want for it sarge?' 'Give us a quid'. I brought it away with me tied up with string.

Well, after finishing with the demob business at Fovant I chugged back to Yeovil; the Yeovil that I'd left five years before. I was five years in Burma and India. I had great mixed feelings, between crying like a baby and being the brave soldier at the prospects of meeting my folks again.

I got off the train at Town Station, only a few hundred yards from my house, shouldered my kitbag and showed my railway warrant; expended. I was off to Earle Street. Now, at this time, late 1919, almost 1920, the thought of demobbing had gone from people's minds and it was so strange to a neighbour in Earle Street. I have never seen a woman run so fast as Mrs. Hill did and she shouted, "My God, Bert, you're back!"

Now, with my heavy kitbag, I couldn't run but she raced ahead of me like a lamplighter and shoved Mother's front door open and said, "Bert's here!" It was a reunion never to be forgotten. Mother and I met in the doorway. I'd come home to a grey-haired old lady, grey with worry about her three sons in the army. The weeping agony of my joining up in '14 turned to tears of joy. It was a contrast. We held each other, spellbound.

I then had my month's furlough; a month on full pay to get things sorted out like. Full Army pay, you reported once a fortnight to the Post Office to draw your pay. And I well remember a young policeman keeping an eye on me and he challenged me: "Not overstaying your leave by any chance are you Corp?" I was in uniform still; in my full Indian regalia and I said to him, "Listen, stop poking your bloody nose in sonny." I could see that he'd hardly shaved more than twice and I settled his hash by making him come back to the Police Station where I collared a sergeant and told him what this youngster was up to.

It wasn't getting any better either, I went back to Petters on the Monday morning and acquainted them as to who I was and told them what type of engines I was on before I went off to the war; VJ twins and triples, damn great engines. I'd only been back a week when I was sacked again, by mistake. There was another Rendall in the factory and he'd been a conscientious objector in the war. They got the names wrong and I was out instead.

Luckily my brother Harold was influential in Yeovil, he worked at the Unemployment Assistance Board in Princes Street. He went, with me, and we tackled Guy Petter about it and he agreed to give me my job back. But even then we were only on 12s. 6d. a week. It was harrowing for some of the ex-soldiers, some of them up to 30 years old and that's all they were paid. I remember that the Government agreed to pay half a man's wages to bring them up to a reasonable level.

I was then on the princely sum of 25s. a week. I wished then that I'd stayed signed on for Indian service.

And with that, having got back into civvy life I terminate the stories of my travels and the Khyber and whatnots. So you've got the lot folks.

91

92

93

94

95

PIANOS OVERBOARD

91
With all the swagger of the British soldier in India.

92
Private Leslie Chant, 19 January 1917. Less fortunate than his elder brother, he fought with the 7th Devonshires at Ypres where he lost both legs.

93
Ed Ewens in later life.

94
John, 2nd Lord Montagu of Beaulieu, in his Brigadier General's uniform, with the Khyber Pass in the background. The painting, by the Hon. John Collier, is displayed in the front hall of Palace House, Beaulieu.

95
The anachronistic Ernest Morely Chant, with the author's grandmother, in the mid-1960s.

In the closing months of 1919 many other 2/5th soldiers, who had been transferred to other units, returned to England from far flung places such as Persia, China, the North West Frontier, India and Burma. The affairs of the battalion were wound up in Taunton and, on 25 February 1920, the 2/5th Battalion (Prince Albert's) Somerset Light Infantry was no more.

The King had commissioned the presentation of a Flag to all the newly raised battalions which had served overseas during the Great War and the 2/5th's Flag was handed to the officers of the battalion by Major General Kennedy, CB, on behalf of the Army Council, on 27 March 1920. The Colour was finally laid up and consecrated in the Parish Church of St. Mary, Ilminster on 9 September 1920. It hangs there today; highlighted by a brass inscription at the base of the flagpole.

The King's Colour
of the
2/5th Battalion
The Prince Albert's Somerset Light Infantry
Formed 1914 Disbanded 1920

Served overseas throughout the Great War.

CQMS E.W. EWENS

Our present day scene now consists of the rolling downs of Dorset on one side and the fertile plains and green hills of Somerset on the other and the majority say 'East is East and West is West but Somerset scenes are still best.'

The final scene of all was the laying up of the Colours in Ilminster Parish Church in September 1920. This was attended by several officers, WO, NCOs and men and was most impressive. A dinner was held after the ceremony at the George Hotel. It was thoroughly enjoyed, several reminiscences being brought out in the speeches and many a laugh was enjoyed.

So here endeth my 'Cook's Tour' and I sincerely hope it has not wearied you, but has been instrumental in bringing to mind a few happenings which in the light of after events we may now smile and joke at, though it would have been most detrimental at the time to have done so.

With the King's Colour safely laid up, the 2/5th (Prince Albert's) Somerset Light Infantry vanished back into the Somerset towns and villages from which the battalion had been drawn six years earlier. The men of the battalion had been lucky, even in the First World War somebody had to have some good fortune. In five years overseas service, they had suffered fifty-one dead, in the drafts sent to Mesopotamia and the rest to tropical disease and accidents; by Great War standards, an insignificant figure. On 1 July 1916, the 10th Battalion West Yorks lost 710 men dead and wounded on the Somme. Britain had lost 760,000 dead in the war and a further 1½ million soldiers had been maimed and wounded. The 2/5th Somersets had been spared.

How would this knowledge have affected the men of the battalion, returning home so late in 1919? How might Morely Chant have greeted his younger brother Leslie, who served with the Devonshire Regiment and lost both legs in a trench at Ypres? It is safe enough to say that a few people, who might have lost loved ones in France and Flanders, would have jibed at their having had an 'easy war'. Assuming the men of the battalion were somehow prescient enough, in 1914, to have known where the various battalions were to be posted; and chosen accordingly. Bert Rendall is ferociously sure that no such feelings were directed at him personally, but he does have a fierce and sensitive defensiveness on the subject of the 2/5th not having served on the Western Front.

And where did he get that from? Was it his own reaction on learning the full history of the war; coming home late in 1919 to find out the terrible extent of the tragedy which had been played out behind his back, so many miles distant from him? Or was it imposed upon him by his peers? A degree of guilt came from somewhere, which he assuages partly with the unassailable logic of, 'We had no choice in where we were sent.'

Certainly King and Country regarded the service of the soldiers who never fought as less meritorious than those who did; the Victory Medal was only awarded to the men who served in the active theatres of the war.

The battalion was very much neglected in the official history of the Somerset Light Infantry in the Great War. Everard Wyrall gave the 2/5th no more than a few cursory lines; almost a sidelong glance. Even today, in the course of writing this book, many observors were of the opinion that the story was not really worth writing about.

The war had nevertheless profoundly altered and interfered with, the lives of over a thousand men who joined the 2/5th. How did it affect the fortunes of the three soldiers who made this book possible?

Perhaps the least dramatic impact would have been on the life of Ed Ewens. In 1914 he was already a mature man of thirty-nine with a ten year old son, Bentley. His roots were well established before the Great War and he was, perhaps, less thunderstruck by the experience than the younger soldiers. Nevertheless, he was away from his wife and son for the five years which elapsed before he returned from India. The family moved back to the Yeovil area on the outbreak of war, having lived in Swindon previously where Ed was the Tory Party Agent.

Ed Ewens went into business with his brothers following the war, trading as E.S. Ewens & Co. The gloving industry was in serious decline in the inter-war years and the family fortunes fell accordingly. They were used to servants and large houses before the war but things became less rosy as the depression of the 1920s cast its malicious shadow. Ed played an active part in organising social and sporting activities in Yeovil; he formed the Yeovil and District Soccer League and the Yeovil Skittles League. He was also the first secretary of the British Legion in Yeovil, after having been a member of the Comrades of the Great War, one of four ex-soldiers' organisations which were amalgamated into the British Legion in 1921.

Perhaps the most important legacy of the Great War for Ed Ewens was the writing of his diary in 1928. 'Cook's Tour of Burma and India' reflects the maturity of his outlook in those years. He viewed the war of the 2/5th Somersets as a travel experience and coined the title for his diary accordingly. CQMS Ewens philosophically trod the middle ground between the officers and men of the battalion, showing a clear perception of the way in which the lot of the ordinary soldier was made worse by the institutionalised selfishness of the Great War officer class, and the thoughtlessness of over zealous NCOs. Equally he was appreciative of the strong bonds of affection and trust which developed between the men and their officers in the field. As a piece of prose 'Cook's Tour' shows a sympathetic command of the English language and an ability to describe the events he experienced, enough as to earn Ed Ewens a good deal of respect as a writer.

Little is known of Ed Ewens' intentions when writing the diary, but it is certain that he intended it to be published in some form. Perhaps it was meant for circulation within the British Legion; he makes several references within the diary to other soldiers who might be reading it. The fall in the fortunes of the Ewens family resulted in Ed working at home, cutting gloves as an outworker, almost up to his death in 1962. In his later years Ed lived with his son and Ollie Ewens remembers his grandfather telling tales of Burma and India, while he worked away at his glove cutting.

You will remember from the background to this book, how the Great War left an indelible stamp of experience on Morely Chant's life. My grandfather was twenty when the 2/5th sailed for Burma, and his experience of the war was to lay conflicts and difficulties with which he would fight for many years.

The lot of the ordinary British soldier in India had always been a peculiar one and it was no different by the time of the Great War. The British ordinary ranker was largely shunned by the English civilian in Burma and India, and lack of money further prevented Tommy from mixing freely outside the military cantonments. But there was an important balancing factor; each British regiment in India was looked after by a large number of camp followers. These were the various wallahs who served the British soldiers: fondly remembered by Morely Chant. The turnout maintained by British soldiers in India was legendary in its smartness and it was largely achieved by the use of cheap native labour. There was a specialised wallah for each and every task, from the punka wallah to the char wallah, the durzai and the dhobi. The British soldier was accorded, and came to expect, a great deal of respect from the camp wallahs. Prolonged service in India led Tommy to think a great deal of himself, 'After about a year in India, they were four feet off the ground.'[33]

It was some small measure of compensation for the way in which they were treated by their own countrymen in India. It was an odd, dual existence, shunned and even despised by the English civilian generally, but treated like lords by the servants, who were usually the only natives the soldiers came into contact with. Morely Chant had four and a half years of this life and it culminated in him becoming a sergeant in the Indian Infantry.

He made full use of the opportunities presented to him by the war, it was an older and wiser Morely Chant who returned to England in the spring of 1919. But the men of the Great War were given no more control of their destiny in 1919 than they had in 1914. On his demobilisation Morely was forced back

33. *Plain Tales from the Raj.* Charles Allen, Century Publishing 1985.

into the industrial and economic trap that he had volunteered to get away from on the outbreak of the First World War. For him it was back to table glove cutting; ten hours a day in the factory, shut-outs instead of holidays and he never earned more than 50s. in a week in his life.

But he had been a soldier for 4½ years, had travelled the world and had learned what it felt like to be accorded respect by other human beings, and he was not going to take it lying down. He was not prepared to accept that the war had been fought for nothing, the clock could not be turned back to pre-1914 no matter how desperately the 'bosses' would have wished it. Morely Chant had not given those years for nothing. The soldiers returning after the Great War were not so naive as to think that any politician really would give them a 'land fit for heroes' but they had given up a lot, suffered much and expected, at very least, some form of improvement in the quality of their lives. So Morely Chant was going to make a fight of it.

He joined the Labour Party and the Trade Union Movement and he was to fight tenaciously for both causes throughout the rest of his life. It was not an easy path for him, in addition to constant economic struggle to keep his wife and family. He married in 1923, Lily Clifton from Leeds, they were to have four children and the 1920s and 1930s were to be one long struggle to retain their dignity. They were lucky compared to many families, Morely was always in work during those years, but their life was nevertheless hard.

Many years were to elapse, and another world war fought, before the working men of this country gained the overall improvement in their condition that many of them felt they should have been rewarded with in 1918. Thousands of men like Morely Chant helped lay the foundations for the more egalitarian material prosperity which we enjoy today.

Bert Rendall's absorption of the Great War was quite similar to that of my grandfather. He was younger than Morely, eighteen when they sailed from Southampton, and on his return in late 1919 he was to sorely regret not signing on for 18 months extra service in India as a driving instructor. The 1920s were very harsh to Bert, the five years of the war had changed him a great deal; he was little more than a boy in 1914, and in 1920 he was allowed to complete his apprenticeship at Petters Engines. He qualified as a fitter and was then promptly sacked as the firm had insufficient work to take him on as a skilled man.

He declined to follow Morely's interest in fighting for the general rights of the working man, preferring a more solitary path in his coming to terms with the viccissitudes of civilian life in England in the 1920s. He married in 1923; Eva Mullins, the girl he had walked out with as a boy before the war. Bert and Eva had two sons, both of whom were to grow up successful Yeovil businessmen, Ivan and Clive. It was a potent legacy of living through the depression of the 1920s that parents strove long and hard to provide for a better material future for their children.

Years of taking any available job followed and Bert's confidence took many knocks as he found it hard to adjust after his years abroad. It seemed that the five years he had spent in the Far East were to count for nothing. However, his driving experience gained him several jobs; he worked for a time as a bus driver and a stone haulier. Then there was a job at the glove factory where his father still worked. Bert threw up several jobs through being all too ready to stand up for his rights against his employers. Other jobs simply disappeared after a short period. Eventually he was to settle down when he was offered a fitter's job at the Westland works.

Bert Rendall lives on today; of all the Somerset volunteers who found themselves onboard the *Ionian*, outward bound for Burma in 1914, he is their last known survivor. He may be found, on most days, in his house in Yeovil. He is 91 years old now and he will gladly recount his reminiscences of the Great War to anybody with the time and interest to listen to him. His living room is full of evidence of those memories; views of the North West Frontier adorn the walls; the Khyber Pass, Ali Musjid, Landi Kotal, the Bolan Pass and a host of other places which have faded into the greying mists of Empire folklore. Brightly polished Indian brassware decorates the room; the cobra candlesticks, Ghurka kukris and engraved vases bear silent witness to the travels of a British soldier.

A wooden sideboard displays sepia images of Bert in his various uniforms, from the red with white piping of the early days of the war, to the khaki serge worn in the Murree Hills and the battledress of the Home Guard. He also made his contribution in the years 1939/1945. His father interposes with uniforms of an earlier hue, the Gordon Highlanders of the 1880s.

Bert remains intense and vital, his health has been kind to him, and in his 92nd year he has more energy than many people half his age. Nevertheless, he has in the past suffered vertigo and he never goes out on his own. His experience of the world today comes mainly through his television set and, in the absence of visitors, he spends his long, lonely hours channel changing with a well thumbed remote control unit. But he finds things to interest him and his understanding of our world of 1987 is very keen indeed. Many things anger him and he shares the opinion of many of his generation that things are worse today than when he was a lad. And when I occasionally protest that, as neither my father's generation nor mine have ever had to go off to a world war, things must surely be better today, he dismisses me with 90 years of wisdom. And of course, in many ways he is quite right.

Veterans of the First World War are now few, and as the years close in they are becoming fewer. Bert Rendall is one of the last survivors of the troopship generation of 1914; men who witnessd more change and bore more suffering than any others in the history of this country. We should salute them now whilst we still have a chance.

Appendix A

MOVABLE COLUMN ORDERS NO. II

(To be read in conjunction with Movable Column
 Standing Orders – below)

SHWEBO

25th April 1917.

Copy No. 5*

PARADE The Movable Column will parade at 4.30 p.m.

KITS: A Blanket and Greatcoat only, will actually be taken on Transport and the Kits will be stacked as per Standing Orders.

RATIONS: Rations for the evening of the 25th. and morning of 26.th instant will only be taken on Transport, and will be arranged for by Coy. Q.M. Sergt. Ewens.

DRESS: Field Service Order. Shirt Sleeves, Tunics in Greatcoat Carriers. Water Bottles filled.

Sgd. F.E. Spurway, Captain
2/5th. Somerset L.I.
Commanding Movable Column.

Copy No   1 to :– The Officer Commanding, Shwebo.
           2   :– Retained.
           3   :– Officer Comdg. Station Hospital, Shwebo.
           4   :– The Staff Officer, Movable Column.
        *5   :– CQMS Ewens, 'C' Coy, 2/5th. Somerset L.I.
           6   :– CSM Gibbs, 'C' Coy. 2/5th. Somerset L.I.

Possibly the *only* documentary record of the 2/5th Somersets in existence today; an order relating to a movable column, Shwebo 1917.

———— Appendix B ————

THE ROLL OF HONOUR

THE 2/5th BATTALION (PRINCE ALBERT'S) SOMERSET LIGHT INFANTRY

Pte.	ADAMS, Albert	Mesopotamia	18.6.16
Pte.	ADAMS, Arthur	Mesopotamia	26.10.17
Pte.	BELLRINGER, Marcel	Mesopotamia	21.12.15
Pte.	BINDING, Ernest William	India	12.10.17
Pte.	BOARD, Fred	Burma	25.1.15
Pte.	BROWN, Henry	India	16.4.19
Pte.	CAREY, Charles Cyril	Mesopotamia	26.1.17
Pte.	CARTWRIGHT, Thomas Bertram	India	31.5.18
Pte.	COATES, Frank Ronald	India	22.6.18
Pte.	COLLARD, Ivan James	India	1.4.18
Pte.	CRIDLAND, Ernest	Burma	17.8.15
Pte.	CRUICKSHANK, Alexander	Mesopotamia	26.11.15
Pte.	DOWDING, Jesse	India	9.11.17
Pte.	DOWNTON, Herbert	Burma	21.3.17
Pte.	ELFORD, George William	India	4.3.16
Pte.	FOOKS, P	India	16.8.19
Pte.	FUDGE, Henry Charles	India	30.5.17
Pte.	GAYLOR, F	India	29.11.18
Pte.	GIBBS, Ernest	Egypt	23.11.17
Pte.	HUTCHINGS, Charles	Burma	23.7.16
Pte.	JENNINGS, Charles	Mesopotamia	25.4.16
Pte.	LONG, Charles	Mesopotamia	28.11.15
Pte.	MORGAN, Reginald	Mesopotamia	9.10.16
Pte.	PARKER, Ernest Albert	India	21.10.18
Pte.	PEACOCK, T	Aden	2.1.19
Pte.	POPE, F	India	27.8.19
Pte.	PIPE, Norman	Mesopotamia	31.12.16
Pte.	RICHARDS, J	India	30.6.19
Pte.	ROWDEN, Mansel	Burma	26.5.16
Pte.	SAUNDERS, Frederick	India	20.7.18
Pte.	SMITH, E	India	25.7.18
Pte.	TAYLOR, Thomas	Mesopotamia	21.12.15
Pte.	TANCOCK, Stanley John	Mesopotamia	8.3.16

Pte.	TURNER, Robert	Mesopotamia	12.8.16
Pte.	WEBBER, Harry	India	22.1.19
Pte.	WELLMAN, Bert	Mesopotamia	22.11.15
Pte.	WESTCOTT, Albert	Burma	24.12.14
Pte.	WHEADON, George	Mesopotamia	8.2.16
Pte.	WILLIAMS, Ernest Charles	At Sea	24.12.14
Pte.	YOUNG, William	India	23.11.17
L.-Cpl.	FROST, CLIFFORD .. .. ..India	India	27.10.18
Cpl.	ADAMS, John	Burma	23.8.17
Cpl.	MAHRENHOLZ, Ferdinand Edmund	India	29.8.17
Cpl.	PARMINTER, Robert	Burma	11.6.15
Cpl.	PARSONS, Hubert	Mesopotamia	13.4.16
Cpl.	SIMPSON, Archibald	Mesopotamia	15.7.16
Cpl.	WEAVER, Henry William	India	21.10.17
Sgt.	FRAMPTON, Thomas John	India	10.5.19
Sgt.	PATTIMORE, Charles	India	26.8.17
CQMS.	DYER, Roy	Mesopotamia	4.10.18
CSM.	PILTON, Frederick George	India	24.5.18

—— Appendix C ——

HONOURS AND REWARDS

MENTION IN DESPATCHES

Broadmead, Lieutenant H.H.
Hunt, Lieutenant W.E.
Paull, Lieutenant-Colonel J.R., OBE, TD

BROUGHT TO THE NOTICE OF GOVERNMENT OF INDIA FOR VALUABLE SERVICES RENDERED IN INDIA

Goodland, Captain C.H., TD
Hood, Quartermaster and Captain T.

REWARDS

OBE

Paull, Lieutenant-Colonel J.R.

MC

Bailey, Lieutenant W.G., 1/72nd Punjabis (late Sergeant 2/5th Battalion).
Price, Captain C.N., 2/76th Punjabis (late 2/5th Battalion).

MSM

Dyer, Company-Quartermaster-Sergeant Roy.
Fry, Regimental-Sergeant-Major W.